HOTEL AND MOTEL PROFESSIONAL MANAGEMENT

HOTEL AND MOTEL PROFESSIONAL MANAGEMENT

M. C. METTI

ANMOL PUBLICATIONS PVT. LTD.
NEW DELHI - 110 002 (INDIA)

ANMOL PUBLICATIONS PVT. LTD.
Regd. Office: 4360/4, Ansari Road, Daryaganj,
New Delhi-110 002 (India)
Ph.: 23278000, 23261597
Branch Office: No. 1015, Ist Main Road, BSK IIIrd Stage
IIIrd Phase, IIIrd Block,
Bangalore-560 085 (India)
Tel.: 080-41723429
Visit us at: www.anmolpublications.com

Hotel and Motel Professional Management

ISBN 978-81-261-3295-9

PRINTED IN INDIA

Printed at Mehra Offset Press, Delhi.

Contents

Preface

The book "Hotel and Motel Professional Management" fills that void. It joins between two covers the findings of the most significant research on services and hospitality services in particular with the best practices of leading hospitality organizations.

A proven principle of hotel and motel management keys each chapter of this book.

Leading hospitality organizations have found these principles to be important, workable, and useful. They represent the key points to keep in mind when putting the book's material into practice. They can guide hospitality organizations and their managers as they seek to reach the levels of excellence achieved.

The book will be very useful to all the professional of hotels and motels. This book will prove to be best friend for those who are in this profession. Students in large will benefit in preparing for there exam.

Chapter 1

The Professional Environment

IMPORTANCE AND NATURE OF CHANGE

A hotel is an establishment that provides paid lodging, usually on a short-term basis. Hotels often provide a number of additional guest services such as a restaurant, a swimming pool or childcare. Some hotels have conference services and meeting rooms and encourage groups to hold conventions and meetings at their location. There is no hard and fast rule differentiating motels from other hotels, although a "Motel" is clearly suggesting that it is aimed at motorists. This may simply mean that it is a hotel with good access to the road network (on a motorway or ring road) so that a long car journey need not be interrupted for long by town-centre traffic. In other cases the designation is simply an attempt to make the most of a poor location inconvenient for town-centre services and attractions.

Classically, though, a Motel is a hotel which is made convenient for people who, for whatever personal reason, wish to be able to have quick access from the outside world (especially from their parked car) to the hotel room - without passing the scrutiny of a receptionist or fellow guests. This is usually arranged by having rooms (sometimes in individual chalets or even trailers) arranged around the car park with room doors opening directly to the outside rather than to an internal corridor. In Australia, the word may also refer to a pub or bar. In the UK similarly, many pubs with "hotel" in their name do not offer accommodation or even food.

In India, the word may also refer to a restaurant since the best restaurants were always situated next to a good hotel. The word *hotel* derives from the French *hotel*, which referred to a French version of a townhouse or any other building seeing frequent visitors, not a place offering accommodation (in contemporary usage, *hotel* has the meaning of "hotel", and *hotel particular* is used for the old meaning).

The French spelling (with the circumflex) was once also used in English, but is now rare. The circumflex replaces the 's' once preceding the 't' in the earlier *hostel* spelling, which over time received a new, but closely related meaning. The practice of lodging people in specialized buildings has great antiquity and has been done by people in various cultures: the Hoshi Ryokan, currently the oldest operating hotel in the world (as far as the Guinness Book of World Records' authors know), was established in Japan in 717; in ancient Rome, inns sprang up by the various roads; Jesus was, according to the New Testament, famously born in the manger of an inn near Bethlehem due to a lack of vacancy in the lodging proper, more than seven centuries before.

Hotel chains were established many hundreds of years later, and hotels today are owned by both small and large businesses. Basic accommodation of a room with only a bed, a cupboard, a small table and a washstand has largely been replaced by rooms with en-suite bathrooms and, more commonly in the United States than elsewhere, climate control. Other features found may be a telephone, an alarm clock, a TV, and broadband Internet connectivity. Food and drink may be supplied by a mini-bar (which often includes a small refrigerator) containing snacks and drinks (to be paid for on departure), and tea and coffee making facilities (cups, spoons, an electric kettle and sachets containing instant coffee, tea bags, sugar, and creamer or milk).

In the United Kingdom a hotel is required by law to serve food and drinks to all comers within certain stated hours; to avoid this requirement it is not uncommon to come across "private hotels" which are not subject to this requirement.

However, in Japan the capsule hotel supplies minimal facilities and room space.

The cost and quality of hotels are usually indicative of the range and type of services available. Due to the enormous increase in tourism worldwide during the last decades of the 20th century, standards, especially those of smaller establishments, have improved considerably. For the sake of greater comparability, rating systems have been introduced, with the one to five stars classification being most common.

"Boutique Hotel" is a term originating in North America to describe intimate, usually luxurious or quirky hotel environments. Boutique hotels differentiate themselves from larger chain or branded hotels by providing an exceptional and personalized level of accommodation, services and facilities. Boutique hotels are furnished in a themed, stylish and/or aspirational manner.

Although usually considerably smaller than a mainstream hotel (ranging from 3 to 100 guest rooms) boutique hotels are generally fitted with telephone and wi-fi Internet connections, honesty bars and often cable/pay TV. Guest services are attended to by 24 hour hotel staff. Many boutique hotels have on site dining facilities, and the majority offer bars and lounges which may also be open to the general public.

Of the total travel market a small percentage are discerning travelers, who place a high importance on privacy, luxury and service delivery. As this market is typically corporate travelers, the market segment is non-seasonal, high-yielding and repeat, and therefore one which boutique hotel operators target as their primary source of income.

Some hotels have gained their renown through tradition, by hosting significant events or persons, such as Schloss Cecilienhof in Potsdam, Germany, which derives its fame from the so-called Potsdam Conference of the World War II allies Winston Churchill, Harry Truman and Joseph Stalin in 1945. Other establishments have given name to a particular meal or beverage, as is the case with the Waldorf Astoria in New York

City, USA, known for its *Waldorf Salad* or the Raffles Hotel in Singapore, where the drink *Singapore Sling* was invented. Another example is the Hotel Sacher in Vienna Austria, home of the *Sachertorte*. There are also hotels which became much more popular through films like the Grand Hotel Europe in Saint Petersburg, Russia when James Bond stayed there in the Blockbuster, Goldeneye. Cannes hotels such as the Carlton or the Martinez become the center of the world during Cannes Film Festival (France).

A number of hotels have entered the public consciousness through popular culture, such as the Ritz Hotel in London, UK and Hotel Chelsea in New York City, subject of a number of songs and also the scene of the stabbing of Nancy Spungen (allegedly by her boyfriend Sid Vicious). Hotels that enter folklore like these two are also often frequented by celebrities, as is the case both with the Ritz and the Chelsea. Other famous hotels include the Beverly Hills Hotel, the Hotel Bel-Air and the Chateau Marmont, in California, Watergate complex in Washington DC, the Hotel Astoria in Saint Petersburg, Russia, the Hotel George V and Hôtel Ritz in Paris, Palazzo Versace hotel on the Gold Coast, Queensland, Australia, Hotel Hermitage and Hotel de Paris in Monaco (in the French Riviera), Peninsula Hotel in Hong Kong and Hotel Leningradskaya in Moscow.

Many hotels can be considered destinations in themselves, by dint of unusual features of the lodging and/or its immediate environment:

Some hotels, such as the Costa Rica Tree House in the Gandoca-Manzanillo Wildlife Refuge, Costa Rica, or Treetops Hotel in Aberdare National Park, Kenya, are built with living trees as structural elements, making them treehouses.

The Ariau Towers near Manaus, Brazil is in the middle of the Amazon, on the Rio Negro. Bill Gates even invested and had a suite built there with satellite internet/phone. Another hotel with treehouse units is Bayram's Tree Houses in Olympos, Turkey.

Desert Cave Hotel in Coober Pedy, South Australia and the Cuevas Pedro Antonio de Alarcón (named after the author) in Guadix, Spain, as well as several hotels in Cappadocia, Turkey, are notable for being built into natural cave formations, some with rooms underground. Capsule hotels are a type of economical hotels that are quite common in Japan.

Ice hotels, such as the Ice Hotel in Jukkasjärvi, Sweden, melt every spring and are rebuilt out of ice and snow each winter. The Mammut Snow Hotel in Finland is located within the walls of the Kemi snow castle, which is the biggest in the world. It includes The Mammut Snow Hotel, The Castle Courtyard, The Snow Restaurant and a chapel for weddings, etc. Its furnishings and its decorations, such as sculptures, are made of snow and ice.

There is snow accommodation also in Lainio Snow Hotel in Lapland (near Yllas), Finland. Garden hotels, famous for their gardens before they became hotels, includes Gravetye Manor, the home of William Robinson and Cliveden, designed by Charles Barry with a rose garden by Geoffrey Jellicoe.

As of 2005, the only hotel with an underwater room that can be reached without Scuba diving is Utter Inn in Lake Mälaren, Sweden. It only has one room, however, and Jules Undersea Lodge in Key Largo, Florida, which requires Scuba diving, is not much bigger.

Hydropolis is an ambitious project to build a luxury hotel in Dubai, UAE, with 220 suites, all on the bottom of the Persian Gulf, 20 meters (66 feet) below the surface. Its architecture will feature two domes that break the surface and an underwater train tunnel, all made of transparent materials such as glass and acrylic. The Library Hotel in New York City is unique in that its ten floors are arranged according to the Dewey Decimal System.

The Rogers Centre, formerly SkyDome, in Toronto, Canada is the only stadium to have a hotel connected to it, with 70 rooms overlooking the field. West Ham United F.C. in the UK now has a hotel with rooms that overlook the pitch and sometimes double as executive boxes for important games.

The Burj al-Arab hotel in Dubai, United Arab Emirates, built on an artificial island, is structured in the shape of a sail of a boat. The RMS Queen Mary in Long Beach, California is the only 1930s ocean liner still in existence. Its elegant first-class staterooms are now used as a hotel. The Oriental Pearl Tower in Shanghai houses an extremely expensive hotel with only 20 rooms.

The tallest hotel in the world is the Burj al-Arab in Dubai, United Arab Emirates, at 321 metres, which however will soon be surpassed by the nearby Rose Rotana Suites at 333 meters (1,091 feet). The Ryugyong Hotel in Pyongyang was intended to reach 330 meters (1,083 feet), but is unlikely to be completed; it has been under construction since 1987 and was abandoned in 1992. The highest hotel rooms are in the *Grand Hyatt* in the Jin Mao Building in Shanghai, the highest floor being at around 350 m. The largest hotel in the world is the MGM Grand Las Vegas in Las Vegas, Nevada, USA with a total of 6,276 rooms as of December 20, 2006.

On December 18, 2006 Guinness World Records listed the First World Hotel in Genting Highlands, Malaysia as the worlds largest hotel. It has a total of 6,118 rooms and is part of the Genting Highlands Resort and Casino. The First World Plaza which is joined to the two hotel towers boasts 500,000 square feet of indoor theme park, shopping centres, casino gaming areas, and eateries. Previously, Guinness had listed the MGM Grand Las Vegas in Las Vegas, Nevada, USA with 5,005 rooms as the largest hotel in the world.

According to the Guinness Book of World Records, the oldest hotel still in operation is the Hoshi Ryokan, in Awazu, Japan. It opened in 717, and features hot springs. The owner, chairman, or CEO of a hotel or hotel group is known as a *hotelier*. A hotel chain is a collection or grouping of hotels under one recognizable brand operated by a management company.

Entering dictionaries after World War II, the word motel (portmanteau of "motor hotel" or "motorists' hotel") referred initially to a single building of connected rooms whose doors face a parking lot and/or common area or a series of small cabins with common parking. Their creation was driven by increased driving distances on the United States highway system that allowed easy cross-country travel. The concept originated with the Motel Inn of San Luis Obispo, constructed in 1925 by Arthur Heinman. The motels are also found along highways in rural and urban areas across Canada.

Unlike their predecessors, auto camps and tourist courts, motels quickly adopted a homogenized appearance. Typically one would find an 'I' or 'L' or 'U' shaped structure that included rooms, an attached manager's office, and perhaps a small diner. Postwar motels sought more visual distinction, often featuring eye-catching neon signs which employed pop culture themes that ranged from Western imagery of cowboys and Indians to contemporary images of spaceships and atomic symbols.

The motel began in the 1920s as mom-and-pop motor courts on the outskirts of a town. They attracted the first road warriors as they crossed the United States in their new automobiles. They usually had a grouping of small cabins and their anonymity made them ideal trysting places (or the "hot trade" in industry lingo). Even the famous outlaws Bonnie and Clyde were frequent guests, using motels as hideouts. The motels' potential for breeding perceived lust and larceny alarmed then FBI chief J. Edgar Hoover, who attacked motels and auto camps in an article he penned called "Camps of Crime", which ran in the February 1940 issue of American Magazine.

Motels differed from hotels in their emphasis on largely anonymous interactions between owners and occupants, their location along highways (as opposed to urban cores), and their orientation to the outside (in contrast to hotels whose doors typically face an interior hallway).

With the 1952 introduction of Kemmons Wilson's Holiday Inn, the 'mom and pop' motels of that era went into decline. Eventually, the emergence of the interstate highway system, along with other factors, led to a blurring of the motel and the hotel. Today, family owned motels with as few as five rooms may still be found along older highways. The quality and standards of every independent motel differ, so it is always wise to cruise around for a good motel before settling in a room.

In seedy areas, motels are sometimes located near strip clubs. These motels sometimes charge an "hourly" rate instead of a "nightly" rate. Motels with low rates sometimes serve as housing for people who are not able to afford an apartment.

In most countries of Latin America and some countries of East Asia, motels are also known as short-time hotels, and offer a short-time or "transit" stay with hourly rates primarily intended for people having sex.

- Bates Motel, a fictional motel from the Universal Pictures horror film *Psycho*.
- Sunshine Motel, a fictional motel outside of Gallup, New Mexico from the Sci Fi miniseries *The Lost Room*, where a strange event erased an entire room and its contents from history.
- Crossroads Motel (later Crossroads Hotel), a fictional motel near Birmingham, England from the British soap opera Crossroads.

The last several years have been a tumultuous period in business from the introduction of new technology to the globalization of economies to the rapid turnover and constant demand for new products and services at lower costs. The rapidly changing conditions in today's business environment have made unprecedented demands on organizations and their leaders that often require radical rethinking of purpose and priorities, vision of the future, and even the structure and function of the organization itself.

In other words, "change" as a constant state has become the norm for the business environment. Organizations that are unable to swiftly change and adapt quickly become obsolete. Change is not uniform between organizations. In fact, it presents itself on a continuum. [1] The most successful organizations are managed by individuals proficient at managing change. For each story of successful organizational change, however, there are two or three or more about failure. Change has become a dilemma for many corporations.

The current business environment is so competitive that changes must be made on a fairly regular basis if the organization is to adapt and be effective (or even remain in existence). In studies of organizational effectiveness, *adaptability and flexibility* continually show up among the top variables that impact on effectiveness as perceived by practicing managers. Adaptability and flexibility are important parts of the change process. Managers in the professional environment are most concerned with change because the ability of the organization to adapt often rests with engineering, research and development, scientific and other professionals that are normally associated with an enterprise.

Change can be defined as any alteration in the established way of doing things. According to this definition, change does not necessarily have to involve technology or personnel. A simple modification of work location in the office or laboratory can cause similar management problems to those caused by larger or more apparent changes. For example, there have been instances where employees' desks were moved away from a window and productivity dropped sharply.

Since the supervision and tasks assigned remained the same, the only thing that had changed was the arrangement of the desks in the room. Although in cases of this kind resistance has an impact on management problems, to the outside observer it is difficult to discern that any change has been made at all. Thus, it is not always major changes involving technology, formal organization, or task that increase management problems.

The movement of desks away from the window modified the social environment. Specifically, the windows were status symbols to the employees and perceived status was lowered among those employees who lost their preferred window location. Their performance deteriorated, and intragroup relationships suffered. Socialization is an important part of the professional work environment and managers of these groups need to examine the social impact of proposed change.

There are many facets to the change process ranging from the previously described rather simple disruption of social relationships to large scale strategic change that involves modifications or transformation of organization culture and managerial value systems. Several years ago Tichy defined this larger type of change as nonroutine-nonincremental, and discontinued change which alters the overall orientation of the organization. He argued that the task of managers regarding change was to deliberately and intentionally change the overall orientation of the organization.

Overall orientation consists of organizational core values, mission, and strategy, and determines the way the organization operates including the alignment among the professional (technical), political, and cultural subsystems.

It is becoming increasingly clear that planned change is an integral part of high performance organizations. Peters and Waterman suggest that "transforming leadership," which they define as leaders that are value shapers and change oriented, is a basic dimension of effectiveness. Similarly, Vail suggests that high performance is related to strong leadership and involves inducing clarity, consensus, and commitment regarding the organizations purpose. He says these necessary leadership skills can be learned and advocates the establishment of learning programmes to provide them to key managers.

There are three driving forces for change: First, internal forces which include strategic choices, creativity, new needs, and anything required for organizations to grow; second, external driving forces which include a variety of market changes that require adaptation for survival; and third, the interaction between internal and external driving forces which creates choices for change and precipitates further change. For example, when an organization creates a new product, this is likely to foster other changes within the organization. There is a continuous dynamic interaction among these forces that produces organizational change.

Managers must lead in an environment that is constantly changing. Employee commitment is needed to make change work, consequently the people orientation is always an important part of successful change. Although professionals may be prone to accept change because of their level of education and accomplishment, these same characteristics may actually increase their resistance tendencies. The large investment in their own training and skill development will cause high sensitivity to how changes affect individual skill application and career development.

Changes that are perceived to impact negatively in these areas are likely to meet strong resistance. Leaders of professionals need particularly strong skills in communication so that needed change is integrated into a future vision of success and growth for both the organization and professional. Additionally, these leaders need to understand the change process and how professionals are likely to react to it.

Many managers delve into the subject of organizational change without fully understanding the theory, principles, or the art of the process involved. They merely attempt, in piecemeal fashion, to copy some general techniques that are reported in the literature, such as work teams, empowerment, visioning, or total quality management. Most often such attempts are disappointing. Frequently the unexpected and unwanted side effects produce results that are the opposite of those intended. Unfortunately, this is often the case when a quick fix is attempted on a complex organizational system.

Organizational change is not a quick fix activity! Effective management of change takes a lot of time and hard work. Change theories and principles must first be studied and thoroughly understood, and the whole organizational system must be pre-conditioned and prepared for the change if future performance is to be high. It may take years to create a change in the entire system and additional years to refine and renew such efforts so that high performance is enduring.

It is important that professionals see structural change as a real benefit to themselves and their careers. Also, the leader needs to be perceived as technically competent, persistent, and in control. Unfortunately strong leadership does not always eliminate or reduce resistance to change. All professionals need to understand the nature of resistance to change so the harmful effects can be minimized. While it is commonly believed that there is a natural human tendency to resist change, there is little supporting evidence.

A major point made in Toffler's *Future Shock* was that changes are taking place faster in America than we can adjust to them. Our society is characterized by rapid change, and a cursory examination of observable events indicates that, in general, change is eventually accepted. The effective manager works to minimize the time needed for the acceptance of change, because resistance is usually costly to both management and employees.

CHANGE THEORIES

Many theories exist regarding the change process. An examination of change theories educates one seeking to implement a change within an organization. Clearly, a good manager is a successful change agent.

Literature about the management of change historically has been characterized by hypothetical practice; and in reaction to previous neglect, has overly focused on the political aspects of the change process. New interest in *the learning organization* provides an occasion to support this bias by developing a theory of change that is more congruent with the requirement to build learning capacity within organizations. The result should be the placement of learning theory centrally within a theory of planned organizational change.

The theory of *planned organizational change* grew to a large extent out of learning theories through the application of *action research* to organizational problems. This research draws upon the Lewinian field theory and related system concepts in addition to a combination of cognitive theory and humanistic psychology.

A. Action Research for Change

Action research focuses on groups to effect change within an organization. This theory examines the role of a group, implicit knowledge, and the locations of learning as centre elements. Action research is a common model used in organizational cultures where participation and equality are the norm. Within this theory, learning is not a change in behaviour, as many define it, but knowledge created through the transformation of experience.

Essential proponents of action research and experiential learning argue that this process of change should involve a critique of the organizational culture, the value system within which people work in the organization, and the societal issues which generate an increased awareness. A key point of learning in an organization is also socialization. The way people construe things and their strategies for action are bound with multiple values developed in, or in relation to, social situations. The focus of action research and change management is therefore people in groups. Similarly, it is within groups that people in organizations learn and develop ordinary work roles.

B. Theorizing about Organizational Change

A review of the diverse literature on organizational change shows the field is at an early stage of theoretical development. There is no one model of organizational change and no agreed guideline for action by change agents or practitioners who have developed frameworks for understanding and directing change based on their practical experiences in organizations. Differing theoretical approaches have been developed to analyze organizational change processes and to deal with alternate problems affecting organizational performance. Theories have been strongly affected by their socio-historical context.

Other approaches, including some managerial fads (i. e., re-engineering, total quality management, core competencies, and empowerment), have proved to be more enduring and became the most useful theoretical approaches in practice. In the field of organizational change, theories are infused with ideology and are value driven due to being grounded in social movements.

While this may be a limitation to theories of organizational change, the fact is that they are not any less relevant or scientifically significant. An important element of organizational change is coming to terms with social reality and how theory building contributes to the integral role of understanding organizations and in guiding change in organizations. The way to develop sounder theories is to disseminate assumptions so that they can be models validated with empirical testing.

C. Components of Comprehensive Change Theory

What then are the components of a comprehensive theory of organizational change? Dunphy defined four elements:

1. An analytical framework or model for understanding the organizational change process.
2. An ideal model of an effectively functioning organization, one that suggests direction for change and the values for evaluation.
3. An intervention theory that specifies when, where, and how to intervene so as to move the organization closer to the desired outcomes.
4. A definition of the role of the change agent.

THE TYPES AND PHASES OF CHANGE

Change takes place as planned, unplanned, or developmental. The first type, *planned change*, is a deliberate action undertaken by an individual or group of individuals. The goal is usually to improve an existing system. By comparison, *unplanned change* is accidental and haphazard; although after the change occurs, hindsight often reveals agents (deliberate or subconsciously) fueling the change.

This type of change is usually an adaptive response to a stimulus that attempts to re-establish balance between a system and the environment in which it exists. The last type, *developmental change*, occurs as an individual, group, or organization progresses from infancy to maturity. The effects on any given individual, group, or organization by any one of these types of change remains the same.

They react to the change and stress inevitably results. Even if the change is desired by the participants and considered "good," stress will still result.

While there are several frameworks for examining resistance to change, an examination of the three phases or stages of the change process is particularly helpful. Since the primary concern of most managers is to reduce employee resistance and increase efficiency, it is important to realize that resistance can occur during any one of the three specific phases or stages that accompany every organizational change.

Specifically, these three phases are the *threat, impact,* and *after-effect* of change. The ability of the manager to plan for change, anticipate problems before they become costly, and understand the present stage of the specific change can be a major factor in determining managerial effectiveness.

A. Threat Phase

The threat phase of change is that time period during which a rumor moves through informal (grapevine) or regular management channels that suggest a change is possible or likely to be imposed. A threat phase may occur even though the change *never actually happens*. If employees *believe* that such a change will happen, they can start resisting it immediately. Employees may quit their jobs or lower their productivity long before a change ever actually takes place. These negative responses by employees are a result of the fact that they believe that a change is actually coming or contemplated.

The length of time and significance of the threat phase is determined by the speed and the magnitude of the change. Changes that are made quickly obviously have a short threat phase, while changes that are large and require a considerable amount of planning usually have a threat phase of a year or more. Examples of these latter types of change include changes in building location, alterations involving technological improvements, or a major change in work procedures.

These changes are usually perceived to be significant by employees, require long lead times, and consequently may have a long threat phase. Managerial ability to deal properly with the threat phase has a direct influence on both the nature and extent of resistance encountered. Involving professionals in change planning, being frank and honest about probable impact in answering questions, and not making misleading promises are important elements of the sound management of change.

B. Impact Phase

The second phase of change, which is commonly referred to as the impact phase, occurs when the organizational change is implemented. Often managers get through the threat phase without difficulty because the company has a good reputation for changes in the past or they have explained the nature of the change adequately. Once the change is introduced, however, serious problems may confront these managers. Why? Many times when professionals are actually trying a new process or building new work relationships, they find that it is actually more difficult than they first realized and they then begin resisting the change.

Also, employees may find that after the change is actually introduced, many of its aspects that they thought would be insignificant in the planning phase actually turn out to be much more threatening than was originally believed. This situation calls for appropriate managerial action designed to minimize the inefficiencies due to resistant behaviour by employees. Increased attention needs to be given to communication with professionals so their true problems with the change can be fully understood and resolved.

C. After-Effect Phase

The after-effect phase of change can involve resistance for several months, a year, or even longer after the change has apparently been introduced successfully. Employees sometimes accept the impact phase of change simply because it is a new stimulating activity that is different from their previous work assignments. Unfortunately, however, the newness wears off, and three or four months after a change has been introduced, workers may decide they prefer to have the "old way" back again.

Resistance in the form of poor workmanship, increased conflict, or lack of tolerance for fellow workers may occur. Thus, the change process is usually long term, particularly for larger changes. In fact, the after-effects phase may occur over a period of several years from the time the change is first contemplated until it has been fully integrated and accepted into the organization. Due to upward communication barriers, employees may not tell their managers the real problem.

Since these managers do not associate sloppy effort or declining morale with a change made several months earlier, it is not surprising that the after-effect phase can be the most troublesome and difficult to resolve. When a change in subordinate effectiveness occurs for no apparent reason, the manager should seek an answer to the following question: *Have any significant changes been made during the past two years that could be influencing my subordinates negatively?* If the answer is yes, practicing communication skills can be helpful in resolving the problem.

CAUSES OF RESISTANCE TO CHANGE

A common cause of resistance in the professional environment is *fear,* specifically, fear of what the change will do to the individuals that have to work with the change.

Managerial action that increases understanding reduces fear and increases acceptance. As was seen in the case involving office window location, changes that are perceived by professionals to lower their social status in the organization tend to be resisted. Feelings of self-worth are often influenced by subtle changes and employees vehemently resist changes that threaten their self-worth.

The method used by specific managers in introducing changes can have as much of an impact on employee perceptions of self-worth as the changes themselves. It is also true that employees may have a genuine concern and feeling of *insecurity*, which occupies their minds when changes take place that cause the environment to appear unstable. Under these circumstances, employees often do not fully realize the impact of their reaction on those around them.

Methods that provide consideration of employee feelings are very helpful in minimizing these kinds of perception problems. As previously discussed, since professionals have a large personal investment in their training, they may be even more concerned than nonprofessionals about proposed changes. Questions often asked by professionals in these cases are as follows:

How will these changes affect my ability to use my specialized training and acquired skill?

How will these changes influence organizational attitudes concerning the importance of my work or profession?

How will these changes impact on my promotional opportunities? What about professional growth and new learning?

Will new changes increase formalization and inflexibility around my job?

Changes that upset valued *social relationships* tend to be resisted. Social needs are often very strong, and when changes are made that upset social relationships and frustrate these needs, they will be resisted. Employee needs for *security* are also strong. When changes are made that are perceived to be threatening either to an employee's physical or economic security, they will be resisted.

Managers should ask themselves the following questions before an attempt is made to integrate change in work environment: What will this change do to (1) the status of the professionals affected by the change, (2) the social relationships of the professionals affected by the change, and (3) the economic and physical security of the employees? If the change has a negative impact on any one of these three variables, then management can predict with a high degree of certainty that these changes will be resisted.

Managers of technical and staff professionals such as engineers and health specialists often overlook the psychological effects of change that appear to be logical and are unprepared for the resistance that follows. In addition, studies have shown that technical specialists often resist changes that do not originate in their own departments. Apparently, these specialists view originating ideas as an index of departmental status and strive to protect the status image of their departments by rejecting outside ideas.

This rejection can be troublesome because it usually is not based on the true value of the proposal. Successful managers will attempt to minimize this resistance either by eliminating its cause or by minimizing its importance to the employees. Emphasizing the value of cooperation with outside individuals and units to the ultimate well being of the professional group can be helpful in stimulating greater acceptance of outside ideas and proposals.

Change can be considered from two points of view, namely, the change agent or manager who implements the change and the people (professional subordinates) affected by the change. Much of the practical and theoretical emphasis has been focused on change agents and how they may best implement proposed changes. The implicit assumption often is that employees have little capability to accept or express positive responses toward planned change. This assumption may cause managers to anticipate resistance from employees which may lead to resistant behaviour that would not ordinarily occur. Specifically, managers may focus so strongly on probable resistance that employees respond as they feel they are expected to, namely, to resist the proposed change. These managerial assumptions are often both unwise and unwarranted particularly in professional work units.

TECHNIQUES FOR REDUCING RESISTANCE

Considerable attention has been directed toward proper ways of introducing change so that resistance is overcome. Many of these techniques have proven value in the professional environment. Often fear of loss in status, security, or destruction of social relationships are imaginary. In these cases, introducing employee participation into the change process can be vital in reducing resistance to the change. Democratic leadership is helpful for managers when these kinds of situations are present.

Resistance to change can be reduced if the manager can "sell through participation" the idea that employees will be better off as a result of making the change. Unless the forces for acceptance are clearly greater than those for resistance, the probability of employees resisting the change is high. The extent and direction of these forces are determined by several variables. The more important of these are the manager, organizational climate, work group attitudes, employee value systems, and the change itself.

The manager can often use participation among professionals to impact favourably on enough of these variables so these employees perceive that a net gain will result from making the change. If the manager is successful with participation, the forces favouring the change would exceed the forces against the change, and resistance will be alleviated as a managerial problem. In fact, participation may be both useful and necessary in implementing change in professional environments.

The process of gaining employee acceptance often involves creating a "we" attitude in making changes. This attitude can result from employee involvement through democratic management. Ideally, employees should feel that part of the substance of the change is their own idea. This is not as difficult as it may at first sound, because managerially promoted changes are usually desirable for the organization, and as the organization benefits, more rewards are available to the individual employee.

Many times it is clear that a change is going to yield direct benefits to professionals (e.g., create better research facilities, new learning opportunities, more pleasant working conditions, or modernized technology). In these instances participation effectively reduces employee resistance, because the improved understanding increases the strength of the forces for acceptance. Resistant employee attitudes do not automatically yield resistant behaviour because attitudes of colleagues and the overall work group often keep employees from expressing their true feelings (peer pressure).

Managers that can convince informal group leaders of the need for proposed changes can minimize the impact of resistant attitudes by specific employees. Professionals are unlikely to exhibit resistant behaviour if it is not supported by the group in which membership is valued. Cohesive work groups can exercise great control over the expression of individual employee attitudes. In effect one of the strongest "we" attitudes that is potentially available to managers of professionals consists of the development of a favourable overall group attitude toward proposed changes.

Creating a "we" attitude involves the willingness to compromise on the part of management. For example, a manager discusses with a group of professionals the idea of introducing new technology into the work process and meets with some resistance such as a suggestion from the group that one piece of equipment should not be purchased as previously planned. This suggestion should be honored if practical.

The "we" attitude emerges when the manager responds positively to these kinds of requests, because the manager is perceived to be both responsive and supportive through this sincere compromise effort and the professional subordinates see that they are impacting on the change process. Conversely, the manager who invites his subordinates in for suggestions on change and gets several suggestions for correction and modification but ignores them loses both credibility and the valuable "we" attitude.

Several research studies including the classic Coch and French study of the late 1940s support the fact that change by decree is likely to meet with a great deal of resistance. Coch and French had changes introduced by three possible methods in a manufacturing environment as follows: First, a group of subordinates were involved in the change on a total participation basis.

Second, employees selected representatives from their group to meet with management and discuss the change. Third, the changes were introduced by decree or with no participation. In surveying the results of the three particular methods, these researchers found that there was less resistance exhibited by the group that experienced total participation.

Apparently, a "we" attitude ensured which had beneficial effects. Introducing change by decree caused the most resistance among the three methods. Autocratic change usually destroys the "we" attitude and unless the change is clearly seen as favourable, employees will resist it.

A. Reasons for Failure

Kotter identified the following eight errors that are common causes for failure of organizational change.

1. Allowing too much complacency.
2. Failing to create a sufficiently powerful coalition.
3. Underestimating the power of vision.
4. Undercommunicating the vision by a factor of 10, or 100, or even 1,000.

5. Permitting obstacles to block the new vision.
6. Failing to create short-term wins.
7. Declaring victory too soon.
8. Neglecting to anchor changes firmly in the corporate culture.

Kotter states "Making any of the eight errors can have serious consequences of slowing down new initiatives, creating unnecessary resistance, frustrating employees endlessly, and sometimes completely stifling needed change."

ORGANIZATIONAL CRISES AND CUTBACK MANAGEMENT

Although many managers fail to plan for it and naturally avoid negative thinking, an increasing part of today's organizational life involves crises situations which include work force reductions among professional employee groups. One of the most frequent aspects of the change process is the occurrence of crisis situations.

Crises often occur because managers fail to identify the need for change or do not implement changes in a timely fashion. Slatter has identified four stages of crisis development and typical management response patterns as follows:

1. *Hidden crises.*. In this stage managers are unaware of emerging major problems, and the need to implement changes.
2. *Crisis denial.* During this stage there are visible signs of crisis within the firm, but managers are unwilling to change. They often suggest changes that have already been implemented or state that existing problems are beyond their control or will be solved without any change. Thus, need for action is denied. Managers may sincerely believe that they are on the correct path or they may feel they are taking a position necessary for self-preservation. According to Slatter, managers often believe they will be blamed and may lose their jobs if previous actions are found

to be wrong. Also, strategic change usually involves alterations in the management power structure, and managers who currently hold power are likely to resist needed change. Managers may take action to make the firm's financial position look better than it really is.

3. *Organizational disintegration.* Since needed changes are not being implemented, the organization exhibits serious problems. While some change is likely to occur, it is often too little and too late. Existing decisions makers become more autocratic, and the full and impartial assessment of alternatives does not occur.

4. *Organizational collapse.* This stage is characterized by partial or total organizational failure. Effective decision making decreases and commitment to organizational goals declines. Managers become even more self-oriented and the mobile employees leave the firm.

Slatter suggests that the earlier the developing crisis is confronted, the less dramatic organizational change is necessary and the greater the chance of successful turnaround. While some managerial action may occur during the "hidden crisis" stage, more often the crisis precipitates the needed changes.

The presence of severe crises causes top management or board of directors to lose confidence in existing leadership. This can lead to replacement of top executives, which increases the probability of successful changes and turnaround for the firm. Once a firm's organization starts to disintegrate, a new chief executive is necessary to bring about a complete change in organizational structure.

Replacement at the top management level is consistent with the need for transformational leadership identified earlier in this chapter. Replacement of personnel at any level is one of the common and effective ways to implement change. While replacement is not necessarily practical in many cases, removal of professionals with negative attitudes is likely to be very effective.

The message to managers in the professional environment is to keep communications channels open both ways. Keep attuned to problems as well as successes. Try to uncover potential crises at the hidden stage and don't allow movement to crisis denial. In fact, crisis denial is a self-defeating position that wills likely lead to both personal and organizational failure. Changes may be needed that involve transfer, layoff, or dismissal of professionals. These kinds of organizational changes are often inappropriate for participation and subordinate involvement.

For example, when a manager is faced with decisions involving employee layoffs (staff reductions) or disciplinary action against specific employees, it is usually not fair or useful to involve subordinates in these sensitive matters. In simple terms, increasing understanding and involvement through participation will not increase the forces for acceptance of these kinds of changes. It is often helpful, however, to obtain employee participation in the formulation of policies guiding layoff or disciplinary procedures prior to implementation.

THE TASK FORCE CONCEPT

Major changes in the professional environment can often be integrated effectively with the use of the task force. This concept simply involves appointing a group of key subordinates and managers to study problems where changes are needed and to recommend the nature and content of changes to be made. Three important steps are necessary in making task forces work.

First, select key group leaders for the task force. These employees should have the respect and support of their co-workers, and should have proven performance records. Second, use democratic techniques in managing the task force so all members will become involved and committed.

Third, once the task force makes a recommendation for change, allow it to continue as a unit to play a key role in implementation and follow-up. The positive results from following these steps will be that major changes are often integrated effectively into the organization with a minimum of conflict.

Obviously, the change must be of significant size and impact so that the cost of formulating and operating the task force will be worthwhile. Many changes that involve new technologies, work procedures, or product lines or services (where the focus of employee activities must be changed), are particularly suited for task force assignment. If the task force is formed early during major changes, especially when the change is initially contemplated, the threat phase of the change is usually minimized or eliminated.

The task force can gather data, field questions, and solicit input so that employees understand and become more involved in what is going to be done. This involvement is particularly important to professional employees because their expertise can make an important contribution to a proposed change. In addition to cutback management and cases involving disciplinary action, there are other changes that, no matter how much participation is involved, the professional employee cannot see that an improved personal position will result from making the change. In these situations there are two avenues to managers.

One is to use other compensating factors to offset the professional's perceived negative impact of the change. Some possible compensating factors are discussed. First, increase the *level of pay* to the employees affected and thereby reduces their dissatisfaction; second, increase the amount of *fringe benefits* or privileges such as travel opportunities or vacation time; and third, make changes in the physical environment, such as improved facilities or adding to support staff.

The amount of control the manager has over many of the above factors varies greatly from one organization to another and within a given firm. However, managers usually have some influence on one or more of these areas (often more than they realize), and the important point is to use it wisely.

Compensating for the negative aspects of the change by increasing some of the hygiene factors or improving intrinsic job design is useful in offsetting negative attitudes about given changes. This approach costs money, and the cost must be weighed against the benefits received. The key question for the manager to ask is: *Will the costs of resistance outweigh the costs of providing these extra compensatory factors?* A positive or negative answer should determine the course of action.

A second approach to reducing resistance when change is perceived negatively and participation is not working is to introduce change on a tentative basis. When making changes on a tentative basis, technical managers should obtain employee agreement to try the changes, but if the changes turn out to be disruptive and dissatisfying, they also collectively agree to withdraw the change. If the tentative change concept is to succeed, managers must be able to reverse decisions regarding change.

Consequently, if a change is made that management does not believe is reversible, it should not be made on a tentative basis. Both personal and managerial integrity is at stake in the change process, and to agree to do things and then not follow through reduces managerial effectiveness. Also, managers should not agree to make changes with employees that are impossible or make other promises simply made to get acceptance of a change.

Professionals will not respect a manager that says one thing and does another. Even proven methods of introducing change such as participation should not be undertaken unless the manager values participation and intends to utilize the input provided by the subordinates. The change situation should be analyzed carefully by the manager before changes are made, and then one of the particular approaches outlined in his chapter may be applied.

If all desirable changes were readily accepted, resistance would not be a problem. Unfortunately, change is often resisted which results in increased costs as well as causing managers both psychological and technological problems of adjustment. Over the next several years many changes will occur in most organizations. Some will be small, but others will be of great magnitude. While some will be planned, others will be surprises. Managers need to pave the way for employee acceptance of these changes, because they are needed if American firms are to survive and prosper in globally competitive markets. Professionals within the firm are likely to be the major contributors of new ideas that emerge in American business. These ideas, which are vital ingredients for most firms, may make the difference between success and failure.

Specific change introduction techniques and the application of other methods to reduce resistance as developed in this chapter will be increasingly important components of the successful professional work environment.

The more important points are summarized below:

1. Effectively handling planned strategic change may be the key to survival for many American firms.
2. Managers of professionals need to be strong leaders who play a "transforming role" and are "path finders" for their units.
3. While some characteristics of professionals suggest they are more likely to accept change than nonprofessionals, in several instances these same characteristics may lead to even stronger resistance.
4. Changes are not automatically resisted, but employees must perceive there are distinct advantages to making a change in order to avoid resistant behaviour.
5. Since resistant attitudes by individual employees do not necessarily lead to resistant behaviour because of environmental pressures, it is important for managers to work with group leadership in order to overcome specific employee resistances. If employees value their group relationships, which is common among professionals, they will be reluctant to resist

changes that have overall group support. Informal group leadership can be an important ally of management in making changes.

6. The extent of employees' trust in management coupled with their own sense of security impacts strongly on acceptance or rejection of change.
7. Resistance to change can occur during any one of three specific phases of the change process.
8. Changes that are not understood often become clouded by employee perceptions of fear and uncertainty, which lead directly to resistant behaviour.
9. Changes that threaten job skills or are perceived to impact negatively on job content or status factors important to the professional staff are likely to result in resistant behaviour.
10. While participation in the change process is one of the most useful ways of reducing resistance, there are several types of change problems where it is ineffective. Management's provision for additional remuneration or making the change tentative can help reduce resistance when participation is not enough. In cases involving cutback management, employee involvement may be dysfunctional and inappropriate.
11. The task force concept is an important vehicle for implementing change.
12. Managers should support promises with action, because management credibility is an important factor in determining the nature and extent of resistance among professionals.

A. Case Study for Organizational Change

Given the present and likely future business climate, the ability of an organization to initiate and implement change is of major importance. The need for effective change to incorporate new technology, new employees, new products and services, new management techniques, and new reward and performance motivation programmes, is a reality of corporate life.

This chapter has discussed the nature of change including the three phases, identified the causes of resistance, and provided methods to reduce resistance to change along with a few supporting theories and useful change practices. All of these points concerning the organizational change process are vividly presented in a sad but true case study.

The reader will be well rewarded for expending the time to review the case study of MIDWEST Consulting Architects & Engineers, a work group of highly skilled professionals with somewhat questionable leadership.

Chapter 2

Hotel and Motel Staffing

PRELUDE TO STAFFING

Staffing is the third sequential function of management. Up until now the executive housekeeper has been concerned with planning and organizing the housekeeping department for the impending opening and operations. Now the executive housekeeper must think about hiring employees within sufficient time to ensure that three of the activities of staffing—selection (including interviewing), orientation, and training—may be completed before opening. Staffing will be a major task of the last two weeks before opening.

The development of the Area Responsibility Plan and the House Breakout Plan before opening led to preparation of the Department Staffing Guide, which will be a major tool in determining the need for employees in various categories. The housekeeping manager and laundry manager should now be on board and assisting in the development of various job descriptions. The hotel human resources department would also have been preparing for the hiring event.

They would have advertised a mass hiring for all categories of personnel to begin on a certain date about two weeks before opening. Even though this chapter reflects a continuation of the executive housekeeper's planning for opening operations, the techniques described apply to any ongoing operation, except that the magnitude of selection, orientation, and training activities will not be as intense. Also, the fourth activity—development of existing employees —is normally missing in opening operations but is highly visible in ongoing operations.

JOB SPECIFICATIONS

Job specifications should be written as job descriptions are prepared. Job specifications are simple statements of what the various incumbents to positions will be expected to do. An example of a job specification for a section housekeeper is as follows:

Job Specification—Example

Section Housekeeper (hotels) [often Guestroom Attendant —GRA] The incumbent will work as a member of a housekeeping team, cleaning and servicing for occupancy of approximately 18 hotel guestrooms each day. Work will generally include the tasks of bed making, vacuuming, dusting, and bathroom cleaning.

Incumbent will also be expected to maintain equipment provided for work and load housekeeper's cart before the end of each day's operation. Section housekeepers must be willing to work their share of weekends and be dependable in coming to work each day scheduled. [Any special qualifications, such as ability to speak a foreign language, might also be listed.]

Employee Requisition

Once job specifications have been developed for every position, employee requisitions are prepared for first hirings (and for any follow-up needs for the human resources department). Note the designation as to whether the requisition is for a new or a replacement position and the number of employees required for a specific requisition number. The human resources department will advertise, take applications, and screen to fill each requisition by number until all positions are filled.

For example, the first requisition for GRAs may be for 20 GRAs. The human resources department will continue to advertise for, take applications, and screen employees for the housekeeping department and will provide candidates for interview by department managers until 20 GRAs are hired. Should any be hired and require replacing, a new employee requisition will be required.

Staffing Housekeeping Positions

There are several activities involved in staffing a housekeeping operation. Executive housekeepers must select and interview employees, participate in an orientation programme, train newly hired employees, and develop employees for future growth. Each of these activities will now be discussed.

Selecting Employees

Each area of the United States has its own demographic situations that affect the availability of suitable employees for involvement in housekeeping or environmental service operations. For example, in one area, an exceptionally high response rate from people seeking food service work may occur and a low response rate from people seeking housekeeping positions may occur. In another area, the reverse may be true, and people interested in housekeeping work may far outnumber those interested in food service.

Surveys among hotels or hospitals in your area will indicate the best source for various classifications of employees. Advertising campaigns that will reach these employees are the best method of locating suitable people. Major classified ads associated with mass hirings will specify the need for food service personnel, front desk clerks, food servers, housekeeping personnel, and maintenance people. Such ads may yield surprising results.

If aliens are hired, the department manager must take great care to ensure that they are legal residents of this country and that their green cards are valid. More than one hotel department manager has had an entire staff swept away by the Department of Immigration after hiring people who were illegal aliens. Such unfortunate action has required the immediate assistance of all available employees (including management) to fill in.

Processing Applicants

Whether you are involved in a mass hiring or in the recruiting of a single employee, a systematic and courteous procedure for processing applicants is essential. For example, in the opening of the Los Angeles Airport Marriott, 11,000 applicants were processed to fill approximately 850 positions in a period of about two weeks. The magnitude of such an operation required a near assembly-line technique, but a personable and positive experience for the applicants still had to be maintained.

The efficient handling of lines of employees, courteous attendance, personal concern for employee desires, and reference to suitable departments for those unfamiliar with what the hotel or hospital has to offer all become earmarks for how the company will treat its employees. The key to proper handling of applicants is the use of a control system whereby employees are conducted through the steps of application, prescreening, and if qualified, reference to a department for interview.

Note the opportunity for employees to express their desires for a specific type of employment. Even though an employee may desire involvement in one classification of work, he or she may be hired for employment in a different department. Also, employees might not be aware of the possibilities available in a particular department at the time of application or may be unable to locate in desired departments at the time of mass hirings.

Employees who perform well should therefore be given the opportunity to transfer to other departments when the opportunities arise. According to laws regulated by federal and state Fair Employment Practices Agencies (FEPA), no person may be denied the opportunity to submit application for employment for a position of his or her choosing.

Not only is the law strict on this point, but companies in any way benefiting from interstate commerce (such as hotels and hospitals) may not discriminate in the hiring of people based on race, colour, national origin, or religious preference. Although specific hours and days of the week may be specified, it is a generally accepted fact that hotels and hospitals must maintain personnel operations that provide the opportunity for people to submit applications without prejudice.

Prescreening Applicants

The prescreening interview is a staff function normally provided to all hotel or hospital departments by the *human resources* section of the organization. Prescreening is a preliminary interview process in which unqualified applicants—those applicants who do not meet the criteria for a job as specified in the job specification–special qualifications—are selected (or screened) out.

For example, an applicant for a secretarial job that requires the incumbent to take shorthand and be able to type 60 words a minute may be screened out if the applicant is not able to pass a relevant typing and shorthand test.

If a candidate is screened out by the personnel section, he or she should be told the reason immediately and thanked for applying for employment. Applicants who are not screened out should either be referred to a specific department for interview or, if all immediate positions are filled, have their applications placed in a department pending file for future reference. All applicants should be told that hiring decisions will be made by individual department managers based on the best qualifications from among those interviewed.

A suggested agenda for a prescreening interview is as follows:

1. The initial contact should be cordial and helpful. Many employees are lost at this stage because of inefficient systems established for handling applicants.
2. During the prescreening interview, try to determine what the employee is seeking, whether such a position is available, or, if not, when such a position might become available.

3. Review the work history as stated on the application to determine whether the applicant meets the obvious physical and mental qualifications, as well as important human qualifications such as emotional stability, personality, honesty, integrity, and reliability.

4. Do not waste time if the applicant is obviously not qualified or if no immediate position is available. When potential vacancies or a backlog of applicants exists, inform the candidate. Be efficient in stating this to the applicant. Always make sure that the applicant gives you a phone number in order that he or she may be called at some future date. Because most applicants seeking employment are actively seeking immediate work, applications more than 30 days old are usually worthless.

5. If at all possible, an immediate interview by the department manager should be held after screening. If this is not possible, a definite appointment should be made for the candidate's interview as soon as possible.

An interview should be conducted by a manager of the department to which the applicant has been referred. In ongoing operations, it is often wise to also allow the supervisor for whom the new employee will work to visit with the candidate in order that the supervisor may gain a feel for how it would be to work together.

The supervisor's view should be considered, since a harmonious relationship at the working level is important. Although the acceptance of an employee remains a prerogative of management, it would be unwise to accept an employee into a position when the supervisor has reservations about the applicant. Certain personal characteristics should be explored when interviewing an employee.

Some of these characteristics are native skills, stability, reliability, experience, attitude toward employment, personality, physical traits, stamina, age, sex, education, previous training, initiative, alertness, appearance, and personal cleanliness.

Although employers may not discriminate against race, sex, age, religion, and nationality, overall considerations may involve the capability to lift heavy objects, enter men's or women's restrooms, and so on. In a housekeeping (or environmental services) department, people should be employed who find enjoyment in housework at home. Remember that character and personality cannot be completely judged from a person's appearance.

Also, it should be expected that a person's appearance will never be better than when that person is applying for a job. Letters of recommendation and references should be carefully considered. Seldom will a letter of recommendation be adverse, whereas a telephone call might be most revealing. If it were necessary to select the most important step in the selection process, interviewing would be it. Interviewing is *the* step that separates those who will be employed from those who will not.

Poor interviewing techniques can make the process more difficult and may produce a result that can be both frustrating and damaging for both parties. In addition, inadequate interviewing will result in gaining incorrect information, being confused about what has been said, suppression of information, and, in some circumstances, complete withdrawal from the process by the candidate.

The following is a well-accepted list of the steps for a successful interview process.

1. *Be prepared*: Have a checklist of significant questions ready to ask the candidate. Such questions may be prepared from the body of the job description. This preparation will allow the interviewer to assume the initiative in the interview.
2. *Find a proper place to conduct the interview*: The applicant should be made to feel comfortable. The interview should be conducted in a quiet, relaxing

atmosphere where there is privacy that will bring about a confidential conversation.

3. *Practice:* People who conduct interviews should practice interviewing skills periodically. Several managers may get together and discuss interviewing techniques that are to be used.
4. *Be tactful and courteous:* Put the applicant at ease, but also control the discussion and lead to important questions.
5. *Be knowledgeable:* Be thoroughly familiar with the position for which the applicant is interviewing in order that all of the applicant's questions may be answered. Also, have a significant background knowledge in order that general information about the company may be given.
6. *Listen:* Encourage the applicant to talk. This may be done by asking questions that are not likely to be answered by a yes or no. If people are comfortable and are asked questions about themselves, they will usually speak freely and give information that specific questions will not always bring out. Applicants will usually talk if there is a feeling that they are not being misunderstood.
7. *Observe*: Much can be learned about an applicant just by observing reactions to questions, attitudes about work, and, specifically, attitudes about providing service to others. Observation is a vital step in the interviewing process.

Perhaps of equal importance to the interviewing technique are the following pitfalls, which should be avoided while interviewing.

1. Having a feeling that the employee will be just right based on a few outstanding characteristics rather than on the sum of all characteristics noted.
2. Being influenced by neatness, grooming, expensive clothes, and an extroverted personality—none of

which has much to do with housekeeping competency.

3. Overgeneralizing, whereby interviewers assume too much from a single remark (for instance, an applicant's assurance that he or she "really wants to work").
4. Hiring the "boomer," that is, the person who always wants to work in a new property; unfortunately, this type of person changes jobs whenever a new property opens.
5. Projecting your own background and social status into the job requirement. Which school the applicant attended or whether the applicant has the "proper look" is beside the point. It is job performance that is going to count.
6. Confusing strengths with weaknesses, and vice versa. What is construed by one person to be overaggressiveness might be interpreted by another as confidence, ambition, and potential for leadership, the last two traits being in chronic short supply in most housekeeping departments. These are the very characteristics that make it possible for management to promote from within and develop new supervisors and managers.
7. Being impressed by a smooth talker—or the reverse: assuming that silence reflects strength and wisdom. The interviewer should concentrate on what the applicant is saying rather than on how it is being said, then decide whether his or her personality will fit into the organization.
8. Being tempted by overqualified applicants. People with experience and education that far exceed the job requirements may be unable for some reason to get jobs commensurate with their backgrounds.

Even if such applicants are not concealing skeletons in the closet, they still tend to become frustrated and dissatisfied with jobs far below their level of abilities. The application of the techniques and avoidance of the pitfalls will be valuable tools in the selection of competent personnel for the housekeeping and environmental service departments.

For many years, the approach of many managers was to write a job description and then fill it by attempting to find the perfect person. This approach may overlook many qualified people, such as disadvantaged people or slow learners. Job descriptions may be analyzed in two ways when filling positions: (1) what is actually required to do the work, and (2) what is desirable. Is the ability to read or write really necessary for the job? Is the ability to learn quickly really necessary?

A person who does not read or write or who is a slow learner can be trained and can make an excellent employee. True, it may take additional time, but the reward will be a loyal employee as well as less turnover. It has been proven many times that those who are disadvantaged or slightly retarded, once trained, will perform consistently well for longer periods. There are agencies who seek out companies that will try to hire such people.

If the results of an interview are negative and rejection is indicated, the candidate should be informed as soon as possible. A pleasant statement, such as "Others interviewed appear to be more qualified," is usually sufficient. This information can be handled in a straightforward and courteous manner and in such a way that the candidate will appreciate the time that has been taken during the interview.

When the results of the interview are positive, a statement indicating a favourable impression is most encouraging. However, no commitment should be made until a *reference check* has been conducted.

In many cases, reference checks are made only to verify that what has been said in the application and interview is in fact true. Many times applicants are reluctant to explain in detail why previous employment situations have come to an end. It is more important to hear the actual truth about a prior termination from the applicant than it is to hear that they simply have been terminated.

Reference checks, in order of desirability, are as follows:

1. Personal (face-to-face) meetings with previous employers are the least available but provide the most accurate information when they can be arranged.
2. Telephone discussions are the next best and most often used approach. For all positions, an in-depth conversation by telephone between the potential new manager and the prior manager is most desirable; otherwise a simple verification of data is sufficient to ensure honesty.
3. The least desirable reference is the written recommendation, because managers are extremely reluctant to state a frank and honest opinion that may later be used against them in court.

Applicants who are rated successful at an interview should be told that a check of their references will be conducted, and, pending favourable responses, they will be contacted by the personnel department within two days. Applicants who are currently employed normally ask that their current employer not be contacted for a reference check.

This request should be honored at all times. Applicants who are currently working usually want to give proper notice to their current employers. If the applicant chooses not to give notice, chances are no notice will be given at the time he or she leaves your hotel.

In some cases, the applicant gives notice and, upon doing so, is "cut loose" immediately. If such is the case, the applicant should be told to contact the department manager immediately in order that the employee may be put to work as soon as possible.

There is no perfect interviewer, interviewee, or resultant hiring or rejection decision in regard to an applicant. We can only hope to improve our interviewing skills in order that the greatest degree of success in employee retention can be obtained. The executive housekeeper should expect that 25 percent of initial hires into a housekeeping department will not be employed for more than three months. (This is primarily because the housekeeping skills are easily learned and the position is paid at or near minimum wage.)

Some new housekeeping departments have as much as a 75 percent turnover rate in the first three months of operation. Certainly this can be improved upon with adequate attention to the interviewing and selection processes. However, regardless of the outcome of the interview, the processing record should be properly endorsed and returned to the personnel department for processing.

A carefully planned, concerned, and informational orientation programme is significant to the first impressions that a new employee will have about the hospital or hotel in general and the housekeeping department in particular. Too often, a new employee is told where the work area and restroom are, given a cursory explanation of the job, then put to work. It is not uncommon to find managers putting employees to work who have not even been processed into the organization, an unfortunate situation that is usually discovered on payday when there is no paycheck for the new employee.

Such blatant disregard for the concerns of the employee can only lead to a poor perception of the company. A planned orientation programme will eliminate this type of activity and will bring the employee into the company with personal concern and with a greater possibility for a successful relationship. A good orientation programme is usually made up of four phases: employee acquisition, receipt of an employee's handbook, tour of the facility, and an orientation meeting.

Employee Acquisition

Once a person is accepted for employment, the applicant is told to report for work at a given time and place, and that place should be the personnel department. Preemployment procedures can take as much as one-half day, and department managers eager to start new employees to work should allow time for a proper employee acquisition into the organization.

At this time it should be ensured that the application is complete and any additional information pertaining to employment history that may be necessary to obtain the necessary work permits and credentials is on hand. Usually the security department records the entry of a new employee into the staff and provides instructions regarding use of employee entrances, removing parcels from the premises, and employee parking areas.

Application for work permits, and drug testing, will be scheduled where applicable. All documents required by the hotel's health and welfare insurer should be completed, and instructions should be given about immediately reporting accidents, no matter how slight, to supervisors.

The federal government requires that every employer submit a W-4 (withholding statement) for each employee on the payroll. The employee must complete this document and give it to the company. Mandatory deductions from pay should be explained (federal and state income tax and Social Security FICA), as should other deductions that may be required or desired. At this time, some form of personal action document is usually initiated for the new employee and is placed in the employee's permanent record.

Note the permanent information that will be carried on file. The PAF is serially numbered, is created from data stored on magnetic discs, and is maintained in the employee's personnel file. When a change has to be made, such as job title, marital status, or rate of pay, the PAF is retrieved from the employee's record, changes are made *under* the item to be changed, and the corrected PAF is used to change the data in the computer storage.

Once new information is stored, a new PAF is created and placed in the employee's record to await the next need for processing. A long-time employee might have many PAFs stored in the personnel file.

When either regular or special performance appraisals are given, the last (most current) PAF will be used to record the appraisal. These forms are usually found on the reverse side of the PAF. Since performance appraisals may signify a raise in pay, the appropriate pay increase information would be indicated on the front side of the PAF. All recordings on PAFs, whether on one side or both, require the submission of data, storage of information, and creation of a new PAF to be stored in the employee's record. The PAF and performance appraisal system should be thoroughly explained to the new employee, along with assignment of a payroll number.

The employer should also explain how and when the staff is paid and when the first paycheck may be expected. The new employee should be provided with a copy of the hotel or hospital employee's handbook and should be told to read it thoroughly.

Since the new housekeeping employee is not working just for the housekeeping department but is to become integrated as a member of the entire staff, reading this handbook is extremely important to ensure that proper instructions in the rules and regulations of the hotel are presented. The handbook should be developed in such a way as to inspire the new employee to become a fully participating member of the organization. Note the tone of the welcoming letter and the manner in which the rules and regulations are presented.

Familiarization Tour of the Facilities

Upon completion of the acquisition phase, a facility tour should be conducted for one or all new employees. For new facilities, access to the property should be gained within about one week before opening, and many new employees can be taken on a tour simultaneously. It is possible for employees to work in the hotel housekeeping department for years and never to have visited the showroom, dining rooms, ballrooms, or even the executive office areas. A tour of the complete facility melds employees into the total organization, and a complete informative tour should *never* be neglected.

For ongoing operations, after acquisition, the new employee may be turned over to a department supervisor, who becomes the tour director. An appreciation of the total involvement of each employee is strengthened when a facilities tour is complete and thorough If necessary, the property tour might be postponed until after the orientation meeting; however, the orientation activity of staffing is not complete until a property tour is conducted

The orientation meeting should not be conducted until the employee has had an opportunity to become at least partially familiar with the surroundings. After approximately two weeks, the employee will have many questions about experiences, the new job, training, and the rules and regulations listed in the Property and Department Handbooks. Employee orientation meetings that are scheduled too soon fail to answer many questions that will develop within the first two weeks of employment.

The meeting should be held in a comfortable setting, with refreshments provided. It is usually conducted by the director of human resources and is attended by as many of the facility managers as possible. Most certainly, the general manager or hospital administration members of the executive committee, the security director, and the new employees' department heads should attend. Each of these managers should have an opportunity to welcome the new employees and give them a chance to associate names with faces.

All managers and new employees should wear name tags. In orientation meetings, a brief history of the company and company goals should be presented. A planned orientation meeting should not be concluded without someone stressing the importance of each position. Every position must have a purpose behind it and is therefore important to the overall functioning of the facility.

An excellent statement of this philosophy was once offered by a general manager who said, "The person mopping a floor in the kitchen at 3:00 A.M. is just as valuable to this operation as I am – we just do different things." The orientation meeting should be scheduled to allow for many questions. And there should be someone in attendance who can answer *all of them.*

Although the new employee will be gaining confidence and security in the position as training ends and work is actually performed, informal orientation may continue for quite some time. The formal orientation, however, ends with the orientation meeting (although the facility tour may be conducted after the meeting).

Finally, it should be remembered that good orientation procedures lead to worker satisfaction and help quiet the anxieties and fears that a new employee may have. When a good orientation is neglected, the seeds of dissatisfaction are planted. The efficiency and economy with which any department will operate will depend on the ability of each member of the organization to do his or her job. Such ability will depend in part on past experiences, but more commonly it can be credited to the type and quality of training offered. Employees, regardless of past experiences, always need some degree of training before starting a new job.

Small institutions may try to avoid training by hiring people who are already trained in the general functions with which they will be involved. However, most institutions recognize the need for training that is specifically oriented toward the new experience, and will have a documented training programme. Some employers of housekeeping personnel find it easier to train completely unskilled and untrained personnel. In such cases, bad or undesirable practices do not have to be trained out of an employee.

Previous experience and education should, however, be analyzed and considered in the training of each new employee in order that efficiencies in training can be recognized. If an understanding of department standards and policies can be demonstrated by a new employee, that portion of training may be shortened or modified. However, skill and ability must be demonstrated before training can be altered. Finally, training is the best method to communicate the company's way of doing things, without which the new employee may do work contrary to company policy.

First training of a new employee actually starts with a continuation of *department* orientation. When a new employee is turned over to the housekeeping or environmental services department, orientation usually continues by familiarizing the employee with *department rules and regulations*. Many housekeeping departments have their own department employee handbooks. For an example, which contains the housekeeping department rules and regulations for Bally's Casino Resort in Las Vegas, Nevada? Compare this handbook with that of the generic handbook.

Although these handbooks are for completely different types of organizations, the substance of their publications is essentially the same; both are designed to familiarize each new employee with his or her surroundings. Handbooks should be written in such a way as to inspire employees to become team members, committed to company objectives.

Training may be defined as those activities that are designed to help an employee begin performing tasks for which he or she is hired or to help the employee improve performance in a job already assigned. The purpose of training is to enable an employee to begin an assigned job or to improve upon techniques already in use. In hotel or hospital housekeeping operations, there are three basic areas in which training activity should take place: skills, attitudes, and knowledge.

A sample list of skills in which a basic housekeeping employee must be trained follows:

1. *Bed making:* Specific techniques; company policy
2. *Vacuuming:* Techniques; use and care of equipment
3. *Dusting:* Techniques; use of products

4. *Window and mirror cleaning:* Techniques and products
5. *Setup awareness:* Room setups; what a properly serviced room should look like
6. *Bathroom cleaning:* Tub and toilet sanitation; appearance; methods of cleaning and results desired
7. *Daily routine:* An orderly procedure for the conduct of the day's work; daily communications
8. *Caring for and using equipment:* Housekeeper cart; loading
9. *Industrial safety:* Product use; guest safety; fire and other emergencies The best reference for the skills that require training is the job description for which the person is being trained.

Employees need guidance in their attitudes about the work that must be done. They need to be guided in their thinking about rooms that may present a unique problem in cleaning. Attitudes among section housekeepers need to be such that, occasionally, when rooms require extra effort to be brought back to standard, it is viewed as being a part of rendering service to the guest who paid to enjoy the room. Carol Mondesir, director of housekeeping, Sheraton Centre, Toronto, states that:

A hotel is meant to be enjoyed and, occasionally, the rooms are left quite messed up. However, as long as they're not vandalized, it's part of the territory. The whole idea of being in the hospitality business is to make the guest's stay as pleasant as possible. The rooms are there to be enjoyed. Positive relationships with various agencies and people also need to be developed.

The following is a list of areas in which attitude guidance is important:

1. The guest/patient
2. The department manager and immediate supervisor
3. A guestroom that is in a state of great disarray
4. The hotel and company

5. The uniform
6. Appearance
7. Personal hygiene

The most important task of the trainer is to prepare new employees to meet standards. With this aim in mind, sequence of performance in cleaning a guestroom is most important in order that efficiency in accomplishing day-to-day tasks may be developed. In addition, the *best method* of accomplishing a task should be presented to the new trainee. Once the task has been learned, the next thing is to meet standards, which may not necessarily mean doing the job the way the person has been trained.

Areas of knowledge in which the employee needs to be trained are as follows:

1. Thorough knowledge of the hotel layout; employee must be able to give directions and to tell the guest about the hotel, restaurants, and other facilities
2. Knowledge of employee rights and benefits
3. Understanding of grievance procedure
4. Knowing top managers by sight and by name

There is a need to conduct ongoing training for all employees, regardless of how long they have been members of the department. There are two instances when additional training is needed: (1) the purchase of new equipment, and (2) change in or unusual employee behaviour while on the job. When new equipment is purchased, employees need to know how the new equipment differs from present equipment, what new skills or knowledge are required to operate the equipment, who will need this knowledge, and when. New equipment may also require new attitudes about work habits.

Employee behaviour while on the job that is seen as an indicator for additional training may be divided into two categories: events that the manager witnesses and events that the manager is told about by the employees. Events that the manager witnesses that indicate a need for training are frequent employee absence, considerable spoilage of products, carelessness, a high rate of accidents, and resisting direction by supervisors. Events that the manager might be told about that indicate a need for training are that something doesn't work right (product isn't any good), something is dangerous to work with, something is making work harder.

Although training is vital for any organization to function at top efficiency, it is expensive. The money and man-hours expended must therefore be worth the investment. There must be a balance between the dollars spent training employees and the benefits of productivity and high-efficiency performance. A simple method of determining the need for training is to measure performance of workers: Find out what is going on at present on the job, and match this performance with what should be happening. The difference, if any, describes how much training is needed.

In conducting performance analysis, the following question should be asked: Could the employee do the job or task if his or her life depended on the result? If the employee *could not* do the job even if his or her life depended on the outcome, there is a deficiency of knowledge (DK). If the employee could have done the job if his or her life depended on the outcome, but did not, there is a deficiency of execution (DE). Some of the causes of deficiencies of execution include task interference, lack of feedback (employee doesn't know when the job is being performed correctly or incorrectly), and the balance of consequences (some employees like doing certain tasks better than others).

If either deficiency of knowledge or deficiency of execution exists, training must be conducted. The approach or the method of training may differ, however. Deficiencies of knowledge can be corrected by training the employee to do the job, then observing and correcting as necessary until the task is proficiently performed. Deficiency of execution is usually corrected by searching for the underlying cause of lack of performance, not by teaching the actual task.

There are numerous methods or ways to conduct training. Each method has its own advantages and disadvantages, which must be weighed in the light of benefits to be gained. Some methods are more expensive than others but are also more effective in terms of time required for comprehension and proficiency that must be developed. Several useful methods of training housekeeping personnel are listed and discussed.

Using on-the-job training (OJT), a technique in which "learning by doing" is the advantage, the instructor demonstrates the procedure and then watches the students perform it. With this technique, one instructor can handle several students. In housekeeping operations, the instructor is usually a GRA who is doing the instructing in the rooms that have been assigned for cleaning that day. The OJT method is not operationally productive until the student is proficient enough in the training tasks to absorb part of the operational load. With simulation training, a model room (unrented) is set up and used to train several employees.

Whereas OJT requires progress toward daily production of ready rooms, simulation requires that the model room not be rented. In addition, the trainer is not productive in cleaning ready rooms. The advantages of simulation training are that it allows the training process to be stopped, discussed, and repeated if necessary. Simulation is an excellent method, provided the trainer's time is paid for out of training funds, and clean room production is not necessary during the workday.

The coach-pupil method is similar to OJT except that each instructor has only one student (a one-to-one relationship). This method is desired, provided that there are enough qualified instructors to have several training units in progress at the same time.

The lecture method reaches the largest number of students per instructor. Practically all training programmes use this type of instruction for certain segments. Unfortunately, the lecture method can be the dullest training technique, and therefore requires instructors who are gifted in presentation capabilities. In addition, space for lectures may be difficult to obtain and may require special facilities.

The conference method of instruction is often referred to as workshop training. This technique involves a group of students who formulate ideas, do problem solving, and report on projects. The conference or workshop technique is excellent for supervisory training. When new products or equipment are being introduced, demonstrations are excellent. Many demonstrations may be conducted by vendors and purveyors as a part of the sale of equipment and products.

Difficulties may arise when language barriers exist. It is also important that no more information be presented than can be absorbed in a reasonable period of time; otherwise misunderstandings may arise. Many hotels use training aids in a conference room, or post messages on an employee bulletin board. Aside from the usual training aids such as chalkboards, bulletin boards, charts, graphs, and diagrams, photographs can supply clear and accurate references for how rooms should be set up, maids' carts loaded, and routines accomplished. Most housekeeping operations have films on guest contact and courtesy that may also be used in training.

Motion pictures speak directly to many people who may not understand proper procedures from reading about them. Many training techniques may be combined to develop a well-rounded training plan. It is possible to have two students sitting side by side in a classroom, with one being trained and the other being developed. Recall that the definition of training is preparing a person to do a job for which he or she is hired or to improve upon performance of a current job.

Development is preparing a person for advancement or to assume greater responsibility. The techniques are the same, but the end result is quite different.Whereas training begins after orientation of an employee who is hired to do a specific job, upon introduction of new equipment, or upon observation and communication with employees indicating a need for training, development begins with the identification of a specific employee who has shown potential for advancement. Training for promotion or to improve potential is in fact development and must always include a much neglected type of training –supervisory training. Many forms of developmental training may be given on the property; other forms might include sending candidates to schools and seminars.

Developmental training is associated primarily with supervisors and managerial development and may encompass many types of experiences. Note the various developmental tasks that the trainee must perform over a period of 12 months. Development of individuals within the organization looks to future potential and promotion of employees.

Specifically, those employees who demonstrate leadership potential should be developed through supervisory training for advancement to positions of greater responsibility. Unfortunately, many outstanding workers have their performance rewarded by promotion but are given no development training.

The excellent section housekeeper who is advanced to the position of senior housekeeper without the benefit of supervisory training is quickly seen to be unhappy and frustrated and may possibly become a loss to the department. It is therefore most essential that individual potential be developed in an orderly and systematic manner, or else this potential may never be recognized.

While undergoing managerial development student and management alike should not lose sight of the primary aim of the programme, which is the learning and potential development of the trainee, not departmental production. Even though there will be times that the trainee may be given specific responsibilities to oversee operations, clean guestrooms, or service public areas, advantage should not be taken of the trainee or the situation to the detriment of the development function.

Development of new growth in the trainee becomes difficult when the training instructor or coordinator is not only developing a new manager but is also being held responsible for the production of some aspect of housekeeping operations.

Whether you are conducting a training or a development programme, suitable records of training progress should be maintained both by the training supervisor and the student. Periodic evaluations of the student's progress should be conducted, and successful completion of the programme should be recognized. Public recognition of achievement will inspire the newly trained or developed employee to achieve standards of performance and to strive for advancement.

Once an employee is trained or developed and his or her satisfactory performance has been recognized and recorded, the person should perform satisfactorily to standards. Future performance may be based on beginning performance after training. If an employee's performance begins to fall short of standards and expectations, there has to be a reason other than lack of skills. The reason for unsatisfactory performance must then be sought out and addressed.

This type of follow-up is not possible unless suitable records of training and development are maintained and used for comparison. Although evaluation and performance appraisal for employees will occur as work progresses, it is not uncommon to find the design of systems for appraisal as part of organization and staffing functions. This is true because first appraisal and evaluation occurs during training, which is an activity of staffing.

Once trainees begin to have their performance appraised, the methods used will continue throughout employment. As a part of training, new employees should be told how, when, and by whom their performances will be evaluated, and should be advised that questions regarding their performance will be regularly answered. Initial employment should be probationary in nature, allowing the new employee to improve efficiency to where the designated number of rooms cleaned per day can be achieved in a probationary period (about three months).

Should a large number of employees be unable to achieve the standard within that time, the standard should be investigated. Should only one or two employees be unable to meet the standard of rooms cleaned per day, an evaluation of the employee in training should either reveal the reason why or indicate the employee as unsuitable for further retention.

An employee who, after suitable training, cannot meet a reasonable performance standard should not be allowed to continue employment. Similarly, an employee who has met required performance standards in the specified probationary period should be continued into regular employment status and thus achieve a reasonable degree of security in employment. Evaluation of personnel is an attempt to measure selected traits, characteristics, and productivity.

Unfortunately, evaluations are generally objective in nature, and raters are seldom trained in the art of subjective evaluation. Initiative, self-control, and leadership ability do not lend themselves to measurement; therefore such characteristics are estimated. How well they are estimated depends to a great extent on the person doing the estimating. Two raters using the same form and rating the same person will probably arrive at different conclusions.

Certain policies on the use of evaluations should be established so that they are understood by both the person doing the evaluating and the person being evaluated. These policies must be established and disseminated by management. In order to establish such policies, the following questions, among others, must be answered and communicated to all those involved in the evaluation: What will evaluations be used for? Will evaluations influence promotions, become a part of the employee's record, be used as periodic checks, or be used for counseling and guidance? What qualities are going to be evaluated? Who is going to be evaluated? Who will do the evaluating?

Reliable evaluations require careful planning and take considerable time, skill, and work. An evaluation must be understood by the employee. Evaluation should be used at the end of a probationary period, and the employee must understand at the beginning of the period that he or she will be observed and evaluated.

Each item, as well as what impact the evaluation will have on future employment, should be explained to the employee. People undergoing periodic evaluations, such as at the end of one year's employment, should also know why evaluations are being conducted and what may result from the evaluation. In both situations, the evaluation should be used for counseling and guidance so that performance may be improved upon or corrected if necessary.

Certainly, strong points should be pointed out. An employee should be made aware of good as well as not-so-good evaluations. Evaluations should be made for a purpose and not for the sake of an exercise. They should ultimately be used as management tools.

Evaluations should be developed to fit the policies of the particular institution using it and the particular position being evaluated. The same evaluation may not be suitable for every position. In certain locales, such as isolated resorts, hotels are tempted to use contract labour because the local market does not support the necessary number of workers, particularly in housekeeping.

Advocates of outsourcing are quick to point out the advantages of the practice. Scarce workers are provided to the property, and there is no need to provide expensive employee benefits. The entire staffing function is assumed by the contractor. There are no worries regarding recruiting, selecting, hiring, orienting, or even training the employees.

Merely issue them uniforms and send them off to clean rooms. Some employers may even be willing to relax their responsibilities regarding employment law such as immigration and naturalization requirements.

Management should never forget that once a contracted employee dons a company uniform, the guest believes (and has no reason not to) that person is an employee of the hotel. The guest also believes the hotel has made every reasonable effort to screen that person in the hiring process to ensure that he or she is of good moral character, who has the best interest of the guest at heart.

Unfortunately, there have been several incidents in which the outsourced employees did not quite have the best interest of the guest in their hearts. There have been more than a few cases in which outsourced workers were wanted felons who inflicted considerable bodily harm on guests during the performance of their duties.

A number of these incidents have resulted in lawsuits, with awards against the hotel in the millions of dollars. This author does not recommend outsourcing in housekeeping, and cautions operators who ignore this advice to keep their guard up and continue to meet their legal and ethical responsibilities regarding employees and employment law.

Staffing for both hospital and hotel housekeeping operations involves the activities of selecting, interviewing, orienting, training, and developing personnel to carry out specific functions in the organization for which they are hired. Each activity should be performed with consistency, dispatch, and individual concern for each employee brought into the organization.

Whereas the major presentation of staffing in this text has been developed for the model hotel where a mass hiring has been performed, each and every aspect of selecting, orienting, and training new employees applies equally to situations in which replacement employees (perhaps only one) are brought into the organization.

Job specifications are the documents that indicate qualifications, characteristics, and abilities inherently needed in applicants. The Employee Requisition is the instrument by which specific numbers and types of candidates for employment are sought by the personnel department for each of the operating departments.

The next step is interviewing, which should be done by people from various departments. Actual selection, however, should only be performed by the department manager for whom the employee will work. The employee acquisition phase is vital to the successful orientation of a new employee and should not be omitted.

Upon acquisition of the new employee, presentation of an Employee's Handbook is appropriate. This handbook should contain major company rules, procedures, and regulations, along with relevant facts for the employee. Orientation is the basis for allowing the new employee to become accustomed to new surroundings.

The quality of orientation will determine whether the new employee will feel secure in a new setting, and it will set the stage for the relationship that is to follow. As training begins, orientation continues but is now conducted by the specific department in which the new employee will work. There are several methods of training, each of which should be used so as to gain the best effect for the least cost.

Employee performance in training should be evaluated by methods similar to those used in evaluating operational performance that will follow. After new employees receive approximately 24 hours of on-the-job training in the cleaning of rooms, they should become productive and be able to clean a reasonable number of rooms (about 60 percent efficient).

Continued application of skills will develop greater productivity as the new employee spends each day working at the new skills. As preliminary training ends, orientation should be completed by ensuring that an employee orientation meeting and a tour of the entire facility has taken place.

Failure to complete an orientation or to provide sufficient training can plant the seeds of employee unrest, discontent, and possible failure of the employee's relationship with the company that might well have been prevented.

Whether conducting training or development, adequate records of employee progress should be maintained. Records of training that have been successfully completed establish a base for future performance appraisal.

Measurement of growth in skills and promotion potential may not be recalled if training records and evaluations are not initiated and continued. Employees have a right to expect evaluations, and usually consider objectively prepared statements about their performance a mark of management's caring about employees.

Chapter 3

Successfully Managing the Professional

THE CHALLENGE

In good economic times or in a severe economic downturn, or in peace or at war, good management skills are critical for the success of any organization. This is about management, but more importantly it is about managing a growing and vital part of American organizations, namely the professional employee. In addition, this book provides a concentrated overview of effective management practice for the person trained as a professional or knowledge worker (e.g., engineer, scientist, physician, or other health specialist), who is or suddenly finds himself or herself thrust into a managerial position. It is clear that professionally trained persons continue to present new and greater challenges to their bosses and organizations, and that many traditional management practices simply do not work.

In fact, incorrect "management knowledge" more often than not is worse than no knowledge at all. One can *not truly learn about management* by simply reading about the unique superstar manager, or the top most successful corporations, or while searching for excellence, or in one minute. The author believes that management skills are earned not given, thus it requires work and individual effort (an old-fashioned idea). This book was written in a most condensed form to minimize reading and study time.

Examples and theories are cited only when deemed essential for clear understanding or necessary reinforcement. It is important to remember that in addition to having correct knowledge about management, *success is only realized by the skillful application of that knowledge!*

The objective of this book is to provide management concepts and knowledge that can be used to manage professionals in such a way that organization effectiveness will be maximized. In order to establish a proper prospective for realizing this objective, management is and briefly reviews how management theory and thought has evolved over time.

Characteristics of the professional work environment will be identified as well as the unique problems of professionals in managerial roles. It is the author's contention that a large gap exists between the knowledge and application of management skills. Managers can make substantial contributions to the effectiveness of their organizations by concentrating and learning from selected management research and then making an ongoing effort to ensure proper application. Thus the link between theory and practice.

WHO IS A PROFESSIONAL?

During the past several decades the term professional has been used to characterize an increasing number of employees. In fact, many employees want to be considered "professionals" by their colleagues and co-workers. Years ago Mary Parker Follett defined a professional in strict terms as one who maintains loyalty to a code of ethics that transcends loyalty to the rest of the organization.

According to this strict usage of the term, very few employees would qualify as a professional. In more popular terms, professionals are likely to be defined as employees with specialized or technical education who utilize that knowledge in performing their regular work. John Naisbitt defined a professional as one who creates, processes, and distributes as his or her primary job. Under these two categorizations many organizations are staffed primarily by professionals. In fact, according to Naisbitt, the second largest group of workers in the United States is professional.

The demand for professionals (knowledge workers) has increased dramatically during recent years. Professional workers and managers are primarily "information people," who include lawyers, teachers, engineers, physicians, software developers, systems analysts, architects, accountants, librarians, newspaper reporters, social workers, nurses, and clergy.

Of this example group, the health professionals exhibit another dimension. In addition to being "information people," they also incorporate a fairly high level of physical work in their normal activities (i.e., they are usually subjected to both mental and physiological fatigue).

Many of today's professionals have a specific code of ethics and formalized licensing procedures. Examples are physicians, lawyers, accountants, nurses, school teachers, engineers, and members of the clergy. There are other specialized employee groups that may not have strict or formalized licensing procedures, but do assume many of the same characteristics as licensed professionals.

Some examples are various types of building trades people (some of whom are licensed), software developers, personnel administrators, and other groups that engage in specialized support activities within the organization. In fact, any attempt to comprise a comprehensive list of today's professionals becomes very voluminous.

Does managing professionals differ from non-professionals? In almost all cases this question should be answered affirmatively. Professionals as a group tend to have a strong sense of self-worth and often possess high mobility. Thus they put pressure on management to manage effectively. Effective management to the professional tends to follow modern human relations guidelines. They expect considerable freedom and autonomy in performing their work. Also, they expect and respond well to interesting and challenging assignments.

This book is concerned with the complex problem of managing professional employees in a way to obtain maximum productivity. Since perceptions determine reality, managers need to be both competent and perceived to be competent. These two occurrences are not always linked together. Since many professionals are often promoted into management positions, they must be prepared to face these managerial challenges (opportunities).

However, a large percentage of these employees have little or no management skills training and are often unprepared to function as an effective manager. This is designed to provide basic managerial skills to the professional newly appointed to a management position and focuses on professionals managing other professionals.

Several recent best-selling books have had a people management theme, and the trend clearly promotes managing and viewing employees as a highly valued human resource. In spite of all the literature on the subject, only traditional approaches are still practiced today by many managers. They often seem easier to apply but in reality do not obtain results for the professional work force.

THE CHARACTERISTICS OF PROFESSIONALS

As stressed throughout, professionals exhibit specific needs that place demands on their managers beyond that of normal supervision. Many of these needs are associated with autonomy, recognition and the desire for interesting work assignments and are common among all professionals. Some differences, however, can be observed when specific professional work environments are viewed more closely. In order to provide insight into these differences it is useful to briefly examine a few of the major types of professionals.

Often one of the major functions of this group is to provide directed creativity within the organization to develop new products, processes, and services. Successful management in this setting requires the establishment of a work climate that fosters free expression and encourages independent thought. Reward systems are needed that evaluate the methodology utilized to produce innovation as well as actual achievements. For example, scientists and engineers who engage in the conduct of experiments for development should be positively recognized even though their efforts do not always result in a meaningful end-product. Appraisal systems that recognize only the end results are not appropriate for this group.

These types of employees usually work best in an environment where managerial control over their work is minimized. Good managers of creative scientists and engineers concentrate their efforts in attaining high levels of support and removing obstacles to effective performance. This managerial climate results in high levels of motivation because good scientists and engineers tend to be high achievers and are almost always internally motivated.

Health professionals often work in a more credentials-oriented, status conscious environment than most other professionals. The elevated position that the physician has historically occupied in America adds complexity to this professional work environment. Physicians often need recognition of their superior status position for continued cooperative effort with other professional groups.

Problems that ensue when this recognition is not realized have increased in recent years with the upgrading of other professionals in the health field (e.g., nurses, laboratory specialists, and administrators). Consequently, effective managers in this environment should be skilled in conflict reduction techniques as well as understanding unique needs of each professional employee group they manage.

As previously mentioned, many health professionals such as nurses have both mental and physical demands in their normal work activities. Consequently, the manager must be sensitive to the needs of the knowledge worker as well as the needs of workers who perform jobs requiring a substantial amount of physical energy expenditure.

There are many kinds of staff specialists in every large organization. One example is the modern human resources personnel administrator. As with most other staff specialists, personnel directors must be particularly skilled at boundary spanning because their work permeates the entire organization. Also, the personnel administrator and other staff managers should strive to develop this skill among the other members of their support departments.

Today, more and more women are pursuing professional occupations. The professional woman is required to make several challenging and sometimes difficult decisions early in her career. The superwoman myth was exposed several years ago, and many professional women realize they cannot assume full responsibility for all traditional family roles in addition to growing career pressures.

Women professionals can maintain solid personal relationships and have well-adjusted families, but it may mean delaying child bearing and applying effective time-management techniques to personal life activities. There is a trend among working couples to postpone having children until their 30s in order to establish themselves in their profession, and to attain increased financial resources to improve their quality of life. In the context of the professional work environment, the following tips are offered to women attempting to move ahead:

1. Keep track of your organizational structure and top management changes, and try to identify and be visible to emerging leaders.
2. Keep most of your discussions at work confined to professional topics and avoid extended discussions of personal items.
3. Avoid negative informal evaluations of your managers. It is particularly undesirable to make enemies in high places.

4. Since most company-sponsored charitable campaigns involve, and are supported by, upper-level management, it is desirable to actively participate in them.
5. Maintain a conservative style of dress. Communicate a strong commitment through both behaviour and dress to both your firm and your profession.
6. Continually monitor your professional environment for opportunities for visibility, new learning opportunities, and promotion. If you're being passed over repeatedly in these important areas, it may be time for a career change.

It is clear from examining a few typical groups of professionals that managers in these work environments need greater managerial knowledge and skill than ever before. This need will likely intensify in the future.

It is usually a difficult transition when an employee is promoted from a doer to planner and organizer. This transition is often most difficult for the professional. An employee who has a large personal investment in academic and/or specialized training is likely to see the application of those acquired skills as the most vital part of their life.

When promoted into the management hierarchy, many of these employees tend to feel that their greatest contribution can still be made through the application of their acquired specialized skills. As a result, the greater portion of their work time is devoted to performing nonmanagerial tasks. Generally, when a manager does this, the organization suffers.

Managerial effectiveness is usually increased as more time is spent on managerial functions, particularly planning, organizing, and facilitating the work of their subordinates. New managers need to shift their work focus away from operative and technical activities and toward the development and application of current "state of the art" management skills. If the individual cannot do this, then he or she should not be a manager.

A. Personality and Managing Oneself

In discussing the knowledge economy, Peter Drucker stresses the importance of managing oneself. One of the keys to managing, and being managed, is to understand one's own personality and that of their superiors and co-workers. There are several aspects of a person's personality that are important in determining their best role in an organization. The first characteristic is understanding strengths of people, including one's own strengths. Another important aspect of individual performance is developing methods for getting things done. Once a successful method is found, it is important to apply that to all facets of business.

People must also identify whether they absorb information better through listening or reading. People also tend to learn in different ways. Some people need to write everything down, whereas others need to talk their way through new material. When working in teams or groups, it is important to know your co-workers so that information can be shared in a medium that can be understood by everyone involved. Other important factors in personality include personal values, finding a place of belonging within an organization, and deciding what types of accomplishments should be contributed by all parties involved.

B. Emotional Intelligence and Hard Work

Daniel Goleman has defined emotional intelligence as self-awareness, self-confidence, and self-control; commitment and integrity; the ability to communicate and influence; and to initiate and accept change. He feels that these competencies are at a premium in the present workforce. Many professionals lack emotional intelligence.

The higher up the leadership ladder one goes, the more vital all aspects of emotional intelligence become, and often determine who is hired and who is fired, and who is passed over and who is promoted. Goleman's research indicates that star performers stand out not only by personal achievement but by their capacity to work well on teams and with people.

The overall effect of emotional intelligence is maximizing group productivity.

The best manager profile while including emotional intelligence also includes intellectual ability and technical know-how to do the job. In addition, there is no substitute for hard work and knowing that you can be successful as a manager. Two individuals are briefly cited as examples of successful managers.

One is from industry and one is from the sports world. Lee Iococca, after his successful career at The Ford Motor Company and Chrysler, said, "I seized the opportunity, but I was no ninety-day wonder. It took me almost forty years of hard work." Nick Bollettieri, after coaching many successful world-ranked tennis players including Andre Agassi, Jim Courier, Boris Becker, Tommy Haas, Monica Seles, Mary Pierce, and Anna Kournikova, said "I know I am the best tennis coach in the world." He did this by years of hard work.

MANAGEMENT DEFINED

Management may be defined as the establishment and realization of goals through the cooperative efforts of all concerned persons. To further explain this definition, additional discussion is useful. The word "goals" usually implies the collective goals of the organization and certain personal goals of participating individuals. Both types of goal realization are required for organizational success. The terms cooperative effort implies that management must be able to obtain the cooperation of persons and direct their efforts toward goal realization.

Management must also be able to measure, evaluate, and control the efforts of all persons and functions within the organization. In addition to individuals within the organization, the term "concerned persons" means that management must be able to properly interface and benefit from individuals outside of the organization that bear influence on ultimate goal realization.

Indeed, management is complex in its structure and activities. It consists of people and physical things. Consequently, the key to successful management is obtaining the proper balance between the theory, principles, and practices of management and human behaviour in organizations. It may be said, the world is management.

Is management an art? Is management a science? Considerable opinion has been set forth concerning the answer to these questions without definitive agreement. An examination of the fundamentals of science and art will be helpful in the understanding of management.

Science relates to knowledge developed from experimentation conducted to determine underlying principles. Commonly, this development of knowledge involves physical experimentation or empirical observation to generate, classify, and analyze data, and formulate statistically valid conclusions. Years ago Berel son and Steiner summarized the important characteristics of science in the outline below:

1. The procedures are public: There is made available to the scientific community a minutely detailed description of the procedures and findings.
2. The definitions are precise: Each important term is clearly delineated, so that common meanings can be universally applied.
3. The data collecting is objective: Regardless of whether data confirm or refute hypotheses or personal preferences, they are accurately measured and treated without bias.
4. The findings must be replicative: Other scientists must be able to reproduce the study and reach the same finding before a hypothesis is generally accepted as validated.
5. The approach is systematic and cumulative: Ultimately the goal is to construct an organized system of verified propositions, a body of theory; individual research projects should be related to

existing theory to achieve an overall theoretical structure; new studies may be indicated by gaps or apparent inconsistencies among findings.

6. The purposes are explanation, understanding, and prediction: The growth of understanding and certainty, the decisions concerning control, creation, or change of conditions are applications of a science; they become part of the science only as they assist in meeting the six criteria discussed herein.

While it is unlikely that management will ever exactly match the characteristics of science, it appears that more science is being incorporated into the ongoing practice of management. A possible reason for this trend is the ever-increasing complexity of most business operations. The scientific approach helps solve management problems relating to productivity and quality enhancement, meeting environmental requirements, technology development, computerization, and cost control, just to mention a few.

Art is defined by Webster's dictionary as "skill in performance acquired by experience, study, or observation." By this definition, a large part of management can be classified as an art. Certainly it is true that managers are many times evaluated on their skill in performance and managers enhance that skill by experience, study, and observation.

It can be concluded that for most organizations, management today should be a combination of art and science. Management should be a mixture of scientific method and analytical techniques, integrated with intuition and judgment derived from experience. In most situations, this combination is necessary to effectively manage change constantly occurring within the organization.

MANAGEMENT THEORY AND THOUGHT

Management can be further explained and better understood by briefly reviewing the major theory and thought approaches developed over the past several decades. Practicing managers and researchers have developed their own views and ideas about management. In some cases overlap and similarity has occurred, causing reinforcement, while at other times a totally different concept was created. This development of different "schools" of management was apparent a number of years ago and has been summarized by Harold Koontz as follows:

There are the behaviourists...who see management as a complex of the interpersonal relationships and the basis of management theory the tentative tenets of the new and underdeveloped science of psychology. There are also those who see management theory as simply a manifestation of the institutional and cultural aspects of sociology. Still others, observing the central core of management is the decision making, branch in all directions from this core to encompass everything in organization life.

Then, there are mathematicians who think of management expressed in symbols and the omnipresent and ever revered model. But the entanglement of growth reaches its ultimate when the study of management is regarded as one of a number of systems and subsystems, with an understandable tendency for the researcher to be dissatisfied until he has encompassed the entire physical and cultural universe as a management system.

The subsections that follow summarize the thought and theory of the classic schools of management and cite a few authors that have substantially contributed to the history of management. It is interesting to note that several individuals initially trained in a professional specialty were among these early pioneers.

The first structured school of management theory and thought, defined as scientific management, evolved from the industrial revolution. An early developer of scientific management was Frederick W. Taylor (a mechanical engineer) in his work at Midvale Steel Company during the late nineteenth century. Taylor believed that management should define specific tasks for every worker to complete in a specified time, select the worker best suited for each task, and be concerned with worker motivation.

In short, he believed that management should solve problems with logical study and scientific research as opposed to relying on rules of thumb and trial and error methods. Indeed, Taylor was the father of scientific management.

A number of others worked to enlarge the practice of scientific management. Henry L. Gantt, an associate of Taylor, worked to improve the scheduling of manufacturing operations, and Frank B. and Lillian E. Gilbreth developed techniques for studying human motions and improving methods (micromotion study). In addition to time study and methods analysis, the early scientific management school fostered several useful and commonly accepted industrial practices including job evaluation, worker training, safety, and personnel and industrial relations.

The management process school, or functional management, treats management more as a profession than does probably any other school of management. This theory states that the basic management function is consistent and independent of the nature of the organization. The theory assumes that once the manager's functions have been defined, knowledge of practical methods of implementing these functions can be systemically observed, evaluated, and taught.

The beginning of functional management was initiated by a French engineer, Henry J. Fayol, who in 1861 published *Administration Industrielle et Generale.* This was not published in the United States until 1949. Based on his own career, Fayol observed that all industrial activities could be grouped into the following six major categories: technical, commercial, financial, security, accounting, and managerial.

The first five categories were relatively well known and encompassed the activities of manufacturing, buying, selling, and record keeping. Consequently, Fayol was most concerned with managerial activities and formulated a number of general principles relating to authority, responsibility, division of work, remuneration, centralization, discipline, and unity of command. A number of other authors helped structure functional management. These included Mooney and Reiley and Dennison for their work in organization, and Tead for his work in leadership.

Another early proponent of the management process theory, R.C. Davis proposed three organic functions of a manager as follows:

Planning: The exercise of creative thinking in the solution of business problems. It involves the determination of what is to be done, how and where it is to be done, and who will be responsible.

Organizing: The process of creating and maintaining the requisite conditions for the effective and economical execution of plans. These conditions are principally concerned with morale, organizational structure, procedure, and the various physical factors of performance.

Controlling: The regulation of business activities in accordance with the requirements of business plans. The control process includes three principal phases: (a) The assurance of proper performance as specified by the plan; (b) the coordination of effort in conformity with the requirement of the plan; and (c) the removal of interferences with proper execution of the plan.

The practice of scientific management during the 1920s and 1930s, while successful in fulfilling workers' economic needs, failed to consider psychological needs. Much of the early work in industrial psychology was based on a book by Lillian Gilbreth. The first major study to examine the psychological factors relating to worker productivity was the Hawthorne experiments conducted by Mayo and Roethlisberger.

The most interesting result of this study was that worker output increased no matter what change was made in physical condition (e.g., noise or lighting levels). The fact that the workers perceived they were a "select" group and were under observation caused increased output. In short, the psychological factors outweighed the actual physical environment considerations.

Human relations knowledge added to scientific management and functional management theories and thought, but there were still short-comings-lacking a more complete understanding of human behaviour. While the detailed topics relating to behaviour in organizations are discussed in later, a historical overview of the behavioural science school of management follows.

A number of persons have contributed to the early theory and thought of behaviour as it relates to management. These include Maslow, Bakke, Dalton, Stogdell, Likert, Sayles, Leavitt, Vroom, Herzberg, Argyris, McGregor, and Bennis. These behaviourists focus on the development of individual and group needs, and the interaction of these needs with the organizational environment. When this approach is integrated into the broader "socio-technical" system, it has become widely recognized as an important part of the effective management of professionals. One of the major purposes of this book is to provide managers with proven managerial and applied behavioural tools that will help increase the effectiveness of their organizational units. Bottom line, a good manager must produce results.

The social system approach views workers from a much less flexible viewpoint than the behavioural theorist. Whereas in behavioural science, motivation is contingent upon each worker's needs and aspirations, the social system theorist relates more to basic motivators relevant to the present culture.

The social system school looks at a corporation as basically an input-output model, with the employees working only when they feel the inducements received equal or outweigh their contributions. March and Simon and Simon and coworkers have outlined the major characteristics of an organization following the input-output model:

1. An organization is a system of interrelated social behaviours of a number of persons whom we shall call the participants in the organization.
2. Each participant and each group of participants receives from the organization inducements, in return for which he or she makes contributions to the organization.
3. Each participant will continue participation in an organization only so long as the inducements offered are as great or greater than the contributions he or she is asked to make.
4. The contributions provided by the various groups of participants are the source from which the organization manufactures the inducements offered to the participants.
5. Hence, an organization is "solvent"-and will continue in existence-only so long as contributions are sufficient to provide inducements in large enough measure to draw on these contributions.

The management science approach has also been defined as the mathematical school, the decision theory school, quantitative methods, and operations research. The modern day foundation for management science began during World War II when mathematical models were developed to solve problems relating to the management of war operations.

The mathematical school attempts to approach each management situation with a parallel mathematic model (either deterministic or probabilistic). The problem is then solved using the precise logical structure of mathematics. If the model does indeed match the business problem at hand and the computations can be completed, the mathematical approach has value. The wide spread use of computers throughout business and industry have increased the usefulness of this approach.

The decision-making process has probably received more attention than any other subject among management scientists.

Traditional decision theory stresses rational thinking, the acquisition of valid data, and quantitative models to arrive at a proper decision. Examples of different business situations may be developed to produce several alternate solutions to a particular problem. There is also an emphasis on objectivity in evaluating different alternatives. Management has borrowed the systems concept from the physical and natural sciences. This approach requires the interrelatedness of all activities within an organization. Norbert Weiner contributed much theory and thought to modern day systems concepts through his work in cybernetics.

The contingency approach came into being because of the individual shortcomings of previously developed schools of management. For example, the behavioural approach works well in many situations involving people problems, but it does not produce results in operations problems requiring the techniques of management science for solution. Similar statements could be made concerning the other management schools. The first authors to observe the need for a contingency approach included Woodward, Fiedler, and Lorsch and Lawrence. The contingency approach requires that the practice and application of management theory should be contingent upon the needs of a specific management situation.

Consequently, behavioural and scientific techniques should be applied along with selected principles and practices from each school or management to solve existing problems. The successful manager must have the ability to recognize which management approach to use in a given situation at a particular point in time.

The major thrust of this book is to familiarize today's professional with management skills that will help ensure personal success (and success for their organization) when they become new or are prospective managers. This is an important challenge because studies show that many technically trained people assume managerial positions within ten years after their first career job assignment. In the case of engineers, it has been found that about two-thirds have managerial assignments within ten years after receiving their bachelors degree. The stresses principles and practices of effective management that professionals need to understand. Particular emphasis is placed on behavioural patterns associated with professionals and their work environment.

Chapter 4

Development of Hotel and Motel

IN SMALL METROPOLITAN REGIONS

Everywhere in North America, suburbanization has caused a relative and, in many cases, absolute decline of downtown areas. The effect on the downtowns of small metropolitan regions (small-metro downtowns) has been particularly severe, for they possess fewer assets than those of larger metropolitan regions to resist the effects of suburban development. This identifies the few healthy small-metro downtowns in order to draw lessons that can aid the other downtowns within this urban size category, all of which are struggling. Our study concentrated on downtowns of North American metropolitan regions with populations between 100,000 and 500,000.

There are 177 metropolitan statistical areas in the U.S. and 25 census metropolitan areas and census agglomerations in Canada in this size range (excluding U.S. primary statistical areas that are part of consolidated metropolitan statistical areas, all with populations exceeding our threshold). In the U.S., these metropolitan areas have a total population of 40.8 million, roughly one of every seven Americans. Small Canadian metropolitan regions register an overall population of 5.08 million, which represents about one sixth of this country's population.

Our objectives in this study were fourfold: (I) identify successful small-metro downtowns across the U.S. and

Canada; (2) explore reasons for their success; (3) from their experience, draw lessons for less successful downtowns; and (4) generate information on a category of downtowns that has been neglected in the literature.

To meet these objectives, we surveyed planners and other urban professionals from the United States and Canada who have an interest in downtown revitalization. Respondents were first invited to define what are, in their opinion, the features that contribute to the well-being of successful small-metro downtowns. Then, they were asked to identify successful ones and justify their selections. As expected, we found that few such downtowns were perceived as successful.

And these districts nearly always cumulate advantages that are exceptional among small-metro downtowns—close proximity of a university, a state capital (in the U.S.), or provincial legislature (in Canada); a strong historical character; and a powerful tourist appeal. The article closes with a discussion of the implications of these findings for the vast majority of these downtowns, which are in a poor state of health. This latter part of the article is based on interviews with informants from the cities whose downtowns were selected in the survey.

DOWNTOWN DECLINE AND REVITALIZATION EFFORTS

In downtowns across North America, whether in large or small metropolitan regions, attempts at revitalization can be grouped into three phases. The first phase concentrated on adaptation to automobile accessibility, the second on head-on competition with suburbs, and the third on the accentuation of a distinct core area identity. Early strategies of the 1950s and 1960s aimed at maintaining the preeminence of the downtown within a changing transportation environment.

Planners sought to preserve or restore the dominant position of the downtown by replacing or complementing transit accessibility focused on the core area with similarly advantageous automobile-oriented access patterns. Radial expressways and widened arterial roads were meant to channel flows of cars towards downtowns, increasingly well provided with parking space.

It soon became clear, however, that accessibility alone would not safeguard the primacy of central business districts.

Policymakers became convinced that to stem the retail hemorrhage towards the suburbs, downtowns had to gloss their image and embrace suburban shopping formulas. This phase, which ran from the late 1950s into the early 1980s, consisted largely of attempts at ridding CBDs of eyesores and tailoring downtown shopping to the tastes of the day.

Sectors seen as blighted or merely obsolete were razed with the hope of replacing them with up-to-date developments apt to fuel downtown growth. This was also the time when indoor retail malls, an already well established suburban shopping formula, were introduced in CBDs. This strategy was grounded in the assumption that by replicating conditions found in suburban shopping centres, downtown areas could compete successfully with suburbs.

The 1970s marked a radical departure from earlier approaches to downtown revitalization. The shift was induced by a growing recognition of the ineffectiveness of previous efforts at reversing CBD decline. In fact, earlier revitalization attempts were often held responsible for downtowns' downward spiral.

For example, in small-metro downtowns, most enclosed retail malls were economic failures, and even prosperous malls tended to generate little retail activity beyond their walls. Also fueling the 1970s transformations were public expenditure cutbacks, the opening of planning to public participation, and a rediscovery of the merits of pre-World War II built environments, most notably the traditional pedestrian-oriented retail street.

Increasingly, planning interventions emphasized preservation or enhancement of the uniqueness of the physical features of downtowns within rapidly suburbanizing metropolitan regions and the targeting of markets where CBDs enjoyed competitive advantages. This reorientation signaled a mounting sentiment that downtowns could no longer compete with the suburb on its own terms and that their salvation rested instead on their distinction from the suburban realm in terms of the nature of their activities, a more compact built environment, and the predominance of pedestrian movement for intradowntown journeys.

The post-1970s attempts at revitalization did not, however, mark a clear break with previous efforts. Large redevelopment projects continued to be a mainstay of revitalization strategies. While redevelopment projects did not lose their allure, the process leading to this outcome underwent transformations. With the demise of large, federally funded urban renewal programmes, reliance on partnership-based approaches gained in popularity.

Projects included, for example, convention centres, professional sport venues, and aquariums. Meanwhile, in downtowns, or portions thereof, that were not subjected to redevelopment, increased importance was given to the preservation of the traditional built environment and its occupation by activities targeting markets congruent with the attributes of core areas—festival places and hospitality and recreational establishments.

In small metropolitan areas, there was a lag in the succession of these phases due to the tendency for revitalization strategies to be first devised and tested in larger metropolitan regions (urban renewal in Pittsburgh, Philadelphia, and New Haven in the late 1940s and in the 1950s, for example). Moreover, the impact of these phases was attenuated in small-metro downtowns by a lesser availability of public- and private-sector resources.

The foremost consequence of limited resources was a weaker involvement in urban renewal and a resulting preservation of much of these CBDs' traditional built environment. Another effect was a tendency in all phases to rely on small- rather than large-scale interventions.

Small-metro downtowns deserve distinct treatment because the circumstances they face are different from those encountered by CBDs of smaller urban areas or of larger metropolitan regions. They are more complex than downtowns of small urban areas (with less than 100,000 residents) and thus require more diversified revitalization strategies. In small urban area downtowns, the problem is often one of main street revival and can lend itself to targeted remedies such as the introduction of a farmers' market, an unusual attraction (such as the carousel in Mansfield, OH), or the adoption of a theme for the street.

At the same time, small-metro downtowns are more often in a state of decline than those of large metropolitan regions. While large-metro downtowns that perform poorly on all fronts (employment, retail, services, housing) are the exception, the opposite holds true for small-metro CBDs. One reason for this discrepancy is the absence in small-metro downtowns of assets widely distributed among their large-urban-area cousins, such as important employment and retail concentrations, world-class attractions, and elaborate public transit networks.

Another factor of decline among these CBDs is the higher decentralization propensity of small-metro downtowns due to their limited critical mass, their near total dependence on the automobile, and the relative ease with which different destinations, including peripheral ones, can be reached from anywhere within these metropolitan regions.

METHOD

With the expectation of poor health generally among small-metro CBDs, we engaged in a study purporting to identify the exceptional ones that are vital, with the intention of drawing lessons that can be of use to less successful CBDs. The study relied on a two-pronged methodology. The first phase consisted of an Internet survey.

Emails with a link to the Internet survey form were sent to the 1,076 persons in our sample: 371 (34.5%) to university planning, urban studies, and urban geography faculty members; 503 (46.8%) to planners employed by the central cities of small metropolitan regions; and 202 (18.8%) to professionals with a possible interest in downtown revitalization who are associated with government agencies (such as regional HUD offices) and economic development and research institutes with an urban focus.

This sample was not constructed with a probabilistic objective, but rather in a fashion that would maximize the information on small-metro downtowns across the continent. Of the sent emails, a total of 859 reached their destination (217 were undeliverable). The number of answered questionnaires after two reminders was 295—a 34.4% response rate.

As do all surveys, this one reflects the values of its respondents. Far from being a challenge to the validity of its findings, we see the expression of these values as an important contribution of our survey. The values it picks up are indeed those of people who are among the best informed on the state of downtowns. Its respondents are also active in the framing and deployment of downtown revitalization strategies and in the advancement of knowledge on downtowns. Directly or indirectly, their values thus become embedded in downtown revitalization policies.

Moreover, in most cases these values have been influenced by firsthand experience of downtowns and past revitalization efforts. Respondents answered the three-question survey on a Web site. Question 1 listed 19 factors potentially influential in the success of small-metro CBDs. Respondents were invited to rate each factor on a scale of 1 to 4, from 1 = very important to 4 = not important at all. Comments were solicited at the end of this question.

The Web site used information about a respondent's state or province to generate, in question 2, a list of all small metropolitan areas in their region, defined as their home state or province and contiguous states or provinces. Respondents were asked to rate each downtown within their region. The adoption of this approach was based on the view that, contrary to the knowledge of downtowns of large metropolitan regions, which is continental or global in scope, awareness of those of small-metro downtowns is mostly regional. Space was provided for comments on each CBD.

Respondents were also offered the opportunity to rate small-metro downtowns within their own region that were not listed in question 2. Because our roster included only the names of metropolitan regions with a 100,000-500,000 population, respondents readily used the space reserved for unlisted downtowns and for comments on enumerated metros to single out the successful downtown within multicentreed metropolitan regions.

In question 3, respondents were asked to mention and comment on any successful small-metro downtown, irrespective of its regional location in North America. There was no limit on the number of downtowns that could be identified as very successful or successful in question 2's list, in the space made available in question 2 for additional downtowns within the region of a respondent, or across the continent in question 3.

The second phase of the study consisted of interviews with urban professionals (mostly planners) from the urban areas identified in the survey. These interviews were intended to cast additional light on the conditions accounting for the healthy state of the selected downtowns, including the revitalization strategies deployed there. We carried out 10 face-to-face and 24 telephone interviews. Two more respondents answered our questions in writing.

Factors in the Success of Downtowns

There was a great deal of agreement among survey respondents about the important attributes of successful downtowns. Together, factors believed to account for the success of small-metro CBDs rated as "very important" by at least half the respondents evoke features of traditional pre-World War II downtown areas: an active, street-oriented retail scene; cultural activities; concentrations of jobs; and a pedestrian-friendly environment with busy sidewalks.

The "important" category adds a further characteristic associated with traditional downtowns: Well preserved neighbourhoods indeed constitute a significant component of traditional downtowns. The other factors ranking high in the "important" category can be perceived as amenities and activities likely to attract and retain people in downtown areas—historical character, distinctive architecture, green space, civic events, and tourist activities.

For 18 of the 19 factors listed in the questionnaire, the sum of the "very important" and "important" ratings exceeds 50%. The exception is the presence of an indoor retail mall, which was rated in these two categories by less than one quarter of respondents. This negative attitude towards indoor malls is consistent with the attachment to the traditional perception of downtowns and with the resistance to attempts at bringing downtowns closer to suburban development norms expressed in the choice of many factors categorized as "very important."

Anti-mall sentiments can thus be construed as a commitment to the preservation of the distinctiveness of downtowns within the contemporary urban environment. Another explanation may be the abovementioned failure of most of these malls. When asked for other factors (i.e., factors not listed by us in question 1), many respondents emphasized the importance of a resident population and of a wide variety of land uses to assure 24-hour activity.

Another common response was the need to find a market niche for downtowns. Some mentioned the importance of distinctive, often locally owned shops apt to create a retail environment that departs from the one produced by chains found in the suburbs. Others stressed the role that food, entertainment, and the arts can play in this regard.

But the most frequently voiced comment concerned the need to properly blend and integrate the identified success factors. Numerous respondents observed that more important than the presence of individual activities is how they interact. In this same vein, many comments concerned the role of small-scale developments, short blocks, and judicious urban design in maximizing pedestrian-based synergy between downtown activities.

Certain attributes are disproportionately present among these downtowns. Seven of them have a large university that is either in or adjacent to the CBD. In five more cases, while not immediately downtown, a university is located within 2 miles of this district; and in two additional cities, Savannah, GA, and Asheville, NC, there is a smaller college in or close to the CBD. Moreover, five of the selected downtowns host a state capital or provincial legislature.

Another common feature among selected downtowns is their historical character. It is noteworthy that virtually none of the chosen CBDs have undergone a profound alteration of their traditional built environment resulting from redevelopment initiatives. This is due to avoidance of or limited reliance on urban renewal in most selected downtowns and a celebration of this historical flavor. (One exception is downtown Boise, ID, where several blocks were torn down to make way for a regional mall, which never materialized.)

Older, architecturally significant buildings have been restored and parts of these CBDs have received historical district designations. In fact, historical flavor has turned many of these downtowns into major tourist destinations. The importance of tourism can be gauged by the presence of unusual concentrations of hotel/motel rooms.

Most of the 19 downtowns register a high ratio of hotel/motel rooms to central-city population. Asheville and Santa Fe have 70 rooms per 1,000 residents, and all but three of the remainder have at least 20 rooms per 1,000 residents. For comparison, central cities within metropolitan regions with a modest visitor orientation register scores in the 5-10 per 1,000 range. For example, the ratio is 6 in Kitchener, ON; 8 in Flint, MI; and 9 in Columbus, GA, and Regina, SK.

Nearly all selected downtowns are further advantaged by the easy accessibility of natural amenities, generally bodies of water, untarnished by defacing developments such as waterside freeways. These amenities have usually been the object of restoration projects intended to enhance their appeal and accessibility, ranging from the creation of large waterfront parks, as in Chattanooga, TN, to the naturalization of the banks of the San Luis Obispo, CA, creek.

As indicated, all chosen downtowns share the presence of continuous street-oriented retail facades. This characteristic is hardly specific to successful downtowns, however. By virtue of its age, this built form is found in most downtowns, whether they are successful or not. But the successful CBDs are distinguished from other such areas by the occupation of street-facing premises by well patronized retail and hospitality establishments and by high levels of pedestrian movement. Chosen downtowns were able to substitute activities targeting niche markets for mainstream retail activity, which historically had dominated these districts but in most cases plummeted in the face of suburban competition.

Department and chain stores have generally been replaced with boutiques, restaurants, bars, cultural activities, and entertainment. The adaptation of these activities to downtown markets—the university community, government employees, and tourists, for example—is a factor of synergy within downtown areas, as is the pedestrian friendliness of their street-level environment. The quality of walking space receives considerable attention in downtowns chosen in the survey. Six of the selected downtowns possess a pedestrian mall, a rare occurrence in contemporary North America, and number ban parking lots.

In summary, in addition to a pedestrian-hospitable environment, all highly rated CBDs possess at least one of the following assets: a university that is in or close to downtown; presence in a metropolitan region with a strong visitor orientation; a well preserved historical district; and a state capital or provincial legislature. In justifying their selection of successful downtowns, respondents also alluded to the presence of cultural activities—art galleries and live entertainment—and natural amenities.

Yet for all their shared features, downtowns selected in the survey present many differences. If all these downtowns are perceived as historically rich relative to the remainder of their metropolitan regions, some of them, Chattanooga, TN, and Savannah, GA, in particular, possess an exceptional historical character.

The markets they cater to represent another difference among downtowns chosen in the survey. While most draw several markets, in some places activities are narrowly focused on university students. This is the case in Athens, GA, and State College, PA. Downtown State College, for example, contains 42 bars and 50 fraternity houses. These downtowns are further differentiated by the extent to which they have suffered the retail assault of the suburbs.

In a few instances, thanks to the underdevelopment of suburban retail establishments or the long distance from the downtown of large suburban shopping concentrations, downtowns were able to retain some mainstream shopping. This happened, for example, in Kingston, ON, Santa Barbara, CA, and Rochester, MN. Finally, a few downtowns—Victoria, BC, and Madison, WI, for example—break from the ranks by posting relatively high public transit patronage.

Answers to question 3, where respondents were asked to name successful small-metro downtowns irrespective of their location in North America, added five CBDs to our list. These are downtowns that were mentioned by a minimum of three respondents, had not been selected in the previous question and approximated our size criteria. All enjoy the presence of a nearby university campus. Portland, ME, and Knoxville, TN, feature well restored historical centres that are popular with tourists. Boulder, CO, has created a downtown pedestrian mall, and downtown Lincoln, NE, is the site of the state capital. Question 3 findings thus confirm those of question 2.

At first glance, observations from this study do not seem to be of much use to the majority of small-metro CBDs, which did not make the list of successful downtowns. It indeed appears that only those downtowns blessed with extraordinary assets that do not lend themselves easily to duplication (such as core area university campuses, seats of government, or exceptional historical character) can aspire to be successful. But closer examination reveals that extensive efforts were made to revitalize these successful downtowns, which served to create or enhance some of their advantages or to extend the benefits of existing assets.

After all, these are not the only downtowns with a built environment that is distinctive within its metropolitan region or with historical merit. Moreover, it is not unusual to find deteriorated downtowns with universities or government employment close by. Somehow, these less successful downtowns have not been able to take advantage of such features to the same extent as those picked by our survey respondents.

Comments from the survey and subsequent interviews reveal six categories of measures used in successful downtowns. Note that none of the downtowns relied on the full roster of revitalization measures and, indeed, that a number of CBDs made very little use of any of them.

In the first category we find initiatives intended to stimulate development, such as public-sector financial support to private investments in the form of tax increment financing, loan guarantees, and different forms of incentive funding. Within this category also fail public-sector involvement in land assembly and brownfield rehabilitation. The second category groups different types of streetscape, urban furniture, facade improvement programmes, and the introduction of public art.

The third category includes the erection of public buildings such as convention centres, courthouses, and municipal offices. The next group deals with transportation and parking issues. We find under this rubric traffic calming measures, the creation of pedestrian malls, the provision of municipally run parking, as well as control—occasionally banning—of parking lots.

The fifth category concerns the restoration of natural amenities, essentially waterfronts, and the opening of pedestrian-friendly corridors to these sites. And the final category groups efforts at increasing the visibility of the downtown through marketing and event programming.

While most of the selected downtowns enjoy the active involvement of a vast array of organizations, including the planning department, the chamber of commerce, downtown business associations, citizen organizations, private foundations, and arts groups, in other downtowns organizational support is virtually absent. This is the case in downtown Victoria where, since the dissolution of the Business Improvement Area for lack of interest on the part of property owners, the planning department is pretty much alone in fending for the downtown area.

We now briefly explore how listed measures and the involvement of different organizations congealed into revitalization strategies. To this end, we rely on the content of interviews to picture the strategies adopted by three of our downtowns—Asheville, NC, Chattanooga, TN, and Kingston, ON—chosen for their representation of different types of approaches. Asheville, NC. Following the 1972 opening of a regional shopping mall in the suburbs, downtown Asheville entered a cycle of decline that lasted into the 1980s. Many buildings were boarded up and remaining businesses were often left struggling.

This situation prompted a broad collaborative approach involving the City Development Office, whose primary function is to assure downtown revitalization; the Downtown Commission appointed by the city; the Downtown Association, which is responsible for programming and retail marketing; the Arts Council; and strong merchant and resident organizations.

From the mid 1980s, downtown issues assumed a prominent position on the municipal political scene and mobilized multiple interest groups. Since then, local government support for downtown revitalization initiatives has been unwavering, with the exception of a hiatus in the early 1990s when municipal leadership was taken by suburban interests for one term.

Asheville has relied on a variety of financial inducements to stimulate private investment in its downtown, and thereby bolster the commercial and residential function of the district and the rehabilitation of historic buildings. For example, loan guarantees from the municipal administration allowed the restoration of 11 adjacent historic buildings and the erection of a parking structure. Overall, the revitalization of downtown Asheville was not so much the outcome of a few major projects as that of numerous local entrepreneurial initiatives and small-scale improvements to the built environment.

Chattanooga, TN. In Chattanooga, as in Asheville, interest in the downtown was triggered by the severe damage caused by suburban retail development. Downtown Chattanooga lost its department and chain stores to the regional mall, but was able to preserve its office employment base.

The revitalization process was initiated in the early 1980s by three distinct initiatives: one focusing on urban design, the second on the waterfront, and the third on the promotion of specific projects in the CBD. The Chattanooga approach to downtown revitalization parallels characteristics of the "urban regime" model documented within large metropolitan regions. This model involves the presence of stable alliances, driven by private economic interests with the means to carry out their own revitalization efforts.

The Lyndhurst Foundation, set up by a pioneer of the Coca-Cola bottling business, has played a leading role in launching and funding downtown renewal initiatives. What is more, banks have been active in the renovation of historic buildings. Like Asheville, Chattanooga has made extensive use of public funding support to leverage private investment in the downtown and has taken a multipronged approach to revitalization. But more than most other downtowns selected in the survey, Chattanooga has relied on large projects.

This is the case of Warehouse Row, consisting of the restoration of eight historic warehouses; Charleston Place, which includes a hotel, conference centre, 30 stores, and an athletic club; the Tennessee Aquarium; and the $120 million waterfront plan presently being implemented. This plan involves the creation of public parks, streets, and the expansion of a museum and the aquarium. The revival of Downtown Kingston began in the late 1960s when railroad lines and derelict industrial structures along Lake Ontario made way for a park, marina, hotels, and luxurious apartment buildings.

Along with the failure of a downtown shopping mall proposal and citizen mobilization against threats to historic structures, this concentration of new developments on the waterfront contributed to the preservation of downtown Kingston's traditional built environment. In comparison to Asheville, Chattanooga, and many other downtowns selected in the survey, the last decades have witnessed little public sector intervention in downtown Kingston.

After involvement in waterfront redevelopment, public sector efforts were pretty much confined to streetscape beautification and an upgrading of the downtown's urban furniture. Still, the district remained healthy and even held on to some of its mainstream retail activity, thanks to the distance of the regional mall from the downtown and a large close-by population. In addition, the Business Improvement Area is effective in marketing the downtown and recruiting new stores to fill empty premises.

And with different community organizations using the downtown as a venue for their events, there are activities programmed over all summer weekends. Asheville and Chattanooga mirror the high level of interventionism shared by most successful downtowns identified in the study. Kingston, on the other hand, figures among selected downtowns where public sector involvement has been lowest.

The contrast between these downtowns can be interpreted as a consequence of differences in the severity of threats confronting them. Again, in a fashion that is common to most downtowns rated as successful in the survey, Asheville's and Chattanooga's revitalization efforts were reactions to manifest signs of downtown decline in the wake of advancing retail suburbanization.

Kingston, on the other hand, is more representative of the minority of successful downtowns where damage inflicted by suburbanization was limited. Many interviewees and a number of comments made in the survey stress the fragility of vital downtowns.

They underscore the need for constant vigilance to safeguard the health of these districts, and thus the importance of durable political support and stable downtown alliances. Sustained mobilization around downtown issues is needed to secure municipal government interest in downtown matters and willingness to tailor interventions to CBD realities. Downtowns indeed require a different approach to planning and development from the remainder of their metropolitan regions, most particularly suburban areas.

Financial incentives are frequently necessary to lure investments to the core, and in contrast to most other parts of metropolitan areas, the vitality of downtowns demands an environment that is stimulating for pedestrians. But the risk always looms that the special needs of downtowns will be overlooked by city councils, especially if they are dominated by pro-suburban interests. The outcome could then be extreme difficulty in attracting investments and, over time, a less distinctive built environment.

In addition, despite the stabilizing effect of universities and government, the replacement of mainstream by specialized retailing and heavy reliance on hospitality and tourism make the downtowns selected in the survey acutely sensitive to economic cycles. Less capable than mainstream suburban retail to withstand recessions, the economies of successful downtowns risk being devastated by a severe downturn.

These downtowns would then require economic rebuilding strategies to take advantage of the subsequent recovery. Successful downtowns must also constantly stay on top of the frequent fashion shifts characteristic of their niche retail markets and of the hospitality and entertainment sectors.

When considering the duplication potential of lessons drawn from our selected downtowns, we must keep in mind that these are the bright stars in the constellation of small-metro downtowns, and that it is unrealistic to expect a generalization of their level of performance across CBDs of similar size urban areas. There are obviously wide variations in the extent to which such downtowns can benefit from the experience of their successful counterparts.

For example, many lessons from the downtowns chosen in the survey are pertinent to other downtowns where the traditional built environment is still in place. In contrast, such lessons are of little relevance to those downtowns where the pre-World War II layout has been severely compromised.

Still, the situation for small-metro downtowns is not as somber as it was in the earlier phases of suburbanization, when the lure of the periphery was fuelled by generalized aspiration for a car-oriented lifestyle. For the many individuals for whom this lifestyle has since lost its luster, the traditional layout of downtowns can be attractive, provided these districts contain activities adapted to their needs and preferences.

Demographic trends are also in part favourable to downtown areas. The prevalence of small, predominantly childless households in downtowns and surrounding neighbourhoods has long been documented. The bulge of aging baby boomers, some of whom are ready to trade their suburban homes for smaller dwellings in a pedestrian-friendly area, provides ample potential residents for core areas. This is also the case for the growing proportion of childless households in all age categories.

What is more, interest in downtowns may be bolstered by present-day environmental and economic development thinking. The compact and pedestrian-oriented characteristics of downtown areas are consistent with smart growth principles presently in vogue. Downtown revitalization figures prominently among measures that the smart growth movement advances to contain urban sprawl and reduce automobile dependence. From an economic development perspective, lively, entertainment- and culture-rich downtowns are depicted as appealing to the "creative class," broadly defined to include people engaged in professional, product development, entrepreneurial, artistic, and management occupations. According to the perspective expounded by Richard Florida, the creative class assumes a leading role in economic growth.

This view therefore implies an enhanced ability on the part of metropolitan regions possessing a healthy downtown to attract members of the creative class and thereby enjoy resulting economic rewards. Revealingly, metropolitan regions whose downtowns were selected in our study figure prominently among urban areas in their size category posting a high presence of the creative class.

The foremost generalizable lesson that can be distilled from our selected downtowns is disarmingly simple: Their success can be attributed to an ability to attract people and assure that they remain in their midst to pursue many of their activities. Chosen CBDs possess magnets (a university, government presence, historical character, and specialized retail establishments) and provide reasons for people to spend time downtown.

Selected downtowns indeed offer a synergy-rich environment consisting of activities that are well adapted to core-area markets and are set within a pedestrian-hospitable environment. In reality, however, it is difficult to distinguish between magnet and retention features, because the presence of many people and of the activities they support itself adds to the allure of downtown areas.

If typical small-metro downtowns cannot improvise the university campus, seat of government, or exceptional historical character commonly found in the downtowns selected in our survey, they can nonetheless make efforts to draw employment and, perhaps with most promise, new housing. Lessons from successful downtowns underscore the need for strategies that are both multipronged and well coordinated. In typical small-metro downtowns, revitalization strategies would at once need to attract employment and housing and create an environment that is hospitable to downtown workers and nearby residents.

Ideally, such an environment will possess historical flavor and lively street life, two characteristics that will differentiate it from the suburbs. It will also harbor retail and services that are suited to the needs and tastes of people who are attracted downtown. For example, to cater to the needs of nearby residents and encourage further housing development, a downtown must provide a variety of food outlets.

Given the nature of the markets they are susceptible to lure, success for typical small-metro downtowns is a function of their ability to provide activities and settings that are unique within their metropolitan regions. These downtowns should attempt to launch a virtuous cycle whereby the attainment of a critical mass of users and activities within a distinct environment will make them attractive to a growing number of visitors. This type of cycle is a major factor in the success of the downtowns selected in the survey.

Our research findings are generally in accord with the transition over the last decades in the perception of the role of downtowns and of appropriate revival interventions. They resonate with the recent literature's emphasis on the preservation and enhancement of the traditional layout and historical character of downtowns. Our results also mirror the importance recent writings give to people places, pedestrian connectivity, variety of land uses, and, generally, quality of life within downtown areas.

Likewise, many of our selected downtowns have adopted revitalization strategies that are consistent with those documented in recent writings. These strategies are inclusive, drawing on diverse constituencies such as property owners, merchants, residents, governments, and historic preservationists and rely extensively on private/public sector partnerships.

Yet, findings from our research are occasionally at variance with the literature. This is mostly a consequence of the scant coverage it gives to downtowns belonging to metropolitan regions with populations of 100,000-500,000. Whereas the revitalization strategies of large-city downtowns can benefit from extensive public transit systems, national- and world-scale attractions, the enduring presence of mainstream retail, large office space concentrations, and the key role of big corporations, most CBDs of small metropolitan regions cannot count on such advantages.

This explains in large part the differences between our findings and previous literature depictions of large-metro downtown revitalization strategies. More than those of their larger counterparts, successful downtowns of small metropolitan regions tend to target niche markets, make use of small- rather than large-scale revitalization interventions, and rely on the public sector.

The results of this research were not surprising insofar as they confirm the observation that the vast majority of small-metro downtowns have not recovered from the severe damage inflicted by suburbanization. Findings also mirror the conceptual turn that has run through the planning profession over the last decades. The emphasis of revitalization strategies on features of traditional downtowns, such as street-oriented and pedestrian-friendly environments, is in agreement with current thinking within the planning profession.

The assets respondents associate with a successful downtown paint the picture of the traditional downtown, harking back to the pre-1950 period. This depiction is consistent with the present popularity of built environment preservation and new urbanism within the planning community. The usefulness of these findings lies in lessons derived from the downtowns identified as successful, which can be of aid to ailing CBDs. The proposals generated by this research stress the need to emphasize the distinction of downtowns from the suburban realm.

First, this type of revitalization strategy should involve an accentuation of historical character and street-level activity, two features that distinguish these districts from suburban-type developments. Second, with the irrevocable loss of mainstream retail activity to the suburbs, downtown revival strategies are compelled to capitalize on the few markets where this sector holds a comparative advantage over suburban locales.

Acknowledgements We acknowledge financial support from the Waterloo Community-University Research Alliance and thank the planners who answered our questionnaire and who agreed to be interviewed. We are also grateful to the anonymous referees for their helpful comments.

Because of the limited literature on small-metro downtown revitalization and considerable overlapping in the nature and sequence of revitalization phases in both large and small metropolitan region downtowns, the following four paragraphs draw on writing pertaining to both categories of downtowns.

The sample was constructed from several sources: rosters of both the American Institute of Certified Planners and the Canadian Institute of Planners; the Web sites of North American university planning, urban studies, and geography departments and programmes; and the Web sites of organizations involved in downtown revitalization and urban research in the U.S. and Canada. All identified academics were included in our sample.

As regards planners employed by small-metro central cities, two names were incorporated in the sample from those administrations with less than seven accredited planners, and where there were more than seven planners, every fourth name was added to our list. All professionals with a possible interest in downtowns who are associated with government agencies or economic development or research institutes with an urban focus were surveyed.

The presence of a retail mall was rated as "not important at all" by 33.9% of respondents, by far the highest score within this category. The second highest factor rated as "not important at all"—abundant parking—was selected by a meager 5.4% of respondents.

Irrespective of the 20% rule, cores that were placed in either of the two categories by less than four respondents were not included. The few cases where the 20% threshold was attained with less than four citations are due to a strong reliance on the "don't know" option. The important proportion of tourist- and university-oriented downtowns within those given highest rankings could be interpreted as an artifact of the method used in this research. The presence of academics in the sample would favour the reporting of downtowns with a university, because of the evident familiarity of this group of respondents with such CBDs.

And tourist destinations are obviously better known by everyone, including our respondents. Two features of the methodology reduce the likelihood of such biases, however. First, academics amounted to only a little above a third of our sample. Second, and most importantly, to assure that as many downtowns as possible would qualify as successful, we set low thresholds—citation by 20% or more for the cores on the regional lists and three mentions or more for the continent-wide selection.

The only selected downtown that does not fully share the historical features and intense street orientation of the highly rated core areas is that of Rochester, MN, where the main focus has been on a modernization of the downtown through the building of an indoor mall and of a skyway and underground passageway system. The hotel/motel room to central-city population ratio was calculated from American Automobile Association and Canadian Automobile Association tour book hotel/motel directories.

This method somewhat underestimates the presence of hotel/motel rooms, because the directories exclude lower-end facilities. In the case of Burlington, VT, the central city was combined with a suburb. This is because while close to City of Burlington boundaries, this metropolitan area's main concentration of hotel and motel rooms is in South Burlington.

There are two explanations for the exceptional presence of pedestrian malls in these downtowns. First, by virtue of their success, we can assume that some of the downtowns selected in the survey are among those that have been most engaged in revitalization efforts, one form of which was the creation of a pedestrian mall.

Second, and perhaps most importantly, these downtowns are among the few that can generate sufficient numbers of pedestrians and activities to bring malls to life, thanks in large part to the presence of tourists and university students. Elsewhere, the use of pedestrian malls as instruments of revitalization has generally failed lamentably.

In Rochester, MN, the Mayo Clinic and the Methodist Hospital attract many visitors—patients and their families—which explains the high hotel/motel room to resident ratio. Rochester ranks fifth in this regard among core areas. Moreover, the Mayo Clinic, with its intense medical research activity, maintains with downtown Rochester a relationship that recalls the one prevailing between centrally located universities and their downtown areas. Respondents listed a total of 170 downtowns in question.

f these, only 17 were part of metropolitan regions that come close to our size criteria and were mentioned by at least three respondents. Twelve of these downtowns were also ranked highly in question 2, thus lending additional credence to this question's regional selections. Of the five additional downtowns mentioned in answers to question 3, two had been listed as options in the previous question, but had not been selected by a sufficient proportion of respondents from their home region to be included among successful CBDs.

Of the remaining three downtowns, one was excluded from question 2's options because the population of its metropolitan region is slightly above the 500,000 limit. The other two are part of larger consolidated census metropolitan areas, Detroit and Denver.

A survey carried out in Kitchener-Waterloo, ON, a highly suburbanized urban area belonging to a 414,284-resident metropolitan region, has revealed that close to half the population would consider living in a neighbourhood close to a downtown.

This interest in central area living was, however, conditional upon the downtown being revitalized into a safe, pedestrian-friendly environment where respondents could find activities compatible with their tastes, and on the availability in central neighbourhoods of their preferred types of housing.

Many of these individuals were attracted to central neighbourhoods by their mature character and the possibility of reducing dependence on the automobile. The results of the Kitchener-Waterloo study are consistent with those of recent studies documenting a housing renaissance in numerous central areas.

Chapter 5

Trouble Management in Hotel

MANAGING TROUBLE

While overbuilding and related declines in occupancies and earnings were apparent a few years ago, the actual failure, foreclosure, and divestment of hotel and motel properties has only recently hit peak levels. As a result, the handling of turnarounds and the sale of such properties now demands that lenders take quicker and more effective action.

In addition to the traditional foreclosure remedy, lenders now frequently seek the appointment of a receiver to protect the property and related business securing the loan.

The lender may not only benefit from the appointment of a receiver but may, in fact, be compelied to take such action in order to protect its future rights. The protective remedy of a receivership action is not new, but-was not often used until recently. Because many attorneys and judges are inexperienced in making such appointments, lenders must familiarize themselves with the process and related issues.

In the present climate, the hotel owner/borrower, when served with a notice of default and proposed foreclosure sale, may resort to filing bankruptcy. This creates a "stay" against creditor actions. Lenders may seek relief from the bankruptcy stay, but that can take considerable time, allowing the debtor to retain possession. This can permit further depletion of the property's funds and deterioration of its physical condition and reputation, and in turn reduce the value of the collateral.

In the event of such a bankruptcy, the lender may find it useful to have the property appraised, particularly if the present value is less than the debt. Proof of the lack of owner equity will strengthen the claim for relief from the stay.

The typical hotel or motel loan is secured by a mortgage or trust deed on the property itself. In addition, the lender usually has the right to exercise some control over the income of the hotel in the event that payments are in default. This right is typically embodied in the "rents and profits" clause of the promissory note. Even if the lender succeeds in gaining relief from the bankruptcy stay, the bankruptcy filing can destroy the lender's right to rents and profits.

In order to exercise its rights to such income before a filing—while avoiding claims of lender interference—the bank may ask the court to appoint an impartial third party to "receive" the property and its income.

The receiver is not an agent for the lender; it is an independent third party hired to protect the property. The receiver is usually selected by the lender or its attorney, who then recommends the person to the judge. In some jurisdictions receivers must be selected from a pre-approved list. The judge has final approval of any receiver, and the receiver's qualifications, actions, and fees are subject to court review, and may be attacked by opposing parties. In the case of most hotel-motel projects, the receiver will hire a management company to oversee daily operations.

A receiver may be appointed on very short notice, even without a hearing involving both parties. The need for such ex parte (where only one side is present) actions must be demonstrated. The proposed receiver and/or management company may be asked for a declaration supporting the lender's claim, say, that the property is being neglected or that funds are being misused.

Both the receiver and the party seeking to have the receiver appointed must file oaths of performance and financial bonds. There are other costs as well. For example, though the property is likely already paying fees to a management company, this expense will likely rise if the receiver engages a new firm. The new firm's fee may be higher because of the short or uncertain duration of the contract, as well as additional demands created in a receivership.

There may be some overlapping fees of receiver and management company for property visits, inspections, court appearances, and so on. Some savings can be realized by appointing a management company executive as receiver.

In a recent case, I was personally appointed as receiver for a mid-sized, full-service franchised hotel in a popular southern California resort area. With the court's approval and the recommendation of the debtor and lender (in this case a large national bank headquartered in southern California), I, in turn, hired Trigild Corp., which I head, as the management company. The receivership order had been carefully drafted to include special conditions. Among these were orders restricting the debtors and the former management company from interfering in the hotel's operation.

Once the judge signed the order appointing the receiver, and the previously prepared receiver's oath and bond were filed, certified copies of the order were obtained. Stepping in. As the receiver, I was responsible for protecting the security for the loan—namely, its improvements, furniture, fixtures, equipment, and its income. I was also responsible for supervising and accounting for all receipts and disbursements and repairs and maintenance. I was also generally charged to protect the business from being damaged or its value being diminished.

Hotel properties present a myriad of issues that require immediate attention, including payroll and employment; tax liabilities; and inventories. In addition, hotels will frequently have other technical issues, such as liquor licenses, franchise agreements, equipment leases, retail space tenants, and vendor or concessionaire contracts.

In this case, within minutes of obtaining the court order, I as receiver and Trigild as operators took the following steps:

1. We went to the state beverage control office to gain control of the hotel's liquor license.
2. We notified the franchise company and transferred the hotel's license to my name as receiver.
3. We went to the borrower's bank to seize all bank accounts.
4. We took possession of the hotel, including cash. After these tasks were accomplished, audits were performed, inventories taken, contracts reviewed, and utilities, business licenses, and vendor accounts transferred.

In this type of situation, vendors, suppliers, and other creditors often put pressure on the hotel for past-due payment. Yet the receiver has no legal obligation to pay prior debts, and not only protects the lender's interest, but is a barrier against such creditor actions as garnishing, attaching, or repossessing any assets without court consent.

The receiver clearly has the authority to spend money to correct serious safety hazards or deterioration. However, dramatic changes to the property or its business operation are not within the receiver's authority, even when such action might improve the property or its business.

A distressed property has often been poorly managed and perhaps had little or no marketing activity. Professional management and aggressive marketing may not only improve the existing income stream, but could increase the hotel's eventual sales price.

Nevertheless, the receiver must be cautious about taking such assertive action. Where will the funds for such changes and improvements come from? Will the owner/debtor object to such expenses in the receiver's final accounting? In many cases the receiver will seek the court's approval for such actions in advance. In most cases where I am named receiver, I ask the court to allow the issuance of "receiver's certificates," which enable me to borrow any funds necessary to maintain the property if the property's income is insufficient. Results.

One week after I was appointed receiver, the previously mentioned hotel was operating normally. Subsequent improvements in management, sales and marketing boosted revenues and trimmed expenses.

Five months later the property went into foreclosure and the lender made plans to sell the property. Yet, because of the soft real estate market and the hotel's improving performance, the lender soon took the hotel off the market, with plans to further improve the property and sell later.

HOTEL FINANCE

Fawlty's problem was his failure to realize that running a hotel is not child's play. Unfortunately for banks financing hotel loans, life in the hotel industry often imitates art.

Indeed, The Wall Street Journal reports that between 350 and 355 hotel properties have experienced financial difficulties annually since 1980. By the end of 1990, the paper estimates, 1,000 properties could end up in foreclosure. Not so simple. Morris E. Lasky, president of Lodging Unlimited Inc., West Chester, Pa., says the misconception that the lodging industry is an easy field which anyone can enter has contributed to the rising rate of hotel loan foreclosures.

Since its founding in 1970, Lodging Unlimited has revitalized over 130 troubled hotels and motels. These properties, which were valued at over $1 billion in total and were threatened with foreclosure or other serious hardships, are brought to Lasky by both lenders and owners. In an interview with ABA Banking Journal, Lasky talked about the pitfalls of the business and how lenders can avoid following borrowers into them. ABA BJ: What future is there for the hotel business? Lasky: We surveyed lenders at a recent workshop on hotel loans. We came up with the projection that there would be over 1,000 hotels and motels foreclosed on in the next couple of years.

Last year at this time, in terms of my own personal experience, we were looking at probably five hotel and motel problems a month. This year we are looking at approximately one hotel property per day. ABA BJ: How do you account for the large number of problems in the industry? Lasky: Probably 95% of the hotels that we've taken on were managed by inexperienced operators.

Many investors come from other fields. They were very successful in those fields, and decided the hotel business was "easy" and invested in it. They were obviously very disappointed. ABA BJ: How does a hotel get into trouble? Lasky: The first time three people sit down and decide they want to build a hotel. They usually have no background in the hotel business. They also have a fourth friend who is a lender, and all agree that a hotel could be built and could succeed in that market.

The first mistake the banker makes is that he never asks the obvious question: Who is going to manage the hotel? If the answer isn't a highly experienced management company or a highly experienced joint venture partner, the banker should consider the deal potentially dangerous. ABA BJ: Why is professional management so necessary? Lasky: People from other fields sometimes enter this industry thinking, "I've stayed in a hotel, so I can run one."

This could not be further from the truth. The hotel business is very complicated. Hotels are open 24 hours a day, 365 days a year. They require a massive amount of skill in specialized marketing—establishing sales quotas, establishing relationships with travel agents and the corporate tour and travel departments of major corporations, and more. Specialized management and accounting skills are also called for. ABA BJ: What other danger signs should a lender watch for? Lasky: The next major mistake involves feasibility—whether the market can support another hotel. In order to satisfy the needs of the lending institution, a study by a feasibility company is requested.

However, most people do not ask who in that company will actually perform the study. In our experience, many of the feasibility companies have their least-experienced employee do the field work. That person has probably just graduated from college and doesn't have all the skills necessary to recognize the issues and problems in the market which could negatively affect the feasibility study.

As a result, many studies are glowing—but they fail to consider the question of other new hotel construction in the same market or what brand name should be on the hotel. ABA BJ: What do you mean by "brand name"? Lasky: A large majority of hotels have some national affiliation, either through a franchise or membership relationship. Generally the investors determine which names might be available in that market and select one.

Lenders should consider whether that name is going to produce business for the hotel. The only reason to buy a brand is to produce business, thus a name should be chosen so it can make an impact and create a positive result for the hotel. Studies can be done to determine the effectiveness of a franchise name in a particular market.

A franchise should produce at least 15% total occupancy to justify its existence. A franchise might cost 6% to 8% gross of room sales plus initial franchise fees. As a result, this can have a major impact on the bottom line. ABA BJ: What other trouble signs should lenders watch for? Lasky: Consider the budget for the hotel. We find that most people who don't have experience in building hotels generally understate budgets by 10% to 20%. And this is assuming they know the basics—the cost of building, furniture and fixtures, and debt.

They generally forget the cost of premarketing a hotel, the cost of prestaffing a hotel, and the cost requirement for operating capital in the early stages of the hotel. They don't realize that operating at a loss for the first year is fairly typical. They also forget the cost of supplies and small equipment, such as the maids' utility carts and their vacuum cleaners. There should also be a fairly reasonable contingency plan for mistakes or delays in construction. In short, a good hotel budget should account for errors in advance.

The hotel industry is not the proverbial "piece of cake." The belief that it is is the reason why so many hotels have been financially derailed.

THE CHALLENGE OF SECURING A BUDGET MOTEL

Family and friends attend the funeral of Ms. X, who was stabbed to death at the Inn Motel. Grasping for straws, police and family members admit they have no clues. Ms. X, a 25-year-old businesswoman and civic volunteer, was in town to be a bridesmaid in her best friend's wedding. The victim's family has filed suit against the motel owner. The attorney for the family says the main issues in the suit are lack of security, nonexistent key control, and prior related security incidents.

Motel management will not comment on the pending suit. Police say the killer gained access to the room with a key. A jury trial is planned. It promises to be emotional and have far-reaching ramifications for the hotel and motel industry. Can this scenario really happen? Yes, and more often than those in the industry care to admit.

Fortunately, most hotels and motels are concerned with security and have measures in place to prevent such violent and unfortunate occurrences. Also, fortunately, many crimes involving hotels and motels do not end up this tragically.

Securing hotels and motels is a challenge because they are open for business 24 hours a day, 365 days a year. Consider a budget motel, where that challenge is increased twofold.

How is it different? Such a motel has

- Exterior entrances to rooms, some with sliding glass doors;
- Numerous remote entrances and exits;
- Parking right outside each room's door;
- Limited staff—usually no security personnel;
- Little or no physical security; and
- Limited capital resources.

Some security basics are inexpensive and can be implemented quickly, while others involve greater capital expenditure. With the volume of litigation against motels today, owners and operators can't afford not to upgrade facilities. Even though they will put a squeeze on already limited funds, certain protective measures are essential. And on new construction, there is no excuse not to employ the latest security design concepts.

With the exception of safe-deposit boxes at the front desk, which limit a motel's exposure to property loss, no codes or laws require a motel to provide physical security. Courts across the nation have mandated that motels merely take "reasonable" precautions to protect guests from physical harm.

The public has also become more educated. In the last few years, for example, guests have insisted on sprinkler systems and 24-hour security. With an overbuilt lodging market, heavy competition, and fewer people traveling because of the recession, hotel and motel owners are being forced to listen to customers and reevaluate security.

This article explores basic security for budget motels. According to the American Hotel & Motel Association, these facilities typically provide no frills, have one to three stories and 20 to 125 rooms, and make up 80 percent of the total domestic lodging community.

Whether a facility is new or 20 years old, basic security programmes must be implemented. They involve time but little cost. Here are the basic steps.

Step 1. Managing by Walking around (MBWA) was first introduced by Tom Peters in his book In Search Of Excellence. It involves getting out in the trenches and seeing what's going on in the business, getting close to customers and employees.

Mom-and-pop operations have practiced MBWA for a while but probably never had a label for it. Multiunit motel chains, however, often lose sight of this key concept, which is essential to running a smooth, successful operation.

MBWA is a caring attitude that is imparted to employees and guests alike. Many security professionals emphasize having a written programme and policy.

Although they are important, without a caring attitude and genuine concern for security, all the programmes in the world will not stop theft or, worse, violent crimes at the expense of a motel's guests, employees, and business reputation.

Any small-motel security management programme should include

- key control to guest rooms and back-of-house areas;
- emergency procedures for fires and other disasters;
- procedures for handling robberies and other disturbances;
- accident management for guests, employees, and property loss;
- access control to guest rooms, the perimeter, and back-of-house areas;
- asset protection, including cashiering procedures, safeguarding of guest valuables, credit policies, and periodic inventories and shopping services;
- records and reporting;
- property inspections, patrols, and follow-up procedures; and
- communications.

If a company needs help setting up a programme, it should contact a reputable hotel or motel security consultant, the ASIS Standing Committee on Lodging Security, or the American Hotel & Motel Association.

Step 2. A background check that includes contacting prior employers should be conducted before employees are hired. This step is important because applicants may have falsified their employment record or reasons for leaving jobs.

Since a motel has maybe two people on duty during the evening shifts—and many times only one person—it is easy to understand the importance of background checks. These are the same people entrusted with the safety and security of guests as well as the livelihood of the owner. They must be able to handle any situation that occurs.

During 1989 and 1990, an Orlando, FL, TV station conducted a series of investigative reports on motel security. Using a hidden camera in a guest room, reporters discovered that when employees were in the room they routinely stole from the guests.

The employees who were stealing turned out to be on state work-release programmes. These same trusted employees who had master keys to every room also had criminal records for assault, robbery, and other offenses.

In addition, for $300, the investigative reporter was able to buy a copy of the master key from an employee. What kind of liability do you think that facility had?

From professional contacts and personal experience, I estimate that 80 percent of thefts from guest rooms are petrated by employees themselves or in collusion with others by providing duplicate keys and other means.

Step 3. Employees need to become involved in security. The American Hotel & Motel Association has a series of video training workshops on the basics of lodging security. Workshops cover everything from awareness to handling disturbances.

Training employees in security and emergency response procedures can go a long way in providing sound defence should an unfortunate incident occur. To keep momentum going, employees should be recognized and rewarded for positive actions.

Some motels have set up performance pay for the amount of work accomplished rather than the amount of time on the job. While controls must be established to ensure quality, motels have reported remarkable gains in productivity. This same performance pay system could easily include safety and security performance factors.

Most lodging security professionals have trouble convincing management of the need for adequate security at small properties. With the recession hitting the travel industry particularly hard, businesses cutting back on expenses, and mass layoffs taking place, consider what will get cut first.

That is why security basics need to be in place. They cost very little up front. All that is required is effort. The owner or operator must possess a philosophy and attitude that protecting assets is essential to remaining competitive in the budget-motel marketplace.

Step 4. Having a liaison with local law enforcement is crucial to the small-property operator. Without adequate police protection, a business is at extreme risk. The property management may want to contact the local crime prevention unit to find out what can be done to improve security at the property. Management also should get to know the police officer on its beat.

Step 5. Motels need to communicate with their neighbours. They need to know what criminal activity is going on around them and its extent. In many locations, courts have established that the level of reasonable care a motel must provide is based on what its competitors in the same location are doing.

Motels should become active in local business organizations, especially the American Hotel & Motel Association. The contacts and information received from such networking can be invaluable.

Step 6. Motels should either designate or hire a security person to patrol the property. This should be the last step in assembling the programme.

In some locations, employing a security person to patrol the property, especially on evening and graveyard shifts, cannot be avoided. Whether a motel uses a guard service or proprietary guards, individuals should be investigated thoroughly. They need to be trained to handle problems so they do not end up creating more.

They also need to be trained in the motel's safety and security policies and procedures and should be introduced to the motel's police contact so they are part of the total security operation.

The safety of security patrols is as important as that of a motel's own personnel. Whoever patrols the property should be given emergency two-way communications equipment, not a cheap citizens band radio. Two-way radios are invaluable for day-to-day operations. Their cost is moderate for small-motel operators but worth every penny.

The one universal concept in the hospitality business is that anything can and will happen. A motel is a cross section of society thrown into a confined space on a transient basis with clashing values and perceptions. Planning is critical.

A motel is smaller than a 1,500-room resort hotel, but its potential for a security debacle is often greater. Why? What can be done to reduce that potential? Where is the biggest bang for the buck?

One security task that is critical to guest protection and is no longer discretionary is controlling access to guest rooms. The courts have interpreted restricted access to such rooms as mandatory. Many motels still have conventional mechanical key and card locks. Many of these lock sets are key-in-knob cylindrical latch sets, which are only 5/8 in long. Case law has determined that this type of latch set does not provide adequate security. Therefore, if a motel does not control keys or regularly rekey locks, it will lose, and lose big, if a lawsuit is filed.

As a rule of thumb, rekeying should occur every time a key is reported lost. It is also a good idea to rekey the whole motel once a year because of the possibility of duplicate keys on the street. Key control is extremely important. Case law has held hotels and motels liable for not maintaining accountability of guest room and master keys.

As the price of electronic motel lock systems decreases, the public demand for them—because of greater security value—increases. Many hotels and motels, even small ones, are requiring them on new facilities, and they are the primary choice in retrofitting new lock systems.

The excuse not to require them on new construction and provide capital improvement funds for retrofitting existing facilities has passed. Motels can no longer defend a security lawsuit involving nonforced entry into a guest room.

Electronic lock systems improve a facility's security by providing the following basic features:

- Automatic reprogramming of a lock to a new key card after every guest
- An audit trail of all key cards made and issued to guests and employees
- A record of recent entries into the room—who, when, and where

Electronic locks also reduce maintenance costs, both in labour and materials. The actual saving has long been debated, but some say a typical electronic system will pay for itself in a few years.

A motel could try to emulate the advantages of electronic systems with a manual system, but the costs and the hassle would be probihitive. The cost and administrative hassle are the main reasons why at some hotels and motels someone can obtain a key to a guest room and gain entry to that same room months later. Mechanical card systems tend to be much better than key types because cards come prepunched in lots of five or a fixed number specified by the motel owner.

Once the cards in a set run out, the motel is forced to recode the lock set. One of the discoveries made by the investigative news team in Florida was that the room kcy it obtained in 1989 still worked in 1990.

Electronic lock systems practically eliminate room thefts by employees and professionals, who look for easier targets down the street.

Before installing an electronic lock set, a motel should consider other important physical security features and measures:

- Solid-core wood or hollow metal entrance doors
- Door frames of welded steel or reinforced knockdown with a security compression anchor
- Door and frame clearance not exceeding 1/8 in.
- All other entrances to the room as secure as the entrance door
- American National Standards Institute Grade 1 (high level of security and durability) mortise lock set with 3/4-in. latch set, 1-in. dead bolt, and automatic retraction of the latch and bolt for life safety
- Wide-angle view port and separate security door guard on all entrance doors
- Emergency graphics on safety, security, and fire precautions and instructions conspicuously posted

Security of the guest room is only as good as the weakest link. Yet a motel need not be a fortress. Another factor critical to the security of guest rooms is site accessibility and opportunity for crime.

An interesting concept was put into practice by a small-hotel owner when he designed a new facility. The building had a U shape, with all doors to guest rooms facing the centre of the U. A small, freestanding building in the centre at the beginning of the U contained the hotel's registration area and lobby. This small building acted as a security checkpoint because all vehicles had to pass by it to exit the site. All parking was contained within the U.

According to the owner, his facility had far fewer security problems than his competitors around him who had traditional motel layouts. Another excellent design involves an enclosed two- to three-story building surrounding a courtyard where all access to guest rooms is through interior corridors. This layout forces visitors to come through the main entrance and pass by the front desk.

Other similar concepts are the traditional four-story or higher facility where all interior corridors, with access through a lobby, pass the front desk to elevators, and emergency fire exits cannot be entered from the outside.

Remote entrances and exits to a building should be minimized. Fire and life safety codes specify the number of exits a building must have. For the convenience of their guests, some hotels and motels permit guests to enter the building through these remote exits. However, they need not serve as entrances.

One way to add convenience and improve security at remote entrances is with readers that accept valid guestroom key cards. In some cases a perimeter door alarm system may alert staff to unauthorized entry or to a door that is propped open. Staff should be trained in how to respond, and the system should be kept in working condition and periodically tested. Although these designs improve guest room security, they do not secure parking lots and pathways.

The number-one deterrent to site crime and improved safety is lighting. Site lighting for a small motel should be a minimum of one footcandle, and the entire site should be uniformly lit. Entrances to the building should have higher illumination levels, around three to five footcandles, to draw attention to them. If a facility has outside entrances to guest rooms, lighting there should be brighter than lighting for walkways, but it does not need to be as bright as it is for the main entrance. Ramps, stairs, and elevator lobbies should be brightly lit.

Landscaping should be minimal and designed and maintained so hiding places and blind spots around the building are eliminated. Each state has some form of liability limits on loss of a guest's property. Laws require that motels provide guests with a safe or safe-deposit box for storing valuables. A motel should be sure to get enough safe-deposit boxes to meet the facility's needs. The boxes should also be of good quality.

Manufacturers usually provide two keys for each deposit box. This second key should be destroyed because some motels have been held liable for the missing contents when it was discovered a second key existed.

If a hotel or motel is in a resort area, room safes may be a worthwhile addition for both security and marketing appeal. In Hawaii in-room safes are a requirement of the innkeepers statutes. In-room safes, however, do not replace front-desk safes or safe-deposit boxes. Physical asset protection in a small hotel or motel begins with good perimeter protection. The more control over access to interior facilities, storage areas, and guest areas, the better.

Inexpensive access control devices can be placed on rear service entrances and high-value storage areas. As a minimum, a secure, restricted-keyway, removable-core commercial lock set with strict key control goes a long way in reducing theft in budget motels. Motels should also consider using an electronic stand-alone access device that provides an audit trail of entries. Some hotels and motels put these locks on storage rooms to control shortages. Armed robbery is a scary experience for roadside motel operators.

Many motels lock their lobbies after dark in the hopes of curtailing crime. Some innovative motel lobby designs have automated check-in equipment, where a guest inserts a credit card, registers, and receives a key card to the room without leaving his or her car. With this approach, however, the human element is lost.

Other facilities have installed bullet-resistive teller windows in the foyer leading to the lobby for after-hours check-in. The lobby should be well lit and open, giving wide visibility to personnel at the front desk. Frequent cash drops and trim safes help reduce dollar loss. Trim safes are small, locked boxes that are mounted under the counter so large bills or excess cash can be dropped inside during high-volume business.

Holdup alarms have pluses and minuses and should be used only after carefully considering all the facts.

Support has grown for CCTV with time-lapse video, both as a deterrent and in documenting events during a robbery. The camera is usually positioned to provide a front view of the assailant, but another good location is a wide-angle view of the front desk and lobby. The use of any of these tools is only as good as the training and instruction of the employees on the front line.

Access to the areas behind the front desk should always be secured with a door and some form of access control device, such as a push-button, reprogrammable lock. The combination should be changed frequently. Drop safes and safe-deposit boxes for employee banks should be contained in a secure workroom, usually behind the front desk. Here, again, key control is a paramount concern.

Often adjacent to this area is the property manager's office, which should have a high-security lock set on the entrance. The front desk acts as a physical barrier, separating the workroom and administrative areas from the lobby. All motels should have an emergency two-way radio system. The system also can be used for day-to-day staff communications.

For a modest investment, three radios with related equipment can be purchased with a somewhat private frequency established and licensed by the Federal Communications Commission. One radio should be placed at the front desk as a base station and the other two given to the property manager and maintenance person.

At night, radios become the primary security and emergency communications between staff on duty and the security officer, if there is one. This small communication system is worth its weight in gold in time saved, in fast response to day-to-day activities, and especially in an emergency.

As security professionals, we tend to notice the extravagant approaches to security at larger hotels and resorts and forget about the small hotel or motel. Being small and located off Highway 1 in Podunk does not denote having small problems. These facilities have just as many security problems as big facilities but with fewer resources to solve them.

As mentioned earlier, 80 percent of the lodging facilities in the United States have fewer than 125 guest rooms. That 80 percent will have the majority of problems. So if your company owns and operates small hotels and motels, make sure they receive a large measure of your expertise.

Chapter 6

Strategic Consistency and Performance

AN ANALYSIS

The past three years have seen the remarkable growth of publicly held real estate companies called Real Estate Investment Trusts (REIT). The industry is still dominated by small, privately held firms but REITs and other large companies are emerging as major players. Organization strategy and structure issues have become very important managerial concerns because they are of concern to W,all Street underwriters. However, evidence suggests that many real estate companies do not have long-term strategic plans. Clearly, this long-term strategic thinking is necessary.

The issue of organizational domain has received much attention in the strategic management literature. This involves the key decision of determining the business or the portfolio of businesses the organization should be in. This domain choice requires the decision-maker's selection of the combination of the organization's specific product(s) and its target market(s).

This strategic choice of product market domain is key because it creates the need for a particular organizational structure and supporting organizational processes to implement the strategy. Consistency between the chosen product market strategy and the supporting structure is a very important ingredient for success. Amburgey and Dacin report the existence of a hierarachial relationship between strategy and structure – strategy being a more important determinant of structure than structure of strategy.

A strategy issue currently facing real estate development firms is how to structure or restructure their organizations in order to improve performance. In a major review of the management literature, in search of lessons for development firms, Bhambri et al. note that real estate development firms take on various organizational structures – smaller firms tend to be project oriented, large firms are either project or functionally oriented, or a mix of the two.

Large firms may be groups of partnerships that are highly decentralized or the firms may be integrated with staff in functional areas and therefore more centralized. The question that these authors raise is: What are the advantages and disadvantages of these alternative organizational structures? As real estate developers begin to restructure and reorganize and add functions such as property management and brokerage, the issue of the appropriate structure becomes very important. This is especially so since a Laventhol and Horwath survey of over 1,000 real estate firms found that most firms tended to operate on a short-term planning horizon, and while 81% of the firms had operating plans that were updated annually, only 59% had long-term (3-5 year) strategic plans.

However, the survey indicates, real estate companies are now becoming more interested in developing business strategies. Other studies of the real estate industry have reported that none of the intended product market domain strategies is either more popular or leads to better performance among development companies. However, the issue of the consistent implementation of the chosen strategy was not investigated. Thus, this paper seeks to form a bridge between the strategic management and the real estate literature by extending Sriram and Anikeeff's findings by investigating the relationship between the consistency of implementation of strategy and performance.

Therefore, the primary purpose of this paper is to see if consistent implementation of strategy – the matching of the appropriate organizational structure to the strategy — results in superior performance. The secondary purpose of this study is to investigate whether this consistency is associated with the age of the organization and its size.

While previous research has found mixed evidence for the relationship between age and strategic choice and size and strategic choice, there has been no research which has studied the association of these two variables (age and size) with the consistent implementation of the chosen strategy.

STRATEGIC GROUP ANALYSIS

Empirical studies have reported on conceptual typologies that are effective in identifying different types of group strategies and organizational structures that are found within an industry. Studies of firms have found that those competing in the same industry often use different types of strategies and organizational structures, but the number of different successful types is limited.

Strategic groups provide a useful intermediate frame of reference between seeing the industry as a whole and seeing each firm separately. The strategic group concept provides a framework for empirical evidence to show that among successful firms a limited number of patterns of strategic behaviour exist. One can see examples of different strategy/ structure types in different real estate firms.

In some firms, the solution is to design diversification strategies and develop approaches for managing the firm as a portfolio of diversified businesses in diversified markets (e.g., the Grubb and Ellis organization). Other firms do not choose to minimize risk through geographic diversification, preferring instead to dominate their local market place (e.g., the Charles E. Smith company in the Washington, D.C. area). Still others prefer one product and diversified markets (e.g., Melvin Simon, a firm which focuses on developing shopping centres in different geographic areas).

Organizational structure, as Bhambri et al. define it, refers to consistent relationships among positions within the organization. They suggest that the best way to structure an organization is a function of firm size, location, product emphasis, and whether the firm intends to handle various activities in-house or use outside consultants.

In the management literature, one model in particular directly addresses the question put forth by Bhambri et al. – the Miles and Snow typology. This typology deals with a firm's product market domain selection strategies and its organizational structure. In this widely tested typology the ideal firm types are classified by the strategic choices made by the firm's decision makers as they adapt the firm's strategy, organizational structure, and administrative processes to the changing economic environment. The underlying assumption is that the firm must adapt if it is to continue to perform and, in the long run, survive.

Miles and Snow argue that determining the business or the portfolio of businesses of the organization is the key strategic choice. The strategic process of adapting the firm to the economic environment requires the firm solve three interrelated problems (discussed next). Their model also suggests that the adaptation occurs in one of three ways.

Miles and Snow believe that the first step in adaptation is the selection by the firm's decision makers of an intended product market domain, which they call the "entrepreneurial problem." The solution of the entrepreneurial problem is followed by the solution of the "engineering problem" – the creation of a system which can implement the product market or entrepreneurial solution using appropriate technology and management information and control systems.

The final step is the solution of the "administrative problem" – the creation of the organizational structure and process that allow for the rationalization and stabilization of activities which solve the other two problems. There are three adaptation strategies, each with its own solution to the entrepreneurial problem, based on the selection of a product market domain. Defenders select a narrow domain with a narrowly defined product and a narrowly defined market.

The Prospector prefers a broadly defined domain with a broad product and a broad market. Analyzers prefer an intermediate strategy with a portion of the firm having a narrow product market domain and the other portion providing multiple products and/or serving broad markets. Miles and Snow emphasize that it is the consistent use of a particular strategy and the selection of the appropriate implementation system, organizational structure, and administrative processes that is important for high performance.

None of the strategies are inherently superior. Miles and Snow define firms that are inconsistent as Reactors. These are the firms where the product market domain is not consistent with the appropriate technology, organization and/or administrative structure. Reactors are generally poor performers. There have been many empirical studies which have found support for Miles and Snow's contention that none of the strategy types, with the exception of Reactors, is inherently superior in terms of performance.

However, Hambrick found that Defenders generally outperformed Prospectors in terms of cash flow and profitability, whereas Prospectors performed better in terms of market share. Returning to our original question: What are the advantages and disadvantages of alternative organizational structures? According to the Miles and Snow model, the answer is contingent upon the organizational structure relationship to a particular strategy.

Several authors have investigated the issue of product market strategies. Gutman found that 98% of the companies he studied chose the sale of existing products in existing markets as the best strategy for growth. Hofer suggests that the current product-existing market strategy is a good strategy if the market is growing, but the new product-existing market is a good strategy when technological innovations require new product introductions. Rumelt found companies that diversified into related businesses were on the average more profitable than other firms.

The Miles and Snow typology provides real estate developers with three stable strategy choices – Defender, Analyzer, Prospector – which yield four product market domain alternatives: (1) sell a narrow range of products in a narrowly defined market (Defender), (2) provide a narrow range of products to a broad market (Analyzer Type A), (3) offer a broad spectrum of products to a narrow market (Analyzer Type B), or (4) provide a broad range of products to a broad spectrum of markets (Prospector).

A previous study of the Miles and Snow framework of strategic group analysis found the typology applicable to the real estate development industry. This study also found that there was no significant difference in the frequency with which the four product market matrix variations were found among single-family residential, multi-family residential, and commercial developers.

By finding no significant difference in average performance (as measured by sales per employee) among the four intended product market strategy categories, the Sriram and Anikeeff study supports Miles and Snow. This lack of difference in performance was found even when controlling for builder type (multi-family residential, single family residential, commercial).

This earlier study demonstrated that various strategies exist among development firms and that no strategy in and of itself could bring about superior performance. However, there was a great deal of variance within each of the categories. The Miles and Snow model would suggest that this is due to differences in the implementation of the selected strategy. According to the model, certain strategies call for certain organizational and administrative processes. Failure to implement these consistently with the chosen strategy will yield poor performance.

Strategic Consistency

Miles and Snow emphasize that whereas none their stable strategic types is inherently superior in terms of performance, it is the consistent use of a particular strategy, coupled with the appropriate implementation system, organizational structure, and administrative processes, which is important for high performance. They label firms that are inconsistent as Reactors. These are the firms where the product market domain is not consistent with the appropriate technology, organization, and/or administrative structure. Reactors are generally poor performers.

While other studies have alerted managers to the importance of the issue of strategic consistency, the issue of strategy in general, and consistent implementation in particular, has received little attention in the real estate literature. This study attempts to close that gap.

This study investigates the benefits of consistency in the implementation of two of the three stable types of strategies – the Defender, with a narrow product market and the Prospector with the broad product market orientation. Ignoring the intermediate Analyzer category allows for sharper differentiation in the classification and greater face validity in the operationalization of the variables.

Also, methodologically it is hard to define and classify a "consistent" Analyzer. This type does not have unique characteristics but rather is a hybrid which has characteristics of both Defenders and Prospectors. This approach of studying only the Defenders and Prospectors in order to test tendencies of extreme strategies is consistent with that followed by Hambrick.

The Defender's problem is to seal off a portion of the total market to create a stable set of products and customers. This is done by aggressively defending a narrow domain and narrow product offering. Technologically, the problem for management is the efficient production of a product. This is accomplished by concentrating on creating a cost-efficient system with a tendency toward vertical integration.

In contrast, the Prospector's strategy is to locate and exploit new product and market opportunities. It does this by avoiding long-term commitments to a single technological process. It has a low degree of routine, it is flexible and gives up efficiency in its production system. The administration problem is how to facilitate and coordinate numerous and diverse operations. There is a tendency toward a product structure with low division of labour and low degree of formalization.

Based on the characteristics of Defenders and Prospectors discussed above, for real estate developers the key determinant of consistency between strategy, structure, and the administrative process is the relationship between the firm and its construction function. Peiser and Schwanke (1992) believe that for real estate developers the two most important decisions are the purchase of the land and the commencement of construction.

The work of the construction team represents the bulk of the project's total cost, and effectively managing their contributions is critical to the success of the development project. McMahan suggests that the development firm may undertake construction in a variety of ways — in-house, on a contract basis with a general contractor, or as a joint-venture partner with a general contractor.

In the real estate industry, a consistent Defender would integrate the construction activity by doing it either in-house or with an affiliated firm in order to maintain control of the organization's core technology and maximize cost efficiency. (This broader definition of integration to include activities performed by close affiliates is consistent with that proposed by Williamson and has been employed by other researchers in strategic management).

On the other hand, a consistent Prospector would outsource its construction activity to maintain flexibility in its ability to obtain multiple technologies. While other studies have confirmed that no one strategy is inherently superior, the empirical evidence on the benefits (if any) of strategic consistency is lacking.

Our contention is that real estate developers who employ a means of performing their construction activity which is consistent with their chosen strategy (Defenders who are vertically integrated for their construction and Prospectors who subcontract it) will outperform ones which are inconsistent (Defenders who subcontract it and Prospectors who are integrated). Therefore, our first research statement (RS) is,

RS 1: There will be a positive association between performance and strategic consistency.

The secondary objective of this study is to investigate whether consistency is a function of the age of the firm or of its size. While some authors have suggested that a firm's strategy and structure change as it progresses through its "life cycle" and that its strategy is influenced by its stage in this cycle, others believe that strategy is not evolutionary. In addition, empirical studies of real estate developers have shown that whether firms choose to be Defenders or Prospectors is not associated with their age. It is therefore likely that consistency of strategy and structure is not systematically related to age either. Therefore,

RS 2: There will be no association between firm age and strategic consistency.

The evidence on the relationship between strategic choice and size is somewhat mixed. The Defender's strategy of focusing on cost-efficient technologies and a tendency toward vertical integration is more appropriate for larger firms since size is necessary to vertically integrate efficiently and to enjoy the economies of scale which in turn drive down costs. On the other hand, Prospectors are smaller and less bureaucratic in order to better respond to market opportunities. There is, however, no reason to believe that size has any relationship with the ability to consistently apply the selected strategy. Therefore,

RS 3: There will be no association between firm size and strategic consistency.

A sample of the largest real estate developers was generated from lists published by Professional Builder (1987) and Building Design and Construction (1988). The person named on these lists (i.e., the chief executive officer or the vice president/director of construction/real estate operation) for each of the companies was sent a mail questionnaire with a cover letter explaining the academic aims of the study and requesting them to respond.

The survey included 391 of the 400 largest homebuilders, the 30 largest retail developers, the 50 largest industrial developers, and 40 largest hotel/motel/restaurant builders. A total of 80 responses were received from the 511 that were mailed, yielding a response rate of 16 percent.

While this response rate is not very high, it is not markedly different from that found in other similar studies. In addition, a visual comparison between respondents and nonrespondents did not reveal any systematic differences between the two groups in terms of geographic location and sales volume. The responding firms varied in terms of age (median 20, range 3 to 78), size (median 65, range 5 to 5,300 employees), and type of product built.

The respondents were distributed among those that received the majority of their sales from single-family residential (n = 31), multi-family residential (n = 17), and commercial (n = 11) development. The remaining firms either could not be classified because of missing data (n = 10) or received their revenue from a mix of product types (n = 11) without a predominant category (i.e., no one product accounted for over 50% of their sales).

Constructs and Measures

Where possible, constructs were operationalized using measurement items generated from existing scales, and others were developed specifically for this study. The questionnaire was pilot tested for its clarity, readability, and to ensure that the theory based items addressed issues of concern to real estate decision makers.

A firm's product market domain was used to determine whether it was a Defender or a Prospector. To measure this product market domain strategy, two sets of questionnaire items were developed: one set to determine the product domain and the other set to determine market domain. Each item was measured on a 5-point Likert-type scale anchored by "strongly agree" (1) and "strongly disagree" (5). Principal component factor analysis was used to determine the underlying concept (product domain or market domain) measured by the set of survey question items. The results provide internal level indices which are used to define the concepts.

Product domain was measured by those items in the questionnaire relating to whether the firm sought new product lines or was limited to existing lines; whether or not it would consider product line expansion in the face of uncertain profit; whether it diversified to balance risks; and whether or not it concentrated on well understood products.

Market domain was measured by those items in the questionnaire which dealt with whether or not the firm planned to expand into new geographic areas even if profit levels were uncertain, whether or not it diversified geographically to balance its risks, whether it concentrated on well understood markets, and whether it would rather concentrate on new product lines in current markets or enter new markets.

A firm's age was measured by the number of years it had been in development. Size was measured by the number of employees in the firm. Performance was measured by sales per nonclerical employee. The total sales of the firm, as reported in the publication from which the firm was identified, was divided by the number of nonclerical employees as reported in the survey.

This measure, rather than sales per employee, was used because in small firms, of which there are many in the real estate development industry, sales per nonclerical employee is a better measure of efficiency. Since all firms need a certain minimum number of clerical employees in order to function effectively and these employees are typically added on less than proportionately to sales increases, they account for a disproportionately high percentage of the total workforce in small firms. Their inclusion would therefore result in a misleadingly low sales per employee figure for smaller firms.

Scale Development

In order to assess the construct validity and unidimensionality of product domain and the market domain constructs discussed above, the multiple questionnaire items used to measure each were subjected to principal component factor analysis, with varimax rotation. Items loading on a factor at a level of 0.4 or higher were included in the scale for that construct. These items were then summed to yield a total score measure for each construct.

These multiple item scales were subsequently assessed for reliability using Cronbach's alpha. Both the product domain and the market domain scales were above the recommended minimum (0.6) reliability. The items used (those with loadings above 0.4) to form each scale, their factor loadings, and the reliability measure for each.

The individual firm's product market domain classification was determined next. The sample firms were divided into groups based on the breadth/narrowness of their product market domains. In the absence of any universally accepted yardstick for determining broad or narrow domains, the relative summed score for each firm on product domain and market domain was used as the basis for categorization. These scores were arrayed in hierarchical order for each of the two constructs. The firms with less than the mean score were identified as having a narrow focus, whereas those that had a higher than mean score were identified as having a broad focus.

Thus, four categories of firms emerged as a result of this classification scheme: 1) Defenders, those with narrow product and narrow market domains, 2) Prospectors, with broad product and broad market domains, 3) Analyzers (Type A), with narrow product domain and broad market domain, and 4) Analyzers (Type B) with broad product and narrow market domain. Defenders had a mean product scope of 12.7 and market scope of 12.3. Prospectors averaged 19.3 and 20.9, respectively on these measures.

In order to determine which firms were consistent, an analysis of their construction activity was conducted (construction was selected rather than building design or property management, for instance, since construction is a function all developers require).

According to Miles and Snow (1978), Defenders would vertically integrate and Prospectors would outsource. In the context of real estate development this would imply that consistent Defenders would use in-house or affiliated companies to undertake their construction activity whereas consistent Prospectors would either negotiate contracts or solicit open bids from outside firms in order to complete this activity.

By extension, Defenders who outsourced their construction or Prospectors who had either an in-house or affiliated construction firm would be inconsistent. Thus, Defenders who did 75% or more of their construction in-house (or with an affiliated company) and Prospectors who outsourced 75% or more of their construction were deemed consistent. The rest were categorized as inconsistent.

In order to test for differences in age, size, and performance between consistent and inconsistent firms, one-way analysis of variance using the F-statistic was conducted. To measure the strength of the association between these variables and performance, the correlation coefficients were computed. For the purposes of hypothesis testing, p [is less than] .05 was taken as the measure of significance of the results.

As indicated by the results, consistent firms, with average sales per employee of $1,434.58, are almost twice as productive as the inconsistent ones ($753.66). These performance differences are statistically significant, with an F-statistic of 4.96 (p [is less than] .03). These results lend support to RS 1, indicating that consistency of strategy is associated with higher performance.

The consistent firms were on average 23.14 years old and the inconsistent ones had an average age of 22.24 years. The F-value of .03 indicates that there is no significant age difference between consistent and inconsistent firms. These findings are consistent with RS 2.

Consistent firms are on average larger (379.14 employees) than inconsistent ones (187.93 employees) but these differences are not statistically significant (F =.38, p [is less than] .54), thus providing support for RS 3.

Strength of Association

While the results presented suggest the existence of a statistically significant association between consistency of strategy and performance, they do not provide a measure of the strength of this association. To assess this, various measures of association were computed. High performers were those firms with sales/employee above the average for the sample and low performers were those firms with below average performance.

As can be seen from the chi-square statistic (6.81, p [is less than] .009), consistency and performance are not independent. The contingency coefficient (0.436, p [is less than] .009, for a two-by-two table, this coefficient's range is 0 to .707) indicates the existence of a positive, moderately strong association between consistency and performance. This conclusion is strengthened by the gamma coefficient (.867) which indicates a strong ability to predict performance based on consistency of strategy.

The results of this study should be of interest to real estate developers. In an industry characterized by a great deal of volatility, the development of longterm strategic plans which incorporate clear product and market domain choices represents one way to buffer the organization from the severe cycles which often occur. However, as these findings suggest, it is the consistent implementation of the chosen strategy which is critical to success. As real estate developers increasingly incorporate strategic management thinking into the organization, they must ensure that their structure is appropriate to their product market strategy.

The results of this study indicate that consistent application of a chosen strategy results in higher performance than if the implementation of strategy were inconsistent. A key finding is the evidence of a moderately strong association between consistency and performance. Among inconsistent firms, the frequency of low performance is much higher than that of high performance. This suggests inconsistency is almost certain to be associated with a relatively lower performance. In short, consistency is necessary but not sufficient for high performance.

This study also found that age and size are not associated with consistency. This is of particular significance in the real estate development industry since many of the firms in it are small and young. Thus, as long as these firms select a strategy and organize their construction activity appropriately, they are likely to perform well regardless of how large they are or how long they have been in the industry. This points to the importance of an early choice of competitive strategy and the setting up of an administrative structure to go along with it.

These findings provide further support to the argument that none of Miles and Snow's stable strategies is inherently superior, provided sufficient care is taken to ensure consistent implementation. While the findings of this study are interesting, the small sample size may make the statistical results somewhat unstable and the results, while revealing, should be interpreted cautiously.

In order to enable stronger conclusions regarding the benefits of strategic consistency, other studies will need to replicate these findings using larger samples and add to their generalizability by investigating other industries. Extending these results will be of particular value to firms in other fragmented industries (e.g., services, retailing, distribution) which, like the real estate industry, consist of many small and young firms which could benefit from the application of business strategies. In addition, longitudinal studies will permit greater confidence in the stability of the results.

Future studies of real estate developers also need to use multiple indicators of consistency (in addition to using degree of integration of construction activity) and assess performance using additional measures in order to validate the findings reported here. The availability of more conventional measures of performance (e.g., ROI, ROE, ROA, etc.) becomes easier as future studies focus on REITs in addition to small, privately held firms. Since REITs are publically held, more accurate and verifiable performance data have become available.

Traditionally, many academic researchers have examined large, well capitalized firms. This study shows that many of the basic findings of the strategic management literature are equally applicable to smaller firms in a fragmented industry. Further examination of small firms across various issues germane to strategy formulation and execution is necessary in order to identify the areas where the lessons learned from large firms can be utilized and those where small firms require separate analysis.

Since 1987/88 the real estate industry has gone through a fairly substantial restructuring as some firms have left the industry and many of the others have reorganized. The reorganized ones have become real estate companies and are not merely developers as in the past. As they have added additional functions (e.g, property management, brokerage) they are having to redefine their organizational strategy.

The findings of this study can help these owners/ managers to properly structure their organizations in order to ensure that this structure is consistent with their chosen strategy. As these results suggest, strategy selection by itself is not a determinant of performance, it is its consistent application which is associated with higher performance.

Chapter 7

Organizational Forms in the International Hotel Sector

CHOICE IN A WORLD OF ALLIANCES

In the new management landscape, interfirm collaborations are common, and control is only loosely correlated with ownership. Firms may collaborate with each other by forming equity joint ventures. However, a large number of interfirm collaborations are based on no equity investment at all, but are contractual or quasi-contractual in nature. The principals have concluded in these cases that the optimal level of ownership is zero. Given several choices, ranging from full ownership to a partial equity position to various contractual modes, such as management service and franchise agreements, the key question tackled by this paper is "What organizational mode is best?"

This study focuses on the global hotel business, which is especially suitable for an investigation of the organizational modal choice question, since non-equity modes are at least as widespread as equity ownership, if not more. Alliances with other firms used to be considered a minor component of overall strategy in many sectors. Today, competitive advantage can equally well be derived from interfirm cooperation in non-equity-based agreements such as management service contracts. This is especially true in service sectors such as hotels, where the capital-intensive elements (such as real estate) can be separated from the knowledge-based or managerial expertise elements of competitiveness.

In the hotels sector, management service contracts (between the owners of the physical capital or real estate and the global hotel company, which supplies the managerial expertise) appear to be the single most common governance mode. Franchising is also ubiquitous. Interfirm cooperation is therefore not peripheral, but central to global strategy.

The global hotels business may be a precursor for other service sectors in terms of the prevalence of non-equity modes of doing business. By covering many foreign markets, our data enable us to examine the extent to which environmental (i.e., market or country-specific) variables, as opposed to firm-specific variables, affect the choice of organizational mode.

With the relaxation of investment controls and the general growth in alliance formation worldwide, managers today face a spectrum of available choices. The key question this paper tackles is: "For a particular foreign operation (a particular hotel in a foreign location), should a firm choose full ownership of the operation, an equity joint venture or contract-specified modes, such as franchising, or management service agreements?" This paper proposes that the choice is not determined by country characteristics or transaction-cost considerations alone. The characteristics of the firm and its global strategy comprise the other leg of the new syncretic theory.

Four literatures have a bearing on the modal choice question. These are.' (i) the traditional market entry literature from International Business. There is a considerable literature on corporate alliances, but less on when it is better for a firm to choose an alliance over its own fully owned operation, or vice versa, and very little indeed on which type of alliance is best, under which circumstances.

The aims of this paper are to advance the theory and testing of the entire spectrum of modal choices, including relatively neglected modes, such as management service contracts and franchising. The latter are more prevalent in service sectors, especially in hotels. The article synthesizes several academic literatures with a bearing on the modal choice issue, and presents a unified framework. The results show that both host country environment and firm strategy influence the selection of organizational mode. They also show that contractual alliances can effectively substitute for equity ownership in several circumstances, and comprise an important part of global strategy.

This paper is organized as follows: A survey of various organizational forms in the international hotel business is followed by a review of the modal choice literature. This is followed by presentation of hypotheses, data, and statistical tests. The paper concludes by examining the implications of the empirical findings for management practice and further theory development.

ORGANIZATIONAL FORMS IN THE GLOBAL HOTELS BUSINESS

One first needs to understand various organizational forms and their idiosyncrasies in the global hotel business before one can formulate hypotheses. Some of the hypotheses this paper will propose are peculiar to the hotel business although most are applicable to other service and manufacturing sectors. Hence we first present an overview of the hotel business.

Since the focus of this paper is the determinants of foreign strategy, we focus only on hotel properties outside the home nation of the firm. Hotel firms listed in the International Hotels Group Directory have more than half a million rooms outside their home nation. From the directory, we first identified firms that listed at least one property outside their home nation as part of their global group of hotels. The directory provides a comprehensive coverage of the business worldwide, but does not show the organizational mode (fully owned, joint venture, management contract, or franchise) for each property. This was obtained from questionnaires.

For the purpose of this paper, therefore, a global hotel firm is defined as one that either has an equity stake in a foreign property, or operates the hotel under a management service agreement, or is a franchisor to the foreign hotel property. Thus, a company could be a global firm without any ownership of a foreign property. However, as a matter of fact, virtually every hotel company in our sample had some equity ownership in at least one foreign property, thus providing a range of organizational choices in the sample.

A questionnaire was sent to all listed firms with foreign hotel operations. The questions covered data on the hotel firm as a whole (e.g., the firm's overall size, international experience, distribution and number of hotel properties worldwide). The questionnaire also asked what organizational mode was used for each hotel property abroad.

The questionnaire response provided a sample that covers 1,131 hotels and comprises over 60 percent of all "foreign" properties and rooms listed in the directory (355,169 out of some half million rooms). Despite reminders, a large firm response bias remains in the sample. Our data base therefore includes the organizational mode chosen for each hotel property, and other details on the global hotel company involved, as well as characteristics of the nation where the hotel property is located.

While the prevalence of management service contracts is high across all major regions where hotels are located, there appear to be variations in equity ownership and franchising by region. Equity ownership is lower, and franchising more frequent in North America. In Asia, by comparison, franchising is less common, and equity ownership modes are most common. Non-equity modes, thus, account worldwide for 65.4 percent of foreign operation properties, and arrangements involving two companies account for as much as 81.2 percent of the total number of hotels worldwide.

But this should not make us jump to the conclusion that managerial control or strategic direction are weak in the joint venture or non-equity organizational forms. In some service sectors, such as hotels, control has been de-linked from equity ownership - but control, and an overall global strategy exist.

What is the dimensions of management "control" in alliances? For both its short and long term strategy, the global firm today must deal with a multiplicity of partners and organizational forms, each having its own degrees of required control. In the international joint venture context, Schaan and Geringer and Hebert described different mechanisms whereby each firm may exercise control over the joint venture.

For alliances in general, the means of control can be classified as "participatory" control (by the act of actively participating in the management of an enterprise), control exercised by "withholding" or threatening to withhold some asset or capability desired by the other partner, and "proscriptive" control (by legal or de facto prohibitions).

We break these down further between (a) daily operational and quality control in each hotel property; (b) control over the physical assets or over the real estate and its attendant risks; (c) control over tacit expertise embedded in the routines of the firm; and (d) control over the codified assets, such as a global reservation system and the firm's internationally recognized brand name.

Equity Investments

In fully owned operations, all four control criteria (a) through (d) are under the strong control of the hotel firm. In equity joint ventures, (a), (b), and (c) are shared, although typically control of the global brand name and reservations system remains with the global hotel company to retain its leverage over the local partner. Since organizational control has many attributes, especially in international business, where culture and national differences prevail, it is difficult to develop an overall measure for control in international joint ventures. The global hotel company may retain strong control over (d) (its reservations system and global brand), but have shared control over day-to-day management, quality, and physical assets.

Tacit expertise (c) is inevitably shared with the local partner, to some extent, which may erode the global hotel company's knowledge advantage over time. Equity investment does provide stronger long-term strategic control compared with management service agreements, for the simple reason that the latter are time-bound and, on expiry of the agreement, subject to cancellation by the property owners. By comparison, an equity stake is not so easily dissolved.

Management Service Agreements

A management service contract is a long term agreement, of up to ten years or even longer, whereby the legal owners of the property and real estate enter into a contract with the hotel firm to run and operate the hotel on a day to day basis, usually under the latter's internationally recognized name.

Quality control, daily management and senior staffing (a) principally rest with the international hotel firm and not the property owners. But the operation is run as if the property were part of the global chain. Customers cannot tell the difference. The international hotel firm, as operator, earns management fees often expressed as a percentage of gross revenues (sometimes with annual minimums and lump-sum payments).

In addition, the global hotel firm may earn extra profit margins on any supplies and material it sells to the particular property. In some cases, there may be bonuses linked, not to revenues, but to profits - as a profit-sharing formula. Finally, in several cases, the property is charged a small fee for every reservation booked through the global reservation system of the global hotel firm. Such codified strategic assets (d) remain in the control of the global firm.

Nevertheless, local partners may not always be content to merely remain as passive owners of the real estate. Since much of the middle management and staff are local personnel, they acquire tacit expertise on the job. There have been a few cases, for example, as the Oberoi Hotels Group, which initially had an agreement with Intercontinental Hotels, but learned the business well enough to launch its own international hotel chain after terminating its partnership with Intercontinental Hotels.

While it is possible that a few minority joint venture investments may provide the firm with lower control over global strategy than a management service agreement, in general we posit that a joint venture equity stake provides superior long-term strategic control, compared with contractual alternatives.

In effect, for the global hotel firm, management service agreements provide strong day-to-day (if not long term) control without ownershi. Moreover, such contracts can amount to surer returns without real estate investment risk. Even ordinary commercial or economic risk is greatly reduced since the hotel operator's take is often a percentage of revenues (akin to a royalty), and not expressed as a percentage of profits, as would be the case in an equity joint venture.

It is axiomatic that over a business cycle, revenues are far less volatile than profits. The latest indicator of this trend is Marriott Corp., which in 1993, split itself into two firms - one a profitable hotel management firm, and the other a debt-laden real estate owning company.

In franchising, (a) daily management and quality control and (b) control over physical assets reside with the franchisee, and not with the global hotel firm. In this case, the international hotel firm does not run the hotel's management, but trains and guides it under a contractual relationship, sharing only some tacit expertise (c). But it would be a mistake to assume that the franchisor exercises no control.

Typically, hotel standards are sought to be zealously enforced. Codified assets (d), such as brands and reservation systems reside with the global hotel company. The franchisor earns fees linked to revenues and profits, additional margins on material supplied to the franchise, booking fees for clients booked via the global reservations network, and training fees for personnel trained.

For the international hotel firm, even without ownership or management involvement, we hypothesize that a network of franchisees enable it to capture at least some economies of global scale in logistics, supplies, architectural design, reservations, training, and brand recognition. Certainly, not all firms replicate hotel architectural designs "cookie cutter" style in every nation; nor do all franchisees purchase from the global hotel firm's central procurement channel. But we hypothesize that enough do so to provide significant economies in a worldwide operation.

The question addressed by this paper is:

"For a firm intending an investment in a particular hotel property located in a particular nation, what determines whether the investment will be fully owned, or an equity joint venture, or whether it will be a non-equity arrangement involving either a management service contract, or a franchise?"

This paper is written from the perspective of a global hotel firm willing to consider different entry modes in various nations. It does not refer to the local owners of a hotel property as franchisees, or as the local partners in a management service agreement.

In this paper we take a syncretic approach to the modal choice question, similar to Hill, Hwang and Kim, or Contractor. The approach is not merely the minimization of transaction costs, with a focus on one transaction or market entry at a time, nor does it treat only the conditions in the host nation (which was the focus of traditional market entry literature). The firm seeks the maximization of profits based on long-term global strategy. This forces a look at the revenue side as well.

Moreover, the maximization of long term global profits is not merely a matter of maximum rent extraction from a particular market, but building the capabilities and knowledge of the company as a whole. Zajac and Olsen describe the modal choice decision as determined by the need to create long-term "value" in the global firm.

Increasingly, the use of corporate allies and partners to create a global network is being seen to be as valid a pathway to building value as an ownership-linked company. Since non-equity modes are more prevalent internationally in the hotel business, this process is well along on its way in this sector. In alliances, the firm must deal with other agents, such as franchisees, local owners of the real estate, and joint venture partners, whose predilections, incentives, and motivations may differ from the strategic objectives of the global firm.

Agency theory also provides some insights into such different objectives. A robust theory of modal choice must therefore incorporate country-specific and transaction-specific variables, as well as factors relating to the strategy of the global company and the agents with which it interacts.

Interest in the modal choice question began in the marketing and international business fields, where the question was couched as the choice between exporting and foreign direct investment (FDI). Root (1994) and Goodnow and Hansz (1985) reflect the traditional marketing focus on conditions or the environment in the host country. This country focus remains as one of the legs of our empirical analysis later in the paper. Locational or country-specific advantages were one part of Dunning's (1988) OLI theory.

However, non-equity forms such as licensing were then considered of lesser interest, and joint ventures were not explicitly considered on the spectrum of governance choices until the mid-1980s. Buckley and Casson (1976) expanded the choice to include licensing as a means of reaching customers abroad. But in their perspective, the multinational firm would usually prefer to "internalize" transactions via direct equity investment rather than license its capability.

The multinational firm's raison d'etre was its superior ability to extract rents from each nation it invested in - a rent that was supposed to be almost always far higher than potential returns via cooperative or contractual modes of entry, such as licensing or franchising. Recent work by Buckley and Casson (1996) considers cooperative modes of organization as far more likely.

Transaction-Cost Explanations

The core of the transaction-cost explanations deal with asset specificity, bounded rationality, the free-rider problem, and opportunism. The principal focus is on one transaction or negotiation - one market entry - at a time. The choice of organizational mode is that which minimizes transaction costs. The other strand of Dunning's (1988) OLI theory, namely Ownership, makes a related argument - that the multinational firm will prefer to "internalize" via equity ownership when the "market" for knowledge transfers "fails."

Transaction-cost explanations will comprise a significant input in the development of this paper's hypotheses. However, since they are sufficiently well known, it would be more useful to discuss how these arguments relate to global hotel operations when formally proposing hypotheses later in the paper. The Organizational Capability Perspective: The Global Hotel Firm as a Knowledge-based Service Company

A useful perspective on many alliances is that they involve the transfer of knowledge between partners over some duration of time, rather than as a transaction. Winter (1987) focused on the creation of knowledge and competence within the enterprise, and on how expertise is embedded in tacit organizational "routines." Ghoshal (1987) has a learning focus, but on cross-affiliate knowledge transfers within the multinational enterprise.

Teece distinguishes between tacit, unwritten or informal knowledge, and formally registered intellectual property which is far more easily transferable or shared with another firm. Contractor points out that intellectual properties, such as patents, trademarks or copyrights, are only of minor strategic importance - as an all-industry generalization. However, in the hotel business, registered brand names, as well as unregistered, but proprietary reservations and logistics systems, are a potent source of control.

Control over codified strategic assets (category (d)) occurs typically in all four modes. The potential threat of withdrawing permission to use the global company's brand, reservations and support systems, moderates the opportunistic behaviour of partners in each nation. In fact, this may be one factor which explains the high prevalence of equity and non-equity alliances in the hotel business.

It is nevertheless true that codified strategic assets are only the visible, formalized tip of a vast iceberg of tacit information embedded in trained personnel and technicians, and in implicit routines. Hence the cost of transferring such knowledge to another partner firm can be protracted, difficult, costly and incomplete. This also partially depends on the "absorptive capacity" of the partner firm learning the new routines.

If the local partner is in a lesser-developed nation (here we connect the transaction-cost argument with a country variable), the transfer of complex tacit knowledge is more difficult, and we hypothesize later that non-equity forms, such as franchising, will be less prevalent in developing nations, ceteris paribus. If knowledge is so extremely embedded, or tacit, as to prevent its accurate valuation by the negotiators, then in the worst case, "bounded rationality" may prevent the "transaction" or partnership itself from taking place.

In the earlier literature such "market failure" left the firm with no choice but to opt for the hierarchical, full-ownership mode. Today, however, the ubiquity of cooperative modes, especially in the hotel business, suggests that such market failure is not common.

Learning across organizational boundaries in partnerships can also be unintended, lack reciprocity, or be unequal. Unequal cross-flows of knowledge can lead to perceptions of "free riding," and unintended leakage of knowledge can lead to opportunism in the form of partners terminating the relationship to become competitors. However, retaining legal or de facto control over strategic assets, such as brands or a global reservations system, can moderate such opportunism on the part of local partners. (Here again, this firm-level literature connects with the transaction-costs arguments.)

Management of knowledge flows within and across the organizational boundary is therefore key to strategic success when dealing with multiple competitors and partners. This leads to the second sub-group of firm-specific factors affecting the choice of organizational mode.

Other Industry and Firm Strategy Variables

Whether a firm will decide to "go it alone" or cooperate with partners, and if so, under what mode of association, depends not just on the intended transaction or on the characteristics of knowledge within a firm, but on the broader structure of the firm and its industry as well. These variables include size and scale, diversification, investment in R&D and training, experience, flexibility, speed, first-mover rewards, and synergies of cooperation.

Each of these variables is complex and is not amenable to easy generalizations as to its effects on the modal choice. For example, Gomes-Casseres indicates that the quest for global economies of scale will discourage cooperative organizational modalities. Yet, in some sectors, economies of global scale may be captured equally well by quasi-integration across national borders.

To capture global economies some firms may grow larger by mergers and acquisitions, or via internal growth; others may join a coalition or network to achieve the same ends, especially if rapid growth is needed for competitive reasons.

How does "knowledge intensity" affect the modal choice? In the manufacturing sector knowledge intensity has been measured by the R&D/Sales ratio. Since hotel companies do not do R&D per se, the ratio of the amount they invest in the training of their personnel, over sales, can provide an alternate measure of knowledge intensity.

Gatignon and Anderson (1988) proposed that when the proprietary content of products or processes is high the choice will tend towards the full ownership end of the spectrum. For hotels, one can operationalize knowledge intensity by ratios such as "investment in training over sales."

Agency Theory and Non-Equity Organizational Modes

Shane applies agency theory concepts to show that non-equity modes of entry can be efficient substitutes for equity investment. Consider the choice between a fully owned foreign hotel operation, where the global company has to hire its own staff, and a franchise. The so-called "adverse selection" and "moral hazard" problems in agency theory focus on the difficulty of assessing the abilities of foreign employees, and monitoring them for performance.

This is more difficult the greater the cultural distance between the firm and the host nation. Equity owners only have residual profit claims on the remnant of the net cash flow from a foreign operation after costs, including those of employees, are met. By contrast, not only does a local franchisee have the better local knowledge to select and monitor employees, but also promises to the franchisor the "first cut" of cash flow collections.

This is because, in franchising, lump-sum fees are paid in advance, and royalties must be paid out of sales revenue collections (regardless of profits). More·specific theoretical arguments will be developed later with the hypotheses.

The Dependent Variable (M): Modal Choice for Each Property

The questionnaire responses listed, for each hotel in a foreign nation, its organizational mode, whether the hotel is a Franchise = 1; Under the company's management in a service contract = 2; Partially Owned (Joint Venture) = 3; and Fully Owned = 4. The dependent variable M is therefore a polytomous measure generally depicting rising levels of equity ownership and overall control. Overlapping categories (e.g., a hotel property under management service agreement and partial equity investment) were dropped, as Discriminant Analysis requires non-overlapping categories. This affected only 6.5 percent of cases.

Two techniques with different objectives and different methodology were used: Discriminant Analysis as a test of the robustness of the group classification based on independent variables, followed by Ordinal logistic regression using a generalized LOGIT model. Discriminant Analysis tests the validity and robustness of the modal choice categories, but is not concerned about their rank ordering. Regression is concerned about by the ordering of categories within the multinomial measure M. The hypotheses developed below relate principally to the regression analysis.

Independent Variables

A complete picture of the organizational choice question needs a syncretic approach combining transaction-cost and agency theory reasoning, as well as country-specific and firm-specific variables, as Contractor (1990) pointed out. This was echoed by Kim and Hwang (1992), and Erramilli and Rao (1993) who used all four types of factors in their empirical studies. Even earlier, while operating under the panoply of transaction-cost explanations, Gatignon and Anderson (1988) had used country indicators, such as country risk, as well as firm strategy variables, such as advertising/sales and R&D/sales ratios, and number of employees, as a proxy for firm size.

The first group relates to the country in which the hotel property is located. We will ask how country-specific variables affect the modal choice. The second groups' independent variables describe the size, international experience, and extent of foreign business of the hotel firm. The third groups' independent variables describes responses from hotel executives on the perceived importance of strategy and control variables.

In diverse international operations, the organizational form is sure to be affected by local conditions. Few companies today follow uniform policies across countries. Assume that a global hotel company is willing to consider in each country either an equity investment (fully or partially owned), or a management service agreement, or a franchise. It assesses each situation, and makes the appropriate choice of organizational mode.

Country Political and Economic Risk: Data for this independent variable were obtained from Frost and Sullivan's, International Country Risk Guide, for each nation where the sample hotel properties are located.

Development of this hypothesis rests on four arguments. The first relates to the size of resource commitments in risky nations. Kim and Hwang (1992), Agarwal and Ramaswami (1992), and Madhok (1994) propose that, ceteris paribus, higher country risk will favour entry modes with lower resource commitments or ownership. Gatignon and Anderson (1988) and Goodnow and Hansz (1985) also suggest that equity investment modes are less likely when country risk is high.

We should recall that in this business, capital investment in real estate is normally high - occasionally approaching $100 million for large resort properties. The second argument deals with "environmental uncertainty" in terms of political and currency volatility. When volatility is high, franchising is preferred over corporate ownership. Agency theory concurs and suggests that franchising can be an efficient organizational mode in risky markets, where the franchisee is responsible for employee selection and monitoring.

Control over the brand name is maintained by the global firm, tempering or eliminating franchisee opportunism. Kim and Hwang (1992) use the term "demand uncertainty" and postulate that when uncertainty is high, equity ownership will tend to be low. This is corroborated by Erramilli and Rao (1993). Third, in the international hotel business, management service contracts enable the firm to exercise a high degree of control over the foreign operation without ownership risk.

Franchising involves an even lesser commitment. Finally, the inclusion of royalty-type payments in alliance agreements, where the earnings of the global hotel firm are linked to sales, and not profit of the hotel property, reduce their risk significantly in volatile environments, because royalties are linked to sales and not profits. Sales are far more stable over the business cycle compared with profits. In Buckley and

Casson's (1996) words, "...as volatility increases so internalization becomes less attractive."

In risky nations then, hotel firms would be more likely to avoid the risks of equity investment and opt for management service contracts or franchising. Hence, our hypothesis:

H1: M (rising levels of equity and control) will be negatively associated with country political and economic risk.

(However, please note that because Frost & Sullivan's "Composite Risk Index" is on an inverted scale of Highest Risk = 0 to Lowest Risk = 100 our hypothesis expects a positive sign for variable CRI).

Cultural Distance: Several studies suggest that "Cultural Distance" between the home base of the firm and the intended foreign market is a powerful determinant of modal choice. There appears to be a consensus in the literature on this topic, namely, that a greater cultural distance between the firm and the foreign nation it is operating in will lead to less equity ownership, and a greater incidence of cooperative modes, ceteris paribus. Gomes-Casseres (1989) explains this in terms of needing more help from local joint venture partners in less familiar environments. Fladmoe-Lindquist and Jacque (1995) posit that "...cultural distance tends to create costly information requirements which encourage U.S. service firms to use lower-cost governance structures."

At the same time, the risk of cultural misunderstandings is higher, especially in a service industry, and one with a high local labour content. Shane's (1996) adaptation of agency theory makes a congruent hypothesis, namely that local partners ease the "adverse selection problem" in selecting and overseeing staff in culturally distant markets.

The global firm needs local partners' help all the more when the culture is unfamiliar. We should distinguish here between cultural distance risk versus political and economic country risk discussed earlier. The two are not necessarily correlated. All in all, ceteris paribus, the higher cost and risk of operating at a greater cultural distance makes the firm less inclined to make large equity investments, especially fully owned ones. Hence, the hypothesis that:

H2: High equity ownership modes will be negatively associated with increased cultural distance (CUL) between the global hotel firm and the nation where the hotel is located.

Level of Economic Development: How might a country's level of economic development affect the modal choice of prospective investors or entrants? In their study of the hotel industry over a decade ago Dunning and McQueen (1981) proposed the hypotheses that the incidence of equity ownership in the hotels business should be positively correlated with economic development. But they did not test this. Moreover, a priori reasoning tends to give greater weight to the opposite hypothesis, that higher income nations will have a relatively larger share of non-equity modes, such as franchising and management service agreements. Why?

First, the lower "absorptive capacity" of franchisees in lesser-developed nations and the consequently higher costs of adaptation and knowledge transfer would tend to support the idea that franchising would be more prevalent the more developed the nation is. Second, while the global hotel company will try to retain legal control over its brand and other intellectual property, enforcement is weaker in developing nations. Many companies which consider intellectual property protection as central to strategy, have concluded that majority or full equity ownership of developing country operations is consequently necessary.

Thirdly, emerging markets are also characterized by weaker competition, faster growth, and higher returns and profits. Recall that contractual modes, such as franchising or management service agreements, constrain the return of the global hotel company to a royalty-type return (a percentage of sales). This is a less volatile cash flow, but one that is inferior to returns on equity in absolute magnitude. In high profit potential areas, returns on equity investments far outstrip royalties.

Moreover, the contractual organization modes are subject to cancellation on expiry of the agreement, whereas a fully owned equity investment is of indefinite duration, in theory at least. For this reason, we propose:

H3: M (rising levels of equity and control) is negatively associated with the level of economic development (GDPCAP) in the country where the hotel is located.

Foreign Business Investment Penetration In The Local Economy: In an earlier study, Dunning and McQueen (1981) proposed that, other things being equal, in nations characterized by a higher penetration of FDI, the firm will choose higher control and equity-based modes.

They stated this as a hypothesis to be tested. Possible explanations involve a "follow the client" abroad hypothesis, based on the assumption that global hotel chains draw an appreciable fraction of their clientele from international business travellers. Hence, in countries whose economies are more open to international investment and trade, there should be a greater incidence of international business travellers who are particularly concerned about quality standards. To be sure, one can question some of these assumptions.

There are no data available per hotel, or per firm, on the fraction of clients who are international businesspersons, so one cannot gauge the extent of their influence. Nor can we assess whether their preferences for quality are different from other classes of customers. However, since Dunning and McQueen's work is the only other empirical study on global hotels, we thought it worthwhile to test this hypothesis. The penetration of FDI into a host nation is operationalized by the ratio of FDI over GDP.

H4: M (rising levels of equity and control) is positively associated with a country's ratio of FDI over GDP.

To summarize, three characteristics of the host nation (where the hotel property is located) are said to influence the mode of organization: Country Risk, Cultural Distance, and

Foreign Business Penetration. We now turn to firm-specific factors.

Firm-specific factors have been divided into two groups. So-called Structural or Objective factors include Firm Size, International Experience, and Degree of Internationalization. The questionnaire also asked executives in the global hotel firm to give subjective Responses to Strategy and Control Questions. The latter are based on a 5-point Likert Scale (5 = Very Important .....1 = Not Important), covering the perceived strategic importance of Global Scale, Intangible Assets such as a Global Reservation System and Brand, Investment in Training and Ability to Exercise Control over Management and Quality.

How does size of the firm relate to the propensity to choose non-equity and contractual organizational modes? The majority of studies indicate that larger firms are likely to prefer high levels of equity ownership. Smaller firms, which lacked the resources or expertise to venture into foreign markets, would prefer shared control modes. This remains the accepted view, and will accordingly be stated as the hypothesis.

Nevertheless, it should be pointed out, that other studies suggest the opposite, namely, that these assumptions may not apply to several service sectors, especially the hotel business, where the advantages of size may equally well be derived by a global network of partnerships and alliances. Gatignon and Anderson (1988) state that "higher control entry modes are less likely for large foreign operations."

They base this argument on the notion that the size of global operations in many industries will force even large firms - or particularly the firms that wish to be large - to accept partners to share in the large total investment and large coverage of a global network. In this strategy, the path to becoming a large global player requires the firm to accept a lot of partners and have lower-control, non-equity relationships (in our case such as franchising). Agency theory suggests that the problems of human resource selection and management may grow even faster than the firm's growth in size, especially in international operations.

We propose to test these contrary views by formally proposing the first viewpoint:

H5: We expect a positive relationship between firm size and M (rising levels of equity ownership and control).

International Experience and Degree of Globalization: More internationally experienced firms have less need for local help in the nation in which they operate and will have a lower tendency to use partners. In longitudinal studies of Scandinavian companies, as well as in Chang's (1995) study of Japanese firms, the company builds its organizational capabilities through sequential experience in overseas markets, initially taking non-equity positions, such as exporting or licensing, and later increasing its equity investment levels.

We may call this the traditional view. (It is worth noting, in passing, that there is a contrary, non-traditional view on the international experience variable namely that with greater international learning, the firm is better able to harness international partners and better assess and utilize the full spectrum modal choices. There is no empirical evidence as to which perspective applies to the hotel business. For testing purposes, the traditional view is stated in the hypotheses.)

We use two independent variables. The first, IEX is the number of years since the firm set up its first foreign operation. This time-based measure, while commonly used as a surrogate for international experience, has some caveats associated with it. For instance, mere length of time in one cultural setting may not prepare a firm for expansion into another country and culture.

For another thing, some firms may have expanded internationally faster than others; a time-based measure may therefore be somewhat biased in a cross-sectional study. For these reasons, a second independent variable, GLOP (number of properties outside the home nation of the firm divided by the global total including the home nation of the firm) was introduced as an alternative measure for the extent of globalization of the firm.

For global optimization purposes, a global company had rather not be hampered by the local preferences of local partners. Hence, a firm with a larger fraction of business globally should prefer majority or full equity ownership. IEX and GLOP are different measures. One is a measure of time since the company's first foreign excursion. The other records the proportion of foreign to total business which the firm has actually achieved.

H6: Rising levels of equity and control (M) and the number of years since the first foreign operation (IEX) will be positively associated.

H7: M and GLOP (ratio of foreign over global total number of properties) will be positively associated.

We now turn from objective data on the hotel firms to subjective responses, on a 5-point Likert scale (5 = Very Important .....1 = Not Important), from responding executives, to questions about the perceived importance of the following strategy variables. Perceived Strategic Importance of Global Scale: One view in the literature is that in order to capture the economies of global scale, a firm is required to have high control and high ownership modes of operation, unhampered by the possibly contrary sub-optimizing concerns of local partners.

The executives of such companies would indicate the need for equity ownership-based control in order for the firm to capture the economies of global scale. On the other hand, we also have a diametrically opposite view expressed in the literature: To become global, a firm may be forced to accept many local partners in various markets.

If what we mean by scale economies in the hotel business relates to logistics, supply, common architectural designs etc., which can be shared with a network of franchisees and local partners at relatively low knowledge-transfer cost, then such economies can indeed be gained without ownership, or even managerial presence. Thus Galbraith and Kay's (1986) "economies of information" as the key ingredient of multinational strategy may be achievable without high equity investment or control. We thus have two diametrically opposite hypotheses in the literature, and propose to formally test the first strategy view, that:

H8: The perceived importance of scale in global hotel operations (PSCA) will be positively associated with M (rising levels of control and equity ownership).

Perceived Strategic Importance of Control Over Management and Quality: Our discussion indicated that management control is a complex and multidimensional concept. We identified Daily Management and Quality Control as one dimension of overall administrative control.

The control by the global hotel firm, in a day to day sense, rises as we go from franchising to fully owned operations. Hence we would expect, in general, that for executive respondents in the global hotel company, who indicate a greater importance for daily management and quality control (on the 5-point Likert scale), the hotel property in question would be more likely to be under a higher equity and ownership mode, ceteris paribus.

This is not tautological. Recall that executive responses indicate the firm's general strategic preferences; but in the "portfolio" of each firm there are likely to be some properties which are fully owned, some under management service contract, some franchised.

The objective here is to test the extent to which the expressed strategy preferences of executives correlates with the actual disposition of each property's management mode, and the strength of this association, statistically speaking as opposed to the influence of the other influences on the choice of organizational mode. We formally propose therefore, that:

H9: The perceived importance of operational control over management and quality (CQ) will be positively related to M (rising levels of equity and control).

Perceived Strategic Importance of Size in Global Hotel Operations: We have already discussed the SIZE variable earlier, based on an objective measure (Worldwide $ Revenue). Here, in the variable PFS, we asked managers to subjectively rate the importance of size as a strategy variable in global hotel operations (on a 5-point Likert Scale).

Our reasoning for this variable is the same as for the objective SIZE, namely that executives placing greater importance on a larger size of global operations will influence, for a particular hotel, a higher level of equity investment and greater overall administrative control (i.e., a higher value for M), with better appropriability of rents, ceteris paribus.

Hence:

H10: PFS will be positively associated with M (rising levels of equity and control).

(We included both the objective measure ($ Worldwide Sales) and the subjective measure (executive responses on the perceived importance of size) conscious that the two may turn out to be collinear. If so, one would be dropped. More on this issue in the section on Empirical Tests and Methodology.)

Perceived Strategic Importance of Global Reservations System and Brand: These are the two principal codified strategic assets, over which proprietary control is usually maintained by the global hotel firm, regardless of the organizational mode.

A global reservation system increases global revenues. In particular, codified assets, such as brands and reservations systems, increase the ability of a firm to have alliances for three reasons. First, codification reduces the "bounded rationality" problem of partners in each nation, who seek to assess the value they will receive from a partnership with the global hotel firm.

Second, by maintaining control (de jure and de facto) over the brand and reservation system, the global firm greatly reduces the opportunism of franchisees or partners in management service agreements, who may be tempted to strike out on their own, on expiry of the agreement. Third, while creation of brand equity and a global reservations system involves large sunk costs, the incremental costs of adding another franchisee, or non-equity partner, is low.

Thus, such strategic assets increase the likelihood of alliances in general, and franchising, in particular.

Hence, we propose:

H11: PRES (Perceived Strategic Importance of Global Reservations System and Brand) will be negatively associated with M (rising levels of equity investment and control).

Perceived Strategic Importance of Investment In Training: Gatignon and Anderson (1988) indicated that when the proprietary content of products or processes is high (operationalized by the R&D/Sales ratio), the choice will tend towards the full ownership end of the spectrum, since rents from this competitive advantage can be best exploited by full or high ownership modes.

The service sector equivalent to "R&D investment" is "investment in training" which upgrades the knowledge and organizational capabilities of the global hotel firm's management and employees. All hotels, especially the large ones, employ complex logistics, dynamic pricing, marketing and inventory control systems for everything from towels to room occupancy rates. Such management skills and their dissemination throughout the company's organization comprises the basis for competitive advantage.

This enables the firm to appropriate higher rents which would lead to a preference for equity, and particularly, full ownership modes. At the same time, the greater the intensity of tacit knowledge in the firm (here we are not referring to codified strategic assets, but tacit organizational routines) the higher the costs of transferring such knowledge to partners, thereby lowering the likelihood of alliance. This hypothesis was verified by Kim and Hwang. Similarly, we propose that:

H12: M will be positively associated with investment in training (PINV).

Two statistical techniques will be used. Discriminant analysis merely tests the validity and robustness of the classification of the dependent variable M into four groups, and reduces the explanatory variables to a smaller number of factors. Ordinal logistic regression (using a Generalized LOGIT model) enables us to test the above twelve hypotheses, and identify independent variables which most strongly influence the choice of organizational mode.

Problems in Using Objective Firm Data, such as Dollar Sales in Research Involving Alliances: As we suspected, the objective SIZE variable (measuring Dollar sales revenues of the global hotel firm) turned out to be collinear with other variables, including PFS.

But SIZE also has other methodological problems, which often hamper its use in alliance research: (i) The sales of minority joint ventures may not be consolidated into the accounts of some of our sample companies, since accounting conventions used in the reported financial data vary across nations; (ii) franchise and management service agreement revenues may not appear under the consolidated sales figure of some companies; (iii) even if they were added to global revenues, this would greatly understate the global total sales of the entire alliance network, because franchise and management service agreement earnings are typically expressed only as a percentage of sales of the hotel property in question.

Hence for both multicollinearity reasons, as well as measurement reasons, SIZE was dropped from the subsequent analysis. Missing Data: The number of usable observations had to be reduced from the 1,131 hotels, to 720, for two reasons. 74 hotel properties were dropped because discriminant analysis cannot accept overlapping categories (typically, a hotel having both part equity investment and a management service agreement). This is a minor loss of only 6.5 percent of the data.

However, another 337 cases had to be dropped because of missing data in various independent variables, but particularly in the cultural distance CUL variable. This variable is constructed from Hofstede's (1980) data on cultural attributes, covering less than 50 nations. No other similar data exist; nor has any scholar subsequently replicated Hofstede's work, or added to his number of countries.

A researcher is thus faced with a dilemma: Either drop the cultural distance variable, considered by many scholars, such as Kogut and Singh (1988) to be a crucial determinant of modal choice, and have a larger data set, or keep the cultural distance variable and work with a reduced data set. In this study we chose the latter option, given the importance suggested for the cultural distance variable. The testing is therefore performed on a data set with n = 720 hotels, which is more than ample for statistical purposes.

Statistical Testing

Before performing discriminant analysis, Variance Inflation Factors for all independent variables were computed, and their low values (not shown) indicated that the discriminant function coefficients can be interpreted with reasonable confidence.

The distances are not inconsistent with the rank ordering of groups within the measure M. The largest squared distance of 4.88 is between categories M = 1 (Franchising) and M = 4 (Fully Owned); followed by the 3.16 squared distance between M = 1 (Franchising) and M = 3 (Partly Owned); followed by M = 1 (Franchising) and M = 2 (Management Service Agreement). The smallest distances are between the pairs M = 3 and M = 4 (Equity-based) and M = 1 and M = 2 (Non-Equity).

The absolute magnitude of the standardized discriminant coefficients enable us (with appropriate caveats) to identify some of the independent variables as being most instrumental in discriminating among groups (Klecka, 1980).tn Function 1, IEX (International Experience) and GLOP (Fraction of Foreign to Total Hotels) have the highest coefficients. An examination of group centroids suggests that Function 1 serves to differentiate M = 1 (Franchising) from the remaining groups.

With appropriate caution therefore, we can venture to say that international experience and geographic reach of the global firm strongly distinguish the equity investment mode from the franchising mode. The coefficients of other variables in Function 1, such as PRES, GDPCAP and PFS are much weaker, and we should not give them as much credence, although they do meet the cutoff of [absolute value of Coefficient] [greater than] .30 suggested by Pedhazur (1982).

It is worth noting that the signs of all the above variables are consistent with the results of the Logistic Regression using Generalized LOGIT, suggesting the convergent validity of results from two separate statistical techniques. Function 2 differentiates the centroid for M = 2 (Management Service Agreement Mode) from other modes. Among the independent variables, PSCA (strategy importance of scale) and PINV (strategy importance of investment in training) stand out as differentiating management service contracts from the rest.

A Posterior Classification was next computed to test the predictive ability of the discriminant functions. Correctly classified cases were 58.88 percent in M = 1 (Franchising Mode); 73.80 percent for M = 2 (Management Service Agreement Mode); 37 percent for M = 3 (Part Equity) and 41.46 percent for M = 4 (Fully Owned). The overall average correct posterior classification has a 58.75 percent rate. Given the four groups under the variable M (a priori p = 0.25), the overall classification rate is good.

ORDINAL LOGISTIC REGRESSION

The results show a strongly significant overall Chi-square value of 380.27, and a Somers' D of 0.61. For the overall model, concordant probabilities were a fairly high 79.6 percent. Seven out of the eleven independent variables are significant at better than .05, and of these, five are significant at better than the .01 level. Country independent variables CRI (Country Political and Economic Risk), and GDPCAP (GDP per capita) both had results congruent with the hypotheses.

The negative sign for the GDPCAP variable confirms the hypothesis that nonequity modes are preferred in high income nations, and equity investment in low income nations, ceteris paribus. This is consistent with other studies which show a positive correlation between country income levels and franchising. In developing nations, the higher knowledge transfer costs to franchisees, and the risks of poor quality, and weaker enforcement of intellectual property rights lead many firms to prefer equity investment and higher control modes there.

The positive sign for the CRI coefficient confirms that, with higher political and economic risk (volatility), nonequity modes, such as franchising and management service contracts, are preferred in higher risk environments, where the real estate investment and business risk is substantially on the shoulders of local investors. Moreover, the royalty-type payments, which comprise a substantial part of the contractual arrangements, are inherently less volatile compared with returns on equity, which in risky nations may disappear altogether.

The results for the country risk and income variables may appear contradictory and paradoxical, but they are not. An explanation which classifies countries into four groups of high and low risk and income levels respectively. It proposes that equity-based modes are preferred in "low risk" and "low per capita income" nations. Non-equity modes are preferred in high income/low risk countries, as well as in high-risk/low income nations. (Incidentally, the fourth quadrant of the typology, namely high risk/high income nations ought not to contain too many countries, as a practical matter, and this common-sensical presumption is confirmed in the scatterplot of countries. Since the risk variable CRI was on an inverted scale with 100 = lowest risk, it has been transformed into CRISK = 100 CRI to conform to the typology.

What explanations apply to for the typology? First of all, in regression, interpretation of each variable is to be taken one at a time on a ceteris paribus basis. On the per capita income variable, virtually every survey of U.S. company global investment by the U.S. Department of Commerce indicates that the profitability of direct investments in emerging and developing nations is considerably higher than in the richer nations. These countries also grow faster.

Higher rents are to be had in emerging nations, rents that can only be captured by dividends and returns on equity investment. By contrast, franchising royalties and management service fees, while less volatile, are necessarily constrained to a small, fixed percentage of sales of the hotel property. Therefore, in potentially lucrative markets, a firm may prefer the (unconstrained) higher returns from equity investments, despite the higher risk.

The normal specification of royalties as a (modest) percentage of turnover, compared with the unconstrained nature of returns on equity investment, also explains the CRI (country risk) result. It is axiomatic that royalties, as a fixed percentage of sales, are far less volatile than dividends. In riskier nations (risk ultimately defined by volatility of sales), therefore, franchising and management service agreements would be preferred, ceteris paribus.

Fladmoe-Lindquist and Jacque (1995), in their report on international franchising indicated that royalties linked to turnover also provide a better protection to the franchisor from currency risk if gross revenues are indexed to inflation. This echoes the findings of Kim and Hwang (1992), who indicated that in conditions of "demand uncertainty," equity ownership tends to be low.

Hypotheses for CUL (Cultural Distance) and FDITOGDP (FDI to GDP Ratio in the host nation) were not supported. Empirical studies using the Cultural Distance variable have yielded mixed results. Madhok explains these inconclusive results by suggesting that the hypothesis of greater use of partners in culturally distant nations, may be countered by "...the inadequacy of a partner's ability (to absorb knowledge at a high socio-cultural distance) or the incompatibility of his routines."

The objective firm variables IEX (International Experience) and GLOP (Proportion of Hotels Outside the Home Nation) yielded strong support for the hypotheses, that equity-based modes will be preferred by companies with considerable experience and existing geographic reach.

These results perfectly echo those of the discriminant analysis. The results for the Management and Quality Control variable (CQ), support the hypothesis that the organizational mode for a property would be influenced towards more equity ownership, ceteris paribus, in firms whose executives place a higher importance on control over daily management and quality. Incidentally, this finding validates the construction of the dependent variable M.

The sign for the PFS (Importance of Size) variable is opposite to the hypotheses (and highly significant). This suggests that the expressed importance of size, as a strategic factor, is not necessarily correlated to the propensity to use high-ownership modes, and supports the conclusion of Gatignon and Anderson (1988) that "higher control modes are less likely for large foreign operations." The high incidence of management service and franchise modes in this business suggests that many firms have concluded that they can be "big," not necessarily via controlled, equity investments, but by building a network of alliances.

The sign for PRES (Importance of Reservations System and Brand) is congruent with the hypothesis. The results suggests that a global reservations system, and brandname, are crucial strategic assets which enable a global hotel company to build and control a network of contractual alliances. Not only do these strategic assets yield additional income (such as a fee for each reservation made through the global reservation system, or separate royalties for the brandname component), but they also reduce the opportunistic behaviour of franchisees and local (management service) partners because of the threat of withholding of these assets. The results for the PSCA and PINV variables were not significant.

The "proportional-odds" model for an ordinal response logistic regression assumes a common slope parameter for the predicting variables. The "Score Test" generates a Chi-square statistic. If the p-value of the statistic is large, then the proportional-odds assumption is valid. However, if the p-value is small (as we found in our case) this does not necessarily mean the proportional-odds assumption is invalid. In brief, a small p-value for the "Score Test" Chi-square does not mean anything, one way or another.

Nevertheless, we ran the multinomial logistic procedure assuming different slope parameters, and showed the maximum likelihood analysis of variance. The results are broadly consistent (common slope parameter assumption) in that all independent variables except FDITOGDP, CUL, and CRI, have a p-value better than 0.05, and even CRI may be marginally acceptable with a p-value of .095.

Consistency of Results In general, the results of discriminant analysis and ordered logistic regression are congruent and lead us to have a high degree of confidence in the validity of the classification and construction of the measure M, and in the explanatory independent variables.

International management today involves the art of selective strategy knowing where to compete, and where to cooperate. An international firm's collection of business ventures will involve some with a high level of ownership or control. Other ventures will be run on a contractual alliance basis, with franchising being a special case of repeated contracting tending towards a standardization of contractual terms and operating procedures.

Management service agreements, whereby global hotel chains manage hotels on behalf of local owners of the property, may today be the single most common organizational mode for global operations. This paper offered a spectrum of alternatives, from franchising to management service agreements, to equity joint ventures, to fully owned investment.

How does a manager know when to choose which mode of organization? This is becoming an important art in the practice of management, since the optimum configuration of global operations is seldom standardized. Until a decade ago, local adaptation by global firms was expressed by varying their business practices and methods in each country, while leaving the ownership and organizational structures fairly invariant across nations. Today, the modal choice issue has gone beyond the "internalize or not" question, and even beyond the "licensing vs. joint venture vs. merger" set of alternatives, to include other types of alliances, such as management service contracts, and franchising.

The general modal choice set now includes varying levels of equity ownership, as well as several alliances of various descriptions. The manager must, today, choose from a larger set of options. This paper offered three groups of explanatory variables: Country-specific variables, variables relating to the international experience and global scope of the firm, as well as perceptual strategy variables, which were shown to influence the modal choice.

The convergent results of discriminant analysis and logistic regression supported the robustness of the model and variables. Higher equity and control modes are preferred by companies with longer international experience and geographic reach. Companies appear to shun equity-based modes in risky nations, preferring to use management service and franchising contracts instead, where royalties and fees provide a surer return compared to dividends.

At the same time, on the per capita income variable, firms appear to prefer equity investments in lower income nations, ceteris paribus. It is an accepted fact that growth in emerging nations tends to be higher, and returns are also higher due to weaker competition in such nations. In all likelihood, this applies to the hotel business as well.

The global hotel business showed results contrary to those found in several manufacturing sectors, with reference to the strategic perceptions of size. In this business at least, high equity and control modes are not seen as crucial for large global operations. In the quest for global reach, hotel firms place considerable reliance on non-equity partners and franchisees. A network of franchisees and hotels under management service agreements enable it to capture some of the economies of global logistics, supplies, architectural design, reservations, training, and brand recognition. It is possible that the findings of this study apply also to other service sectors. This remains an area for further research.

One general conclusion that can apply to other sectors is that contractual relationships can effectively substitute for equity ownership when the fear of partner opportunism is reduced by the global company's ongoing control over key strategic assets. The threat of withdrawal of an international reservations system or brand name moderates the behaviour of local partners in each nation.

Moreover, these same strategic assets enable the firm to earn additional royalties (together with royalties for providing management services) in franchising and management service agreements. Such contract-specified royalties and fees often tip the balance towards alliance-based participation in risky nations, where equity-based investment may be precluded. This study has made a beginning towards understanding modal choice in the context of the dynamic interaction between the risk/return framework. This remains an area for further research.

What are the implications of this study for theory development? A theory of modal choice cannot rest only on conditions in the country market or host foreign environment. Similarly, the nature of the "transaction," or entry conditions negotiated with a prospective corporate ally, can provide only a partial explanation, Why? Because the global firm is more than a collection of national organizations; it is more than a set of discrete transactions. The global company has an overall long-term strategy. A robust theory of modal choice is therefore necessarily syncretic, and includes country, transaction specific, agency theory, as well as firm strategy factors.

Chapter 8

The Evolution of Hotel Populations

A THEORY

The simple but powerful idea that institutions form the constraints that shape human interaction has had a dramatic impact on economics and political science and is gaining influence in sociology. Institutions, in this view, are formal and informal "rules of the game" that, with associated enforcement mechanisms, provide the structure for economic action. In this paper, we examine the coevolution of a set of institutions in response to a collective action problem and two populations of organizations. The institutions are rules that developed in response to a tragedy of the commons at Niagara Falls resulting from overexploitation, and the organizations are the hotel populations in Niagara Falls, New York, and Niagara Falls, Ontario, which were leaders in the effort to establish these institutions at Niagara Falls.

We first examine the historical development of tourism in the two hotel communities at Niagara Falls to explain how and why hotels responded to collective action problems. We then present dynamic analysis of hotel failures and foundings to show how institutional structures and interpopulation competition affected population dynamics.

This study, therefore, attempted to address two research questions: How do collective action problems among competitors lead to the development of institutional solutions, and how do interpopulation rivalry and institutional structure affect failure and founding rates? This study contributes to both organizational theory and the new institutional economics. Organizations are the principal actors in institutional economics, but the theory suffers from a general inattention to the realities of organizational action. The recognition in institutional economics of organizations as the agents of institutional change is a critical insight, but the characterization of organizational agency has been too simplistic. North referred to organizations as "players" in the game defined by institutions, and the treatment of organizations as unitary, rational actors is common in the literature.

As we show in our historical analysis, the contributions of organizations to the creation and change of institutions can depend on factors that do not fit neatly into a rational model of collective action. Further, although North claimed that institutions fundamentally influence organizational evolution, this idea has not been tested in institutional economics. Organizational theory has sophisticated methods for studying the evolution of organizational forms, and by applying them here, we demonstrate that institutions affect organizational populations in surprising ways.

In organizational theory, it is well established that organizations are influenced by the institutional structure of their environments and that they affect their institutional environments. Often, institutions provide a structure of incentives that is a benefit to a set of organizations, even if some or all of those organizations did not contribute to the creation of the institutions.

This creates an opportunity for organizations to free-ride on the institution-building efforts of others and makes critical the question, "Why do organizations contribute to the creation of institutions when other organizations that did not contribute can also benefit?"

Unlike the few other historical studies that have examined jointly the creation and influence of institutions, we consider this problem of collective action. We examine this collective action problem in this study of the dynamics of the populations of hotels at Niagara Falls. By hotels, we mean all organizations that host transient overnight visitors, including organizations called houses, inns, and motels.

Hotels at Niagara Falls had a collective action problem that was solved by the establishment of institutions. At the same time, intergroup rivalry - the cross-border competition between the Niagara Falls tourism industries in Canada and the United States - played an important role in overcoming the collective action problem associated with creating institutions. We begin with a historical analysis of the problem, from which we derive testable hypotheses about the evolution of these hotel populations and the effects of the institutional structures of their environments.

INSTITUTION BUILDING

Niagara Falls, a cataract on the Niagara River, has attracted visitors since Father Louis Hennepin first described it to Europeans in 1683. The Niagara River forms the border between two cities at Niagara Falls: Niagara Falls, Ontario (hereafter Ontario) on the western bank and Niagara Falls, New York (hereafter New York) on the eastern bank. In each city, since early urban development, there have been various types of firms such as hotels, taverns, restaurants, and tour-guide companies that serve the visitors who come primarily to see the falls.

Each city has tried to develop institutions that would regulate activities immediately surrounding the falls and enhance the attractiveness of the falls as a place to visit. The first attempts were relatively small-scale community efforts, but the eventual result was elaborate public parks in both cities. Among the most visible of those pushing for the development of these parks were hoteliers, who had much to lose if the parks were not created and much to gain by their development.

Hotels within each of these cities compete with each other. A hotel in New York competes for tourists with the hotel down the block. All hotels within a community, however, share rivals: they compete with the hotels across the river for tourist business and with any type of organization that threatens the development of tourism in their community. Although two hotels in New York are competitors, they would both prefer that tourists come to New York, where the two hotels would have the opportunity to compete for them, than that tourists go to Ontario. Hotels in Ontario are in an identical position with respect to New York hotels.

Likewise, hotels in each community share concerns about confidence men, tourist abusers, and even industrial firms that become eyesores. Hotels within each community have also undertaken cooperative activities throughout their history, such as groups formed to establish standards for the treatment of hotel patrons, and neighbourhood hotel associations have been common.

One such group - the Niagara Promotion Association - even ran a school of hospitality for the benefit of member hotels. Hotels have often undertaken joint advertising efforts as well. Hoteliers in New York cooperated to publish what was at the time the only daily tourism newspaper in the world. Almost all of these activities were within communities, either among New York hotels or Ontario hotels, not between communities. Intergroup rivalry in many forms has characterized the relations between hotels in the two communities during the last 150 years.

At its fiercest moments, the rivalry between the two hotel communities has involved direct attacks. In the late-nineteenth century, New York hoteliers secretly funded carriage drivers to go into Ontario and entice tourists into their cabs with the promise of a ride through the Niagara Gorge but then take them across the border and leave them on the New York side.

Similarly, Ontario hoteliers were accused of tempting tourists bound for New York to get off trains on the Ontario side of the falls. More recently, New York hoteliers claimed that Ontario hoteliers were conspiring with bus companies to dump tourists on the Ontario side of the falls. Hotels also maligned their cross-border rivals in advertisements.

The Tragedy of the Commons

The collective action at Niagara Falls was in response to a "tragedy of the commons," a term offered by Hardin (1968) to describe situations in which actors have unrestricted access to a common asset and overuses it. The tragedy that developed at Niagara Falls during the early 1800s was that peddlers, hucksters, con artists and sideshow men on both sides of the falls became extremely aggressive in their attempt to profit from tourists.

Particularly on property close to the falls, it was impossible to have a free, undisturbed view of the natural scenery. The properties close to the falls, including hotels, built elaborate walls and fences enclosing all viable spaces from which to see the falls; they charged admission to their properties, not only for the privilege of a view, but also for the privilege of encountering the hucksters who had negotiated to work within the confines of these spaces.

These activities generated externalities that hurt all tourist organizations by giving the area a reputation for corruption that scared away tourists. The offending organizations eventually overstepped their boundaries by threatening the economic viability of other tourists organizations. As Way described the problem: "since it is almost a truism that uncontrolled enterprise in any sphere is apt to mistake liberty for license, it is not surprising that the falls [became] the scene of unprincipled exploitation of the tourists by rapacious cabmen and others practiced in the art of polite robbery."

One incident illustrates as well as any the excesses of commercialism around the falls: the highly publicized Michigan event of 1827. This involved an irreparably leaking Lake Erie schooner that the property owners on both shores of the falls transformed into a crowd-gatherer by announcing that it would be retired by sending it over the falls - loaded with exotic circus animals. Fifteen thousand spectators reportedly showed up to witness the event. According to the editor of a local newspaper, on both shores "there were show men with wild beasts, gingerbread people, cake and beer stalls, wheel of fortune men, . . . the tavern-keepers cleared a great deal of money".

Because of the entrepreneurial success of such events, all varieties of spectacle followed. A colonv of starving dogs was placed on "a small barren island in the great rapids, to be wept over in the distance by crowds of sympathetic tourists". Advertisements were floated over the falls. Men brought explosives to detonate near the falls to see if they could rival the water's thunder. Daredevils rode over the falls in various rigs; they jumped over the falls, they tightrope-walked over the falls.

Other built precarious observation decks and bridges off the precipices surrounding the falls. The New York Times editorialized, "it is high time for the hotel owners to take the matter in hand and protect themselves from the worm that is eating them to death." The majority of hoteliers were particularly alarmed that a few hotels (those immediately overlooking the falls) were in the thick of the abuse.

The Table Rock House, one of the closest properties to the falls on the Canadian side, and its proprietor, Saul Davis, were investigated and found guilty of extortion of tourists. Their common practice was to pay cabbies to advertise to tourists the museum and tours offered at Table Rock House as either free or nearly free.

Once tourists had their fill of the sights available within the confines of Table Rock's walls, they were told they must pay several dollars (an exorbitant amount then) before they could leave and were confronted by "enormous ushers" at the exit should they choose not to pay. Threats of murder were common. Other hoteliers called for an investigation, and the Ontario premier commissioned one in 1873. It was the first step in the institution-building process, with the aim of cleaning up around the falls, and it required the cooperation of local hotels.

The structure of commensalism. The structure of organizational populations at Niagara Falls illustrates two important preconditions for cooperation between organizations of the same type (hereafter, commensalism). The first is a common interest in some resource. The degree of competition between organizations is determined by the overlap of the resources they require. Organizations of the same type rely on the same resources and therefore compete intensely. Competing organizations, however, share an interest in having common resources protected or increased. Competition and commensalism are both driven by reliance on shared resources.

The second precondition for commensalism is an opportunity for relative advantage. Competitive advantage is relative, so merely increasing or protecting a shared resource does not necessarily provide a benefit to competing organizations. If all competitors have equal access to the enhanced resource, the results of commensalism may be competed away.

In many instances, relative advantage can be obtained because there is a broad range of competitors for a given resource. If competitive groups can be differentiated, legal and other mechanisms can be used to exclude some of them from accessing enhanced resources. In the simplest example, resources are usually geographically localized, and distant competitors will not benefit (or will benefit less) from the protection or enhancement of local resources.

Applying these arguments to institution-building efforts of Niagara Falls hotels results in the prediction that there should be two competing subpopulations of hotels. Organizations within a population or subpopulation share an interest in resources, satisfying the first precondition for commensalism, and the presence of two subpopulations makes it possible for one group to gain a relative advantage over the other, satisfying the second precondition.

Hotels on each side of the border could potentially gain relative advantage by solving the tragedy of the commons and thereby attracting more tourists to their side. Hoteliers at Niagara Falls felt there were two competing subpopulations, but it is not obvious that there actually were. The border at Niagara Falls was extremely permeable for tourists over the period that we examine, which allows the possibility that hotels at Niagara Falls were undifferentiated in their competitive relationships. For testing, we formulate our hypothesis as the hoteliers would have:

Hypothesis 1: There are two subpopulations of hotels at Niagara Falls, and there is competition between them.

There was no clear single solution to the tragedy of the commons at the falls. In each community, private efforts by hoteliers and others resulted in some progress, but not enough to solve the problem entirely. These efforts were most important as precursors to the stronger institutions that would grow out of the community efforts.

For example, the Niagara Falls Business Men's Association was formed in Niagara Falls, New York by "the proprietors of the leading hotels, and the local business men, [who] gradually saw that the abuse and robbery of the public . . . were killing the place". The association's initial action was to develop a new system of ordinances and means of enforcing them. Most notably, these efforts included forcing the hackmen (carriage drivers) to sign an agreement to follow a code of behaviour. Those who violated the codes would lose their licenses.

This did nothing, however, to combat the equally large problem of hucksters and peddlers hawking around all of the spots from which to view the falls. At the same time that it became clear that this local effort was not enough, there was discussion in the press and in New York's state government about the possibility of creating a state-run park at Niagara Falls. The Niagara Falls Business Men's Association immediately began a lobbying campaign to further this cause by organizing a statewide petition.

The result was the formation of a larger, more cosmopolitan organization, the Niagara Falls Association. The stated goal of this organization was to "promote legislative and other measures for the restoration and improvement of the natural scenery of Niagara Falls".

On the Ontario side, there were also private efforts to free the falls from hucksterism. As early as 1832, hoteliers and other businessmen on the Ontario side developed schemes to buy the property around the falls to create a park in which commercial activity would be strictly controlled. The earliest recorded scheme, in 1832, was the City of the Falls plan to purchase 400 acres on the Canadian shore for such a purpose. Invariably, these plans ran into obstacles, including failure to raise enough funds, but most importantly, the inability to compel all property owners around the falls to sell their land.

The plans for a private park were most nearly achieved by a real estate developer and hotelier named William Oliver Buchanan. In the 1870s he began efforts to convince the Ontario premier of the importance to the province of a park at Niagara Falls for tourism development purposes. In his view, the park should be established using the land acquisition powers of the government, but should be managed privately. Not only was protecting the falls from hucksters a selling point in Buchanan's arguments to the premier, but competition with New York was important as well.

While Buchanan's plans came very close to being realized, they were finally scuttled by others in the community. An 1885 petition from citizens of Ontario to the premier asked him to support a government park rather than a private one. While there was a strong public outcry by hoteliers and others for a park, public officials also got the message that to make such an institution fair to all, it must be developed as a government entity. The issue had become what kind of institution would best solve the problem.

Interpretation: Choosing among institutional alternatives. The solution to the tragedy of the commons suggested by economics' theory of the firm would be to give control to entrepreneurs: An entrepreneur who acquired the tourism assets at the falls would have the incentive to maximize present and future returns, which would mean not abusing tourists for short-term gains.

Further, it would be in the entrepreneur's interest to monitor employees to discourage the abuse of tourists. It is noteworthy that despite some aggressive campaigns, nobody succeeded in implementing this solution. The best explanation for the failure of the entrepreneurial solution at the falls is Holm's (1995) observation that political and economic activity takes place in a hierarchy of institutions, and what is possible and reasonable at a lower level depends on higher-order institutions.

A concrete example of this is the Canadian government's lease clauses on property at the falls, which gave the government the right to revoke the lease at any time and thus denied entrepreneurs sufficient property rights to make the huge investment necessary to privatize the falls. Holm's (1995) observation that the preferences of individuals are influenced by higher-order institutions is reflected in the bias of the citizens of the falls against an entrepreneurial solution. The New York Times attributed the failure of privatization schemes at the falls to the fact that they each "savored too much of a private speculation which would result in less benefit to the public than to its individual promoters."

Voluntary organizations such as the Niagara Falls Business Men's Association are an alternative for solving the tragedy of the commons.

These voluntary associations are designed to encourage behaviour that benefits the collective and threaten penalties for organizations or individuals who defect. The problem with voluntary associations is that they rely on mutual monitoring. It is costly for one tourist organization to monitor another, and if defection is detected, it is costly to punish the offender. Rational members of the voluntary organization will be tempted to free-ride when it comes to monitoring and enforcing the association's rules. These problems with private institutional alternatives for managing the tragedy of the commons at the falls allow an opportunity for government institutions to be implemented.

The idea of governments establishing parks free of commerce around the falls had been first offered publicly by Lord Dufferin, Canada's governor-general from 1872 to 1878. Dufferin offered the park as a solution to "the various squatting interests that have taken possession of every point of vantage at the falls; who tax the pockets and irritate the nerves of the visitor". He proposed an international park in 1878 to Lucius Robinson, governor of New York.

The plan was for each country to acquire suitable lands on its side of the border. Hoteliers manipulated the planning process by lobbying to make their interests salient to legislators. Their efforts included local politicking and testimonials before various legislative committees.

The potential establishment of a state park at Niagara became the hot issue in the races for assemblyman and senator in the region surrounding the falls. The family that owned the principal newspaper in Niagara Falls, New York was originally opposed to the park idea because it also owned nearly all of the property that had views of the falls (including a hotel); they editorialized against the park proposal and those who favoured it. Counter-campaigning by members of the Niagara Falls Business Men's Association and the larger Niagara Falls Association helped win enough votes for the candidates who campaigned in favour of the park idea.

The petitioning and statewide lobbying was equally matched by local efforts to persuade voters that the park was in the interest of Niagara Falls residents. Hoteliers appeared prominently in hearings to determine the potential cost and impact of forming the park; all who testified were in favour of the idea. According to the New York Times, hoteliers in New York became even more vigorous in their private efforts to rid the falls area of hucksters as the state began to respond to the public outcry for a park. In particular, the International, Cataract, Spencer, Prospect, and Clifton hotels were given credit for this crusade to clean up the area. These were among the larger hotels, and the implication of the reports is that they were trying to distinguish themselves from other hotels so that when the park was finally established, they would be given credit for their efforts, bringing more tourist business to them.

An institutional solution to the tragedy of the commons. A government park would solve the tragedy of the commons by establishing a buffer around the falls, protecting the area most attractive to tourists from the individuals and organizations that had been defiling it. The establishment of laws against commerce in the area immediately surrounding the falls reorganized the incentives of tourist organizations.

With the parks, anyone in the area immediately around the falls who tried to engage in the activities that had been discouraging tourists would end up in jail. With the establishment of the parks, and their subsequent development, more tourists could be attracted to the falls. North argued that "what organizations come into existence and how they evolve is fundamentally influenced by the institutional framework"; because parks at the falls had a positive effect on the resources that hotels rely on, they positively influenced the evolution of the hotel populations there:

Hypothesis 2: The development of parks at Niagara Falls positively influenced the evolution of the local hotel populations.

Recognizing the usefulness of parks at the falls did not completely solve the collective action problem. Even though government parks could solve the tragedy of the commons, it was costly to lobby for their establishment. There was a second-order collective action problem because rational tourist organizations could be tempted to free-ride on the efforts of others to establish the parks. The organizations at Niagara Falls, however, had motivations to contribute to efforts to establish the government institutions. Foremost among them was intergroup rivalry.

The establishment of the Canadian park was hindered by a battle of jurisdiction between the federal and provincial governments, but residents on the Ontario side of the falls became confident that if the New York side acted, their own government would follow suit. While the park concept evolved out of a desire to restrict the activities of aggressive entrepreneurs, as both sides realized the value of such an enterprise in enhancing the attractiveness of their side to tourists, the focus shifted to cross-border rivalry over who would build a park first and better.

One official, in favour of establishing a park on the New York side first, made the plea in a public debate that New York "must not be outdone in so noble a rivalry". The rush to be the first to open a park created a stir in the two communities, such that rhetoric and bravado became standard modes of dialogue across the falls. The day the park opened on the New York side, local hotels raised their flags for the occasion as a sign of victory. New York's progress in establishing a park finally stimulated the public park movement on the other side of the falls to take serious action, and the first meetings of the Ontario Niagara Falls Park Commission coincided with the opening of the New York Park.

The commission's first head was Casimir Gzowski, who with Canada's first prime minister, Sir John A. MacDonald, was a co-owner of a prestigious Toronto hotel. There was no public opposition to Gzowski's appointment, despite his being a hotelier, because the commissioner was an agent of the province and not working on behalf of his own interests. Moreover, because there was no way for him to gain personal advantage in this position, he was the perfect representative for the community's hoteliers on this commission, which would determine the park's future scope.

And, fittingly, the first meeting of the commission was hosted at Prospect House, a prominent hotel, rather than in a government office. Perhaps the most important issue to hoteliers, an issue on which they sought and gained guarantees, was that no hotels would operate in the park.

Hoteliers and others also lobbied successfully to have the park boundaries drawn to come close to their properties without including them. The Ontario park opened in 1888, three years after the New York park.

The rivalry that created the race to open the first park maintained momentum in subsequent years. When the commissioners of the Ontario park wanted to expand the territory they controlled along the Niagara River, they made the provocative claim that businessmen from Buffalo were planning to lease historic land on the Canadian side of the river and build a golf course.

The commissioners could not "refrain from expressing [their] hope that a more honorable and worthy disposition shall yet be made of this hallowed ground, the scene of many sanguinary battles in 1812-1814 and where many of our honored dead still lie buried". Not surprisingly, the image of American businessmen golfing on the graves of Canadian heroes stirred up patriotic sentiment, and the Ontario commissioners were given the capital to purchase the land in question for their park. Intergroup rivalry had been used to advantage in motivating collective action.

Interpretation: Intergroup rivalry and collective action. Research on the social psychology of groups has shown that the presence of a rival group increases cohesion and cooperation within a group, which suggests that actors may be sufficiently motivated by the process of collective action to forego the opportunity to free-ride. The idea that intergroup rivalry increases intragroup cooperation was demonstrated compellingly by Sherif et al. in their "Robber's Cave" experiment. When their two groups "met in competitive and reciprocally frustrating engagements, in-group solidarity and cooperativeness increased".

This could be because the presence of a rival increases group identity: Common features of the focal group may become more salient with the introduction of "others" with whom to draw contrasts. Bornstein, Erev, and Rosen (1990), in a laboratory experiment, and Erev, Bornstein, and Galili

(1993), in a field experiment, have demonstrated that intergroup rivalry decreases free-riding in collective action.

The implication of these experimental results for Niagara Falls is that intergroup rivalry may have added to the willingness of hoteliers, other tourist organizations, citizens, and politicians to make the contributions to collective action that were necessary to establish the parks.

The intergroup rivalry explanation is also consistent with the instances of institution building on one side of the border being spurred on by institutional progress on the other side of the border. The actors involved believed that by building a park they were helping their side and developing a local competitive advantage in the cross-border rivalry. From this perspective, the hotel subpopulations should have derived benefit from the development of their parks because a developed park would attract tourists, in particular, to the focal population rather than to the competing population. The correctness of this belief can be tested in our analysis of the effects of the institutions on the hotel populations.

Thus, we hypothesize:

Hypothesis 3: Hotel subpopulations benefited more from the development of the park on their side of the border than from the development of the park across the border.

The creation of the parks restored the public's interest in Niagara Falls as a tourist destination. The superintendent of the New York park estimated that the park caused the number of tourists to the falls to double immediately. Creation of the parks alone, however, was not a panacea for hotels. The parks needed to survive, if not thrive, if they were to be helpful in the long run. It quickly became clear on both sides of the falls that this would not be a simple matter.

The New York park was officially called the Niagara Falls State Reservation and represented the first time a state had used public money to preserve a natural setting. The federal government had recently created the first national park at Yosemite, but for a state to make such a commitment was unprecedented. The legislation establishing the reservation stipulated that after the appropriation for the purchase of lands, the state would have to make annual allotments to the reservation for capital improvements, maintenance, administration, and other expenses.

Between 1885 and 1900, the state spending for the reservation was frugal, with expenditures on basic infrastructure such as roads, bridges, walkways, and grading. When electrical generation became available shortly after the turn of the century, arc lights and an inclined electric railway were added. After these additions, some shelters, and a lookout point, very few major capital improvements were made to the reservation itself. The state acquired more land when the reservation was expanded into the Niagara Frontier State Park in 1935, but it was at a considerable distance from the falls.

When the Ontario park was established, a bond issue provided funds for land acquisition, but all operating funds were to be provided by minimal tolls for the use of optional features, such as bridges to the islands and an elevator to the foot of the falls. The original intent was in the same spirit as the New York reservation: to set aside the land surrounding the falls so that there would be as little evidence of human intervention as possible.

Almost immediately this plan proved unrealistic. The revenues from the tolls were not nearly enough to cover expenses. By the end of the fourth year, a large operating debt had accumulated. The park commissioners, holding up the New York reservation as a model, asked for an annual provincial appropriation to cover expenses, but it was denied.

The struggle to keep the park open during the next year forced the commissioners to make plans to cover the financial shortfalls through entrepreneurial venturing. In particular, they would reverse the original plans for the park by leasing out the rights to electrical generation, electric railways through the park, and other forms of concession. This provided enormous revenue windfalls through the next century.

By the 1950s, the Ontario park had experienced impressive expansion: A scenic highway was built along the length of the Niagara River; Fort George, a strategic site in the War of 1812, was restored and opened to the public; a floral clock 40 feet in diameter was erected; and an observation plaza, a school of horticulture, and a golf course were all opened.

Not all of the developments the parks engaged in served the interests of hoteliers. Electrical power generation, in particular, had two distinct negative impacts. First, any water used to generate electricity is diverted from the falls, making the spectacle less grand. Rules were set allowing up to half of the Niagara River's volume to be diverted away from the falls during tourist season, and up to 80 percent during the off-season. Perhaps even more important was the secondary impact of the diversion. The electricity that was generated attracted energy-intensive industries, such as chemical and metallurgical producers.

These industries have by-products that are antithetical to tourism: noxious fumes, ugly air pollution, and toxic waste dumped directly into the river (though there are now restrictions on this). By most accounts, these by-products have overwhelmingly hurt the New York side more than the Ontario side, which is further evidence of the differences in institutional evolution on the two sides of the river. Interpretation: Embedded interests, inertia, and environmental control.

Institutional evolution tends to be path dependent: "The consequences of small events and chance circumstances can determine solutions that, once they prevail, lead one to a particular path."

For the parks at the falls, the initial funding arrangements interacted with unforeseen events, and the result was eventually an elaborate, wealthy, and powerful park in Ontario, facing a smaller, more government-dependent park in New York. The potential for electricity generation at the falls was the key factor in this process. The Ontario park has the right to rent out the water of the Niagara River for electric generation, but in New York, the state holds that right.

Given the engagement of hotels and others in collective action to create the parks, it is notable that there were not subsequent efforts to revise the institutions. New York tourist organizations could have lobbied for a change in the funding system, or both tourist communities could have tried to change the parks to be more responsive to tourism. In her examination of institutional solutions to common-pool resource problems, Ostrom (1990) noted that although appropriators (those who use the common-pool resources) are capable of supplying their own institutions, they do not always change institutions when it would be beneficial to do so.

Ostrom argued that appropriators are biased by a short-term perspective on the creation of institutions. Costs of institution building are immediate and calculable, but benefits often are long-term and uncertain. Add to this the fact that potential losses carry more cognitive weight than potential gains, and the result is that unless the common-pool resource problem can convincingly be presented as a crisis, collective action is difficult to motivate. So the chronic hucksterism of the nineteenth century could rally tourist organizations, but the slow invasion of heavy industry in the twentieth century did not.

The differential development of the parks that were created by cooperative action is related to the differential development of the tourism and hotel communities in New York and Ontario. At the time the parks were created, New York received 300,000 visitors annually and had about 45 hotels. Ontario received 200,000 visitors annually and had fewer than a dozen hotels. Now the positions of the two communities are reversed. In 1991, Ontario had 12 million visitors and 170 hotels; New York had 8 million visitors and 80 hotels. Next, we quantitatively examine the relationship between the parks and the evolution of these two hotel populations.

THE EVOLUTION OF HOTEL POPULATIONS

The evolution of organizational populations is studied by estimating rates of founding and failure. Organizations become more common as their founding rate increases and as their failure rate decreases. Benefits of the parks to the evolution of the hotel populations would be represented by a decrease in the failure rate and an increase in the founding rate. We expect that as the parks develop, failure rates will decrease and founding rates will increase (hypothesis 2) and that these effects will be stronger for the park on the same side of the river as the focal hotel population (hypothesis 3).

Data for these analyses came from a number of archival sources and represent the population of New York hotels from 1885 to 1991 and the population of Ontario hotels from 1904 to 1991. We relied primarily on city directories in both Ontario and New York and used phone directories, travel directories (Where to Stay in Ontario, 1945-1965 and Accommodations, 1966-1989, both published by the Ontario Department of Tourism), the Hotel Redbook, and the Directory of Hotel and Motel Systems to check the primary data source and provide additional information about the hotels.

Analysis of Hotel Failure

The unit of analysis here is the individual hotel, and our goal was to determine the risk of a hotel failing in any given year, as affected by the influence of the parks, population density, hotel characteristics such as distance from the falls, and control variables. We define hotel failure as occurring when the hotel ceases operation, but not when it changes ownership or changes name. One reason for not classifying changes of ownership and name as the failure of one organization and the founding of another is that there is no reason to conclude that the "organization" changes at all.

Names and ownership can change while the same participants continue to carry out the same routines. We have reason to believe that this definition of failure is the most appropriate one to use in investigating the influence of the parks on the evolution of the hotel population at Niagara Falls. Outright failures are clearly negative events for the population, while name and ownership changes are difficult to interpret and may even be more likely when the population is thriving.

We modeled hotel failure using r(t), the instantaneous rate of failing. This hazard rate of failure is defined as the limiting probability of a failure between t and t + [Delta]t, given that the hotel was operating at t, calculated over [Delta]t:

Parametric estimates of the hazard rate require assumptions about the effect of time (in these models, age) on failure. There is disagreement about appropriate parameterizations of age dependence in organizational mortality, so we used a piecewise exponential model, which allows the rate of failure to vary in an unconstrained way over preselected age ranges.

The age range in the model is divided at k points ([a.sub.1], [a.sub.2], . . ., [a.sub.k]), which, with [a.sub.k+1] = [infinity] creates k age periods: [l.sub.l] = {t[where][a.sub.l] [less than or equal to] t [less than] [a.sub.l+1]}, l = 1, . . . k. Constants (baseline mortality rates) are estimated for each age period. So the piecewise exponential model we estimate is of the form:

r(t) = [e.sup.[Beta]X] [e.sup.[[Alpha].sub.1]], if t [element of] [l.sub.l], (2) where X represents the vector of covariates, [Beta] the associated vector of coefficients and [[Alpha].sub.1] is a constant coefficient associated with the lth age period. The life histories of each hotel were broken into one-year spells to incorporate time varying covariates, yielding 14,280 spells. The reported results are maximum-likelihood estimates obtained using the statistical package TDA.

Besides the institutional and density variables that are needed to test our hypotheses, we included variables in our models that we expected to influence the risk of hotel failure significantly. These include hotel size and age, type, and variables capturing spatial distribution.

Park Development Variables

To operationalize the development of the parks, we used expenditure data for the Ontario Niagara Park, from the annual reports of the commissioners and for the State Reservation in New York, both from the Laws of New York

(1886-1974) and directly from the Niagara Falls State Reservation in Niagara Falls, New York. To make the expenditure figures comparable, they were converted to constant 1983 U.S. dollars.

The expenditures were accumulated over time and depreciated to represent in each year the current value of past capital investments in a park. We were not able to identify the capital investment component of expenditures in all years, so we calculated the proportion (52 percent) of expenditures that were for capital investment in the years in which we could make the distinction and applied this to all years to estimate capital expenditures. We chose an annual depreciation rate of 10 percent, which was reasonable given the range of capital investments that the parks made; 10 percent would be fast depreciation for buildings but slow for roads and landscaping.

Park development over time for both the Ontario and New York parks and is consistent with our understanding of the influences on the growth of the parks. The U.S. park has three intense periods of growth, 1923-1925, 1943-1950, and 1955-1967, bracketed by periods of neglect. Since reaching its peak in 1967, the park has atrophied.

This pattern of sequential attention and neglect reflects the political nature of the New York park's funding. The Ontario park exhibits consistent growth from its founding in 1888 to the present. This reflects the increasing power and resources that accrued to the Ontario park as it continuously gained control over its environment.

Density and Population Dynamics

Hypothesis 1 predicts two subpopulations of hotels that compete. To determine, for the purposes of density dependence and population dynamics, whether there is one undifferentiated population of Niagara Falls hotels or two subpopulations, we began by modeling "own" subpopulation and "other" subpopulation effects for the relevant variables. Then we tested to see if the coefficients for own and other variables are the same to determine the appropriate level of aggregation at which to model density and population dynamics.

A number of studies have found that density and population dynamics results differ over levels of aggregation, often with competition being more intense at the local level. The theory of density dependence holds that population density, defined as the number of organizations in the population, influences the vital rates of organizations through the processes of legitimation and competition.

Legitimation, in the sense of taken-for-grantedness, increases with density but at a decreasing rate. Rates of organizational failure decrease and rates of organizational founding increase with legitimation. Competition increases with density at an increasing rate. Organizational failure increases and organizational founding decreases with competition. The prediction that density will have a nonmonotonic effect on failure and founding has been supported in a number of empirical tests.

We expect that density will operate according to the theory within the subpopulations of hotels at Niagara Falls. We predict that the failure rate will decrease with own density (density within the focal hotel's subpopulation) and increase with own. While hypothesis 1 predicts that competition extends across the border, it is less likely that there will be cross-border legitimation.

The history of the rivalry between the two tourism communities includes repeated attempts to de-legitimize the rival community. Therefore, although we include other density and other to test for a possible nonmonotonic effect, we predict that the influence of other density will be to increase the failure rate.

Carroll and Hannan suggested an extension of density dependence theory to include density at the time of the focal organization's founding. They argued that high density at the time of organizational founding will permanently increase the risk of failure. If organizations are founded in environments of intense competition, they may be forced into unattractive niches and may lack the initial resources necessary to establish the organization properly.

For example, Niagara Falls hotels founded at times of high density may be forced to locate farther from the falls and away from train stations and highway interchanges. Unlike tourists, the resources necessary for founding a Niagara Falls hotel (e.g., bank financing, legal permission, and managers) have historically been partitioned by the border, and much of the relevant strategic space (particularly geographic location) also exist in two distinct sets (i.e., a hotel can be close to the falls on either the Canadian or the American side).

Therefore, we expect that the influence of founding density will be from founding density in the hotel's subpopulation and predict that own founding density will increase the failure rate, but other founding density will not influence failure. The rate of failure (or founding) may depend on the number of recent failures (or foundings). Like density, recent events have been found to have a nonmonotonic effect on vital rates. The number of recent failures in a population provides a signal that the environment may be less hospitable for the organizational form, but recent failures also liberate resources that can increase the survival chances of other organizations.

A recent review found that most tests for a nonmonotonic effect of past failures on the failure rate showed that the rate either simply increased, or first increased, then decreased with failures in the previous period. Further, past foundings usually had the same pattern of first increasing then decreasing the founding rate. We predict that own failures at t-1 will increase and own [failures.sup.2] at t-1 will decrease the failure rate. Both signaling and resource implications of past events should extend across the border, so we predict the same pattern for other failures at t-1, and other [failures.sup.2] at t-1.

Hotel-level Variables

Size. Organizational size usually decreases failure. It may represent slack resources and economies of scale. In preliminary analysis, we explored alternative functional forms for the size variable and found the number of rooms to be best for explaining the failure of Niagara Falls hotels, which is how we measured size in the models we report. We also estimated models using the natural logarithm of the number of rooms as the size measure, and the results of the two operationalizations are very similar.

Finding the number of rooms for Niagara Falls hotels was difficult. We often had to rely on advertisements or listings in selective directories. Ultimately, we found size data for 85 percent (6356/7516) of Ontario hotels but only 31 percent (2126/7065) of New York hotels. We reasoned that the hotels for which we were unable to find size data were likely to be smaller, since they advertised less and were not listed in selective directories. Therefore, we assigned a size of 30 rooms to the hotels that left no record of their size, which is about half the average size (58.1 rooms) of other Niagara Falls hotels. We have some support for the accuracy of our assignment from a test we conducted on New York hotels that existed in 1991.

In that year, our archival sources provided size data for 24 hotels, and their average size was 81.21 rooms. We were able to contact 13 of the hotels for which we had no size data to ask them their size, and the average was 31.38 rooms. We have run models without the size variable, and the results for other variables, including those associated with the parks, are the same as when the size variable is included.

Although the initially accepted position was that there is a liability of newness, and organizations become more robust as they age, more recent evidence indicates that the failure rate increases with organizational age and that earlier findings supporting the liability of newness were due to the omission of organizational size as a covariate. We predict failure will increase with age, but confidence in any result for age in our models has to be tempered because we had to estimate size for many spells.

Several types of hotels have existed during our period of observation. The major types include the "house" (now a virtually extinct type), "hotel," "motel," and "inn"; other types, such as the "lodge," have so few instances that we categorized them all together as "other." Dittmer and Griffin stated that "the public tends to associate different characteristics with the various terms used and to select or avoid lodging establishments on the basis of their interpretation of the terms." The stated goal and marketing strategy of each firm is distinctly linked to its particular form.

Firms that end their name with house (e.g., The International House) are more similar to firms with the same naming strategy in their pricing and services offered than they are to other firms. Houses link themselves to a tradition of European hostelries that traditionally have served guests of wealth and nobility for extended stays (serving as a "house" away from home). At Niagara Falls, until relatively recently, houses operated as expensive summer resorts for wealthy North Americans and Europeans.

Likewise, firms that use a hotel naming strategy are more similar in form to firms with the same naming strategy than they are to other firms. They have typically operated year-round and are usually larger in terms of numbers of rooms than any other lodging form. Similar distinctions are found for inns (small and inexpensive) and motels (inexpensive and geared toward automobile travellers).

We classified lodging firms that do not use any of these naming strategies, and therefore have no clearly categorizable form, as having a form that is other. We expect that being one of the four categorizable types of establishment decreases the failure rate of the firm relative to those that choose an alternate, less well-known type.

"Economies of geography result from proximity to activities from which the need or demand for an organization's services are derived". Proximity to relevant attractions should help hotels, so we expect that the failure rate of Niagara Falls hotels will increase with distance from the falls.

To test this, we used the variable distance to the falls, which is the Euclidian distance in miles between the hotel and the falls. We also expect that the advantage of proximity to the falls will decrease with time, because proximity to the falls should be less important as transportation becomes easier over the years. To test this idea, we included an interaction between distance to the falls and calendar time.

Although proximity to the falls should help hotels, it is also associated with proximity to other hotels. Consideration of the location of competitors suggests two predictions for hotel failure. First, the degree of competition between two organizations should be a negative function of the distance between them. The idea that organizations that are closer to each other in some way are more competitive than more distant organizations is referred to as localized competition and was tested for physical space by Baum and Mezias.

They found that the failure rate of Manhattan hotels decreased with the average of the Euclidian distance between the focal hotel and all other Manhattan hotels. To test for localized competition, we use the variable distance to competitors, which is the average of the Euclidian distance in miles between the focal hotel and all other hotels that existed in the year.

For hotels on different sides of the Niagara River, we calculated the distance between them by way of the major bridge. Like proximity to the falls, we expect the advantage of distance from competitors will decrease with time, since transportation became easier during the period of observation, so we included an interaction between distance to competitors and calendar time, for which we predict a positive coefficient.

The second way that the locations of competitors matter is in the production of agglomeration economies. There may be advantages to locating within a cluster of similar organizations. For example, tourists in Niagara Falls may minimize search costs when looking for a hotel by going first to an area with a high concentration of hotels.

Baum and Mezias found that the failure rate of Manhattan hotels decreased with the number of other hotels within three avenues and 25 streets of the focal hotel. We test for agglomeration economies using the variable half-mile agglomeration, which is the number of other hotels within a half-mile of the focal hotel. We expect that the failure rate will decrease as half-mile agglomeration increases.

The means of the distance measures for New York and Ontario hotels are similar, indicating that the spatial structures of the two areas were comparable. Difference of means tests done in each year in which a comparison was possible, however, indicate a number of significant differences. New York hotels were significantly farther from the falls, the bridge, and competitors starting in 1957. New York hotels had larger agglomerations from 1904 to 1963, while agglomerations were larger in Ontario in 1967 and from 1970 to 1991.

Control Variables

Ontario is coded one for hotels on the Ontario side of the border. This variable will capture any basic differences in the failure rate resulting from, for example, a better view of the falls from the Ontario side. Left censored is coded one for hotels that were founded before the beginning of our observation period, to control for the possibility that these hotels may be different in an unobserved way because they had survived selection before our analysis begins.

Calendar time is the year of the observation minus 1885. This variable is included to capture trends in the failure rate that are a function of historical time.

The results of the failure analysis. Model 1 includes age, size, and the variables capturing density and population dynamics. The model is a significant improvement over the baseline model that posits a constant rate of failure (not shown). To test for the presence of subpopulations, we estimated a version of model 1 in which the coefficients of own and other variables were constrained to be equal [e.g. [Beta](own density) = [Beta](other density)].

If a log-likelihood test indicated that the unconstrained model was not better than the constrained model, it would mean that density and population dynamic effects are the same regardless of which subpopulation they occur in and, therefore, that they should be modeled at the aggregate level. The test indicated that there was a difference between the constrained and unconstrained models, indicating that there are two subpopulations, as predicted by hypothesis 1.

Size had a negative coefficient, indicating that larger hotels are less likely to fail, as predicted. Also as predicted, own density had a negative coefficient and own had a positive coefficient. At the subpopulation level, the theory of density dependence is supported. The effects of the other subpopulation's density change slightly in the full model, so we will wait to comment on them. Own founding density has the predicted positive coefficient.

Surprisingly, the coefficient of other founding density actually decreased the failure rate. We had reasoned it would have no effect. Failures in the previous period in the own subpopulation had the predicted nonmonotonic effect, first increasing then decreasing the rate of failure. Failures in the previous period in the other subpopulation had the opposite effect, first decreasing then increasing the failure rate. The failure rate was lower for Ontario hotels and increased with calendar time. The control for left-censored observations is not significant.

We estimated constrained models to test the significance of differences in the age coefficients. At the .05 level, the initial increase at two years ([[Lambda].sup.2] = 4.02, 1 d.f., p [less than] .05), the subsequent decrease at five years ([[Lambda].sup.2] = 18.06, 1 d.f., p [less than] .01), and the increase at sixty years of age ([[Lambda].sup.2] = 5.52, 1 d.f., p [less than] .05) are significant. Different from our prediction and past findings, the failure rate first increases then decreases with age, remains constant for a large range of ages, then increases again for organizations over sixty years of age.

This unusual pattern of age dependence is fascinating, but the fact that we had to estimate size for a large percentage of spells makes it unadvisable to put high investment into interpreting the pattern. Briefly, the pattern of age dependence may be due to the fact that hotels represent large capital investments: If the hotel passes an early hurdle of feasibility (i.e., if it is not an immediate flop), then heavy sunk costs may facilitate its persistence until the physical asset begins to break down, apparently at around sixty years of age. Model 2 adds the type variables.

The model was a significant improvement over model 1 [[Lambda].sup.2] = 124.62, 4 d.f., p [less than] .01). As predicted, each of the modeled types, Hotel, Motel, House and Inn was less likely to fail than the omitted category of Other. Tests for differences between the estimated coefficients indicate that the ordering of types by failure rate, from highest to lowest, was as follows: Other [greater than] House = Hotel [greater than] Inn [greater than] Motel.

Model 3 adds the variables that test for economies of geography and agglomeration and for localized competition and was a significant improvement over model 2 ([[Lambda].sup.2] = 14.64, 5 d.f., p [less than] .05). As predicted, distance to falls increased the failure rate and the interaction of distance to falls and calendar time showed that the disadvantage of being far from the falls decreases with time. The interaction overwhelms the basic coefficient in the 77th year.

Distance to competitors had the predicted effect of decreasing failure, and this effect also lessens with time. Coincidentally, the interaction with time overwhelms the basic coefficient in exactly the same year as it does for distance to the falls. Initially, hotels that were close to the falls and far from competitors were less likely to fail, but these advantages decayed with time, and starting around 1962 (1885 + 77) hotels were less likely to fail if they were farther from the falls and closer to competitors.

Half-mile agglomeration had the predicted effect of lowering the failure rate. So, although for most of the history of the population, hotels are less likely to fail if they are on average far from other hotels, they are also less likely to fail if they are located in a cluster of hotels. We tested and found no evidence for a nonmonotonic effect of half-mile agglomeration (model not shown).

Model 4 introduced park development and improved significantly over model 3 ([[Lambda].sup.2] = 7.42, 1 d.f., p [less than] .01). Park development had the effect predicted by hypothesis 2 of reducing the failure rate of Niagara Falls hotels. Because the effect of the density of the other subpopulation was monotonic in model 4, model 5 was estimated without the second-order term, other [density.sup.2]. Model 5 was not significantly less powerful than model 4 ([[Lambda].sup.2] = 2.28, 1 d.f., p [approximately equal to] .13).

Other density is positive in model 5, so, as hypothesis 1 predicted, there are two hotel subpopulations at Niagara Falls, and there is competition between them, but no legitimation.

Model 6 breaks park development into own and other to test hypothesis 3 that hotels will benefit more from development of their own park than they will from the development of the other park. The difference between the coefficients for own park development and other park development was not significant ([[Lambda].sup.2] = .08, 1 d.f., p [approximately equal to] .78), so hypothesis 3 was not supported. The failure rate of Niagara Falls'hotels was lowered by the development of the parks, but the effect was the same for development of the hotel's own park as it was for development of the other park. Coefficients of other variables remained the same in models that included the park development variables, except the variables representing own failures, which were no longer significant.

Analysis of Hotel Founding

Since there is no identifiable organization before a founding, an aggregate unit of analysis is necessary to study processes of organizational founding. The dependent variable is the number of foundings in a year in one of the hotel subpopulations at Niagara Falls, to be explained by park development, density and population dynamics, and control variables. We considered modeling founding processes using Poisson regression, which is applicable when the dependent variable is a count of events in a discrete period. Poisson regression requires that the mean and variance of [Y.sub.i] given [X.sub.i] are equal.

In many models, the variance exceeds the conditional mean, a situation referred to as over dispersion. Overdispersion has an effect similar to heteroscedasticity in the linear regression model, allowing for consistent estimations of parameters but inconsistent estimates for standard errors, invalidating hypothesis testing. We performed Cameron and Trivedi's (1990) tests for overdispersion on Poisson regressions using the variables described below and found evidence of it.

Apparently, there is some unobserved heterogeneity - variance in the founding rates that our covariates are unable to account for. A negative binomial model responds to this problem by adding a parameter to model overdispersion. The overdispersion we found was of a variance-mean ratio that is linear in the mean: [Mathematical Expression Omitted]. We used Cameron and Trivedi's (1986) type of negative binomial model, referred to as Negbin II, for this form of overdispersion and estimated negative binomial models using the statistical package LIMDEP.

All of the variables used in the failure analysis that are independent of a focal hotel can be used in the founding analysis. The accepted position is that founding and failure are antipodal, so we predict that density variables will have the opposite effect on founding as they do on failure. Own density should increase and own [density.sup.2] should decrease the founding rate, and other density should decrease the founding rate. As noted, studies of the effects of past foundings on the founding rate have found a nonmonotonic effect, with founding first increasing then decreasing, so we predict that for both own and other subpopulations, foundings will increase and [foundings.sup.2] will decrease the founding rate. Ontario and calendar time are included as controls.

Model 7 is a basic model to test whether density and population dynamics should be modeled at the subpopulation level. It was a significant improvement over the baseline model of a constant rate of founding (not shown) ([[Lambda].sup.2] = 55.08, 9 d.f., p [less than] .01). A log-likelihood test leads to a rejection of the null hypothesis that own and other coefficients are the same ([[Lambda].sup.2] = 23.2, 4 d.f., p [less than] .01). As with failure, in founding models there is evidence of the subpopulation distinction predicted by hypothesis 1. Model 8 dropped own [foundings.sup.2], other foundings, and other [foundings.sup.2], which were not significant in model 7. Own density and own [density.sup.2] had the predicted effects. Own foundings had a monotonic effect of increasing the founding rate, while other variables were not significant.

Model 9 added park development to test hypothesis 2 for foundings. The model was a significant improvement over model 8 ([[Lambda].sup.2] = 21.56, 1 d.f., p [less than] .01), and total park development had the predicted effect of increasing the founding rate. Since other density and other [density.sup.2] both had negative coefficients in model 9, we dropped the second-order term and estimated model 10. In model 10, other density was negative and significant. As predicted by hypothesis 1, and as we found in the failure models, there is a competitive effect of the density of the rival subpopulation, but no legitimating effect.

Model 11 breaks park development into own and other to test hypothesis 3 for foundings. As in the failure models, in founding models the difference between the coefficients of other park development and own park development was not significant ([[Lambda].sup.2] = .30, 1 d.f., p [approximately equal to] .58). Hypothesis 3 is not supported. As the parks develop, the founding rate of Niagara Falls hotels increases, but it does not matter on which side of the river the development takes place.

The results of the failure and founding models are in perfect correspondence with respect to our hypotheses. In both founding and failure, there is evidence of two subpopulations of hotels, and there is competition, but not legitimation, between the subpopulations. Thus, Niagara Falls hotels satisfied the preconditions for commensalism, with organizations sharing reliance on resources but differentiated such that it was possible for a group of organizations engaging in commensalism to derive a relative advantage over other organizations. The parks that were established in response to the tragedy of the commons at the falls benefited the hotel populations by lowering the failure rate and raising the founding rate.

This evidences the potential of institutions to promote the growth of populations by regulating the self-interested action of individual organizations. Surprising to us, the effect of the parks on both founding and failure rates is the same despite the border. A park benefits hotels across the river as much as it does those in its own community. We consider this finding compelling in light of the historical evidence that the parks were supported as a means to provide relative competitive advantage to their communities and that inter-community rivalry was a critical motivation in the collective action project to create the parks.

The nondifferentiated effect of the parks suggests that expectations of the institutional entrepreneurs about the competitive implications of the institutions were not accurate and that by contributing to the establishment of the parks, institutional entrepreneurs were not providing a relative advantage to their group. Actors operate in response to their expectations, but when their actions are based on complicated predictions such as what effect institutions will have on organizations, the results are often not what they expected. Errors in the expectations actors have for the effect of institutions may be systematic. Perhaps actors systematically underestimate the response rival groups will make to institutional developments of the focal group. Actors may also tend to do a poor job of extrapolating institutional structures into the future, failing to account fully for path dependence.

Our interpretation of the role of inaccurate expectations in the institution-building process reinforces the importance of considering the context in which institution building occurs, and not just the outcomes of institutions. This is one way that the historical study of the creation of the parks complements the quantitative study of their effect. The best evidence of the expectations of the interested actors is what they said and did at the time the parks were created, not the ultimate outcome of their actions.

It is also possible that the parks did provide a relative advantage that our models failed to capture. It could be that the Ontario park provided a benefit to Ontario hotels that was a constant over the period we studied and is reflected in the dummy variable for Ontario hotels in the failure models. Another explanation for the coefficient of the Ontario variable is the popular belief that the view of the falls is better from the Ontario side, but it is interesting to note that before the creation of the parks, the popular perception was that the view was better from the New York side. The survival advantage of Ontario hotels could also be a function of greater industrialization on the New York side. The relationships between the tourism and heavy industry sectors at Niagara Falls could form the basis for a fascinating study of community ecology.

The institutional history of the falls supports the arguments of economists such as North (1990) and organizational theorists such as DiMaggio (1988) that organizations in the pursuit of their interests are a driving force behind institutional creation and change. The institutional history of the falls also demonstrates the limitations of a simple rational model of behaviour for explaining institutional creation and change.

Organizational actors at the falls were motivated by nonpecuniary interests such as intergroup rivalry, were overly influenced by the temporal near-term, and may have miscalculated how the institutions they established would develop and operate. The interests of organizational actors with regard to institutions are often ignored within organizational theory and are treated as a standard rational feature of actors within the institutional economics framework, so these findings move our understanding of organizational action forward.

Relatedly, the examination here of cross-border competition is the first that we are aware of in organizational theory. We predicted and found cross-border competition, but not cross-border legitimation. This adds a new dimension to the active debate on the nature of legitimacy in the theory of density dependence. Historical accounts and the results of failure and founding analyses support the idea that attacking the legitimacy of rival groups was a strategy for tourist organizations at Niagara Falls.

Finally, some of the other variables from our failure analysis generate notable results. Our findings on economies of agglomeration and geographically localized competition are consistent with Baum and Mezias (1992). We extend their study of geographic space and competition in two ways. First, the falls are a clear centre of attraction, allowing us to test economies of geography in a way that was not possible in the Manhattan hotel industry studied by Baum and Mezias (1992).

Second, we find that the relevance of spatial location changes with historical time, which we attribute to improved transportation. We also found significant differences in the failure rates of Niagara Falls hotels as a function of their type. We are fascinated that such strong results could be obtained from a variable operationalized from the information in the names of the organizations we studied.

Clearly, hotel organizations do better if they take the form of one of the legitimated types - house, hotel, inn, or motel - rather than represent some other, less known form. Additionally, it is compelling that at Niagara Falls the humble forms of motel and inn were more robust than the grander forms of hotel and house, after controlling for size and other features of the organizations.

The overall findings here do more, though, than simply illustrate the dynamics of hotel populations or the complexities associated with organizational collective action. The structural conditions that led to commensalism at the falls are generalizable and can be used to predict the occurrence of commensalism in other contexts. Intergroup rivalry may facilitate collective action in the many circumstances in which differentiated groups of organizations are in competition with each other.

This study shows that competing organizations can be affected by the same ingroup-outgroup effects that are fundamental to understanding individuals in groups. One testable prediction of this is that commensalism is more common in industries with greater levels of foreign competition. As international trade increases, institutions may become the principal weapons in a competitive environment in which the level of selection moves from the organization to the commensalistic group.

We used a number of unpublished sources to develop this history, in addition to the published sources reported in the references. The Niagara Falls Public Library in Niagara Falls, New York has an excellent local history department that holds city directories and local newspapers, including the Niagara Falls Gazette, from 1854 to the present. That department also holds the earliest annual reports of the commissioners of the State Reservation, and other rare materials related to tourism around the falls. The Niagara Falls Public Library in Niagara Falls, Ontario holds city directories and phone books and is a good source for local papers from the Canadian side, such as the Niagara Falls Review and the Welland Gazette.

That library also holds all of the annual reports from the Ontario park and has a clipping file on the local hotel industry that includes items from the late nineteenth century. The Niagara Parks Commission in Ontario keeps a collection of historical material on its own development, and the State Reservation in New York has some early material on the tourism industry in New York, including some documents of the Niagara Falls Association and at least one early copy of In the Mist, a newspaper published by Niagara Falls hotels from 1894 to at least 1919.

The Archives of Ontario in Toronto has extensive records on the Niagara Parks Commission, including correspondence of the Ontario premier and that of the first head of the park commission, regarding the establishment of the park. The American Hotel and Motel Association archives in Washington, D.C., has complete holdings of the Hotel Redbook, and the Directory of Hotel and Motel Systems.

We also investigated a localized competition measure based only on distances to hotels on the same side of the river, and the results were comparable to those using distances between all hotels.

Chapter 9

Motel and Hotel Taxes

ABOUT THE TAX

The use of hotel/motel taxes to fund cultural programmes and facilities in the United States now is widespread and considered a popular way of dedicating tax dollars to the arts. The arts programming supported with these funds boosts local tourism and has a significant impact on local economies. Nationally, the arts are a $36.8 billion industry, which supports 1.3 million full-time jobs and generates $790 million in local government revenue. Expenditures by arts audiences on restaurants, hotels, parking facilities, and retail uses spur even more economic activity.

There are tremendous differences in the ways in which hotel/motel taxes have been established, the levels of taxation that have been allocated to the arts, and the purposes for which funds have been disbursed. This article examines the emergence of the hotel/motel tax with a general overview and a series of case studies from across the country. Each of these cases is unique, yet common themes and experiences can provide insights and direction to agencies and local governments now considering the hotel/motel tax as a funding source for cultural development.

The hotel/motel tax (also sometimes called a bed tax) has emerged over the last 15 years as a means of financing activities that attract tourists and visitors. With the phenomenal growth of tourism in the 1980s and the declining fiscal situation in many regions, communities have soughtnew means by which to promote and develop their tourist industries, without placing an additional burden on residents.

American and foreign visitors now are spending close to $450 billion ear in the United States. At the same time, federal contributions to cities and counties have dropped by more than two-thirds since 1980. Not surprisingly, then, state and local governments around the country have created and/or raised taxes on meals, rental cars, alcoholic beverages, and hotel and motel rooms.

The hotel/motel tax is considered the major generator of tourism taxes. A 1'992 survey by the National Conference of State Legislatures (NCSL) shows that 42 states have a local-option accommodation tax, meaning that local governments in these states can elect to add a hotel tax. The local tax usually is collected and disbursed by that _jurisdiction. Ill a 1991 survey by NCSL, the hotel tax in 25 cities ranged from a low of 6 percent in Sioux Falls, South Dakota, to a high of 19.25 percent in New York City and averaged 11.1 percent (these rates include state taxes).

Hotel/motel taxes, together with other tourism taxes, historically have been used for a broad range of services and activities, from operating support for visitors' bureaus to funding for summer concerts and fireworks displays.

For the arts, hotel tax funding can be dedicated to a specific facility, to re-granting of programmes, or to events with some relation to local tourism. Funds also can be forwarded to the local arts agency or paid directly. to arts presenters and producers by a local commission, which manages fund distribution. The level of funding also can be fixed by statute or be left to the discretion of the taxing body. With these profound differences, it is best to consider specific examples.

"The arts are an important economic component in San Diego," says jack McGrory, city manager for the past five years. "They create an attraction in and of themselves. By supporting these organizations and helping them to grow, they in turn give something back to the city."

For many years, San Diego has had a transient occupancy tax. Starting in the 1980s, a portion of that tax revenue has been allocated to the San Diego Commission for the Arts and Culture for re-granting to local arts and cultural programmes. In 1988, in conjunction with the increase of the tax to 9 percent, the city council awarded the arts commission a more substantial portion of the tax revenue. From 1988 to 1993, annual allocations ranged from $4.5 million to $6 million.

In 1994, the arts commission received a one-cent dedication of the tax, which concurrently was increased to 10.5 percent. This amendment has taken effect recently and likely, will result in a 10 percent increase in local arts funding. The 1995 allocation was budgeted at $5.6 million.

The commission splits funding into four pots: I percent is a public art fund, which is in addition to capital improvement projects funded elsewhere; 2 percent goes to neighbourhood arts programmes; 7 percent goes to administration of the programmes; and the remaining 90 percent is re-granted to local arts organizations as organizational support ($5 million in 1995). Of the 90 applicants for these funds in 1995, 84 will receive support.

According to the commission, the key to getting the increase and the dedicated income stream from the occupancy tax was a strong relationship with the convention and tourist bureau, which made a number of joint presentations with the commission to the council and has maintained a close relationship. The commission also maintains a standing committee on cultural tourism.

"Historically, our room tax has been spent principally on areas where the city could promote itself, particularly with respect to tourism," says McGrory. "We think the arts and cultural life in the city are key components to attracting people to it."

To receive room tax funds, local arts organizations and individuals must go through a rigorous evaluation process that involves an initial application, screening by a 15-member commission appointed by the mayor and council, and final council approval. Not only says McGrory, has this process brought the arts community together "but the council has a process they. can rely on. I think [the room tax] has helped our city. We're proud of the arts and cultural organizations that we have and the level of support that they get reflects that."

A 2 percent bed tax was established in 1978 by state enabling legislation, a local referendum, and a county ordinance. By ordinance, 20 percent of the annual proceeds from the tax are dedicated to the Dade County Cultural Affairs Council. Another 60 percent goes to the countywide convention and visitors' bureau, with the balance going to the city of Miami for renovations to the Orange Bowl.

Funds are delivered to the Cultural Affairs Council to support a full range of cultural activities. Bed tax revenues to the council in 1995 will total S1.5 million, roughly 35 percent of its annual budget. More than 700 individuals and organizations apply annually to the council's competitive grants programmes; on average, 350 applicants are awarded grants.

The council has managed the administration of this significant funding initiative successfully on behalf of the county, earning praise and support from county and community leaders. The arts council also has developed a strong relationship with the local tourism industry. The council and the industry have worked together to secure this funding stream, to pursue other dedicated revenues, and to build numerous programmes and services that link culture and tourism in Dade County. Representatives from the Cultural Affairs Council and the convention and visitors' bureau sit on each others' committees and boards.

Currently, these two groups have joined with economic development interests in Dade County to pursue the establishment of a food and beverage tax. This will provide an additional dedicated source of funding for the county's cultural activities, for its tourism advertising and promotion, and for economic development initiatives.

Finally, the county has committed proceeds from the convention development tax (an additional 3 percent bed tax) to plan, develop, and construct the new performing arts centre in downtown Miami. This revenue is anticipated to yield $140 million in bond proceeds.

Columbus began arts funding in 1973 through the Greater Columbus Arts Council (GCAC). In 1978, the source of these funds was changed from general funds to hotel/motel tax funds. In 1982, the city revised its tax code to increase the municipal room tax and to dedicate a 20 percent portion to the GCAC and its grants programme. These changes resulted from an intensive advocacy effort undertaken by the GCAC and its member organizations.

In 1985, the allocation to the arts was increased to 25 percent, and the total tax climbed from 4 to 6 percent. Funding for the arts has continued to rise since the beginning of the programme. The 1982 allocation to the GCAC vas $425,000. For 1995, that allocation has risen to S2.2 million, which represents some 50 percent of the total GCAC budget.

Funds are distributed to approximately 50 organizations each year. Grants are available for projects, management assistance, and operating support. Funds also help the GCAC deliver such services as technical assistance, training, information services, and residency programmes.

The GCAC maintains a close relationship with the tourism industry, in Columbus. Their premier annual event is the Columbus Arts Festival, which brings 500,000 people to the downtown. The industry and the GCAC also fund a number of downtown special events for residents and visitors. Arts council board members and staff also sit on boards of the convention and visitors' bureau and the chamber of commerce, acting as conduits between the arts and tourism industries.

Though there is no legislation that guarantees the arts allocation of the hotel/motel tax, the income stream is relatively secure, thanks to the benefits that this allocation provides to the arts, the tourism industry, and the community as a whole.

Creating, increasing, or dedicating a room tax to the arts has proven to be a popular means of funding the arts as a basic city or county service. These arts programmes increase tourism and have a significant economic impact on the community. Because the Source of these funds can be identified specifically and because the funds are dedicated to a particular purpose, the tax is politically attractive, as it is not collected from local residents/taxpayers/voters but from renters of a city's local hotel rooms. This dedicated revenue stream is also less competitive than a city s general fund, which supports core services like policing, fire protection, and garbage collection.

For a local government official or an arts advocate to obtain a portion of a local hotel tax requires a strong argument that the arts contribute to local tourism, either through arts programmes or facilities. To make this argument, a close relationship between the arts and the tourism industry is mandatory. This is a real challenge, as the hotel operators who collect the tax must be convinced of its long-term benefit to their businesses.

The downside to a dedicated income stream is that funds can vary from year to year with the varying health of the local tourism industry. Yet, if properly, managed by a local arts agency, as one of several funding sources, room tax revenue can provide meaningful support for local arts groups, as well as capital and/or operating funds for arts facilities.

This article is based on a report by AMS Planning and Research for the National Assembly of Local Arts Agencies' (NALAA) Institute for Community Development and the Arts, of which ICMA is a partner. The purpose of NALAA's Institute is to educate local arts agencies, elected and appointed local government officials, and arts funders about the important role of the arts as community change agents for economic, social, and educational problem. NALAA's Institute also will identify innovative community arts programmes and nontraditional funding sources to enable local arts agencies and local civic officials to adapt these programmes to their own communities.

HOTEL LENDING

Banks are dipping their toes back into the hotel-lending business. But inexperienced owners and operators need not apply. Banks are interested in financing people who have proven track records. Financing for construction of new hotels and motels, however, is frequently difficult to obtain. And where credit is being extended, bankers are striking tougher deals, putting more of the onus of bad performance in the borrower's lap.

Yet to the hotel industry, this is good news. "Lenders are no longer hanging up when they hear the word 'hotel'," says Kyle Draggoo, director of hotel brokerage at Merimark Corp., Houston. "They'll at least listen to you."

Prices on the rise

Many banks are still smarting from the hotel overbuilding of the 1980s that turned lenders into landlords.

It wasn't long ago that experts were suggesting the best thing that could be done with hotels involved dynamite and a detonator. Though some banks still have a fair share of seized properties to unload, prices are beginning to firm for hotels, and demand is up.

In September, Hospitality Valuation Services, Inc., Mineola, N.Y., released its latest "Hotel Valuation Index." The lodging consulting firm's study found that U.S. hotel values increased an average of 15% across the country in 1993. This compares to an 8% increase in 1992 and a 14% decrease in 1991. The HVS index is based on analysis using occupancy and average daily room rate data to compute value.

The strongest comebacks were seen in Atlanta, which gained 39% in value; Phoenix, 31%; Denver, 28%; and

Washington, D.C., 23%. On the other hand, Orlando, Honolulu, and Los Angeles saw values based on occupancies and room rates drop. Stephen Rushmore, president of HVS, sees the overall strengthening value of the business to be an indication that interested buyers should move now to obtain the properties still on lender's books.

"The beauty of lending to hotel operators today is that the downside risk has been taken away," says Rushmore. Besides the improvements in value, the consultant notes, "there is virtually no hotel building taking place." (The one exception in 1993 was the construction of three mega-hotels in Las Vegas. People in the hotel trade believe they were an anomoly. The Hotel & Motel Brokers of America estimates that if Las Vegas is subtracted from rooms opened in 1993, the total for that year comes to 23,500, which it says is a six-year low for new construction.)

What contributed to this improving picture? Business is better. In 1993, U.S. hotels annual occupancy rates hit 64%, according to Hospitality Directions, a quarterly journal of the national hospitality group at Coopers & Lybrand. This was the highest occupancy rate reached by the industry since 1984, Coopers & Lybrand notes. The firm predicts steady improvement at least through 1996, when it expects occupancy rates to approach 70%. Average daily room rates and growth in demand for rooms have also been steadily improving, though the firm observed that they were still behind the rates of growth seen before the recession.

Small Banks More Active

"Financing for hotel real estate acquisitions and new construction was more attainable in 1993 than at any time since the late 1980s," stated a mid-1994 report by the Hotel & Motel Brokers of America. "Currently activity is not widespread, but there is sufficient volume to speculate that the credit logjam is breaking up, and the future holds more promise."

The report, Transactions by HMBA, is based on a survey of the activity of HMBA members. Brokers belonging to the organization account for about 25% of all hotels sold nationwide and about 35% of the middlemarket segment of the business. Thus the study is considered a good proxy for the industry's experiences.

The HMBA survey indicates that the bulk of activity is actually centreed in the nation's community banks, rather than among the large banks.

"For loans of $4 million and under, local community banks were primary resources in 1993," states the HMBA report. "These lenders, who have a stake in building their local economies, treat the financing as a business loan, requiring personal guarantees from owner/operators. Rates and terms are generally more favourable than those offered by credit companies. Lower debt coverage ratios often can be negotiated, especially if the loan carries a Small Business Administration guarantee."

LTV ratios are down

Generally speaking, however, bankers from institutions of all sizes are playing harder ball.

"They're definitely trying to be more conservative in this recovery," says Merimark's Draggoo. He (and others) points out that underwriting has become much stricter than it had been during the 1980s. "We're finding that lenders are typically lending no more than 75%," says Patrick H. Ford, Sr., a principal with National Hotel Realty Advisors, Portsmouth, N.H. Others say they've heard of lenders going as low as a 60% loan-to-value ratio. By contrast, lenders were frequently willing to go to 90% and beyond during the 1980s.

"As lenders get back into business, they are being much more prudent," says Mark Woodworth, national hospitality industry chairman for Coopers & Lybrand. "They are basing decisions on current hotel earnings, rather than on prospective earnings."

As mentioned at the outset, this is a difficult time for newcomers to the lodging business to obtain financing.

Lenders are much less likely to entertain a newcomer's application than someone who knows the business. In fact, says Woodworth, just knowing the hotel business isn't always considered sufficient.

Nowadays lenders look for expertise in the particular type of hotel being financed: luxury, upscale, mid-price, economy, and budget. In addition, lenders are paying more attention than ever to the track record of the particular brand name a hotel has decided to affiliate itself with, according to Woodworth.

Most of the financing referred to thus far consists of making loans to purchase existing hotels from current operators or from lenders. Other credits include renovations to an aging hotel and refinancing of outstanding debt. Loans for construction of new hotels are scarce to nonexistent, except in some pockets of unusual growth. Las Vegas is one, Branson, Mo., is another.

This is as much a matter of market demand as lender willingness. Coopers & Lybrand's Mark Woodworth notes that while hotel values are rising again, it is only beginning to make as much sense to build a new hotel than to buy one that's already up. Woodworth doesn't expect to see any meaningful amount of construction in the mid-price range for another year or so, and generally expects little construction of luxury hotels for another three.

As more than one expert noted, large-bank lenders still have a ways to go before they finish unloading the big hotels they got stuck with after the debacle of the late 1980s. Thus, most of the big domestic banks remain on the sidelines.

"A couple of them are talking about getting back into the market, but they haven't yet," says Tom Arasi, executive vicepresident of finance and development at Tishman Hotel Corp., a subsidiary of Tishman Realty & Construction. "There has been a great deal of equity trying to get into the hospitality business," says Arasi, "and it is way ahead of the debt side."

A particularly hot source of equity funding in recent times has been real estate investment trusts dedicated to hotel properties. Much of what debt financing is available has come from hotel mortgage conduits set up by major hotel companies to provide financing to their franchisees.

Among big commercial bank lenders, says Arasi, what activity there has been has chiefly come from European banks operating in the U.S. Even they are very selective, however. Roderick Rohrbach, vice-president at Credit Lyonnais, New York, points out that even fast-growing markets can be risky. A property in a market where hotels still sell out on many nights of the year has appeal, he says.

But a hot market will attract new development, which could lead to a glut that would upset the economics that make a loan appealing at first glance. As a result, in some circumstances Credit Lyonnais would find the proposed acquisition of a high performer in a satisfactory market to be preferable to lending for acquisition in a roaring market. (In no event does it finance construction.)

While loans for big hotel projects remain elusive, the hospitality industry has begun going directly to the credit markets with the assistance of Wall Street investment banks.

These players are forming hotel mortgage conduits, similar in principle to the secondary mortgage market for residential loans. The Hotel & Motel Brokers of America report cited earlier makes these observations about the relatively new conduits:

"The terms are restrictive and the loans are for only the highest-performing hotels, but the availability of funds is most welcome. Total loan volume, however, is only a trickle of the traditional flow of funds that it is replacing. Nonetheless, these loans are an important and needed interim step prior to the expected return of conventional sources of financing over the next few years."

One example of the technique is Richfield Hotel Management, Inc.'s partnership with Lehman Brothers. In June the two companies introduced a programme that Richfield clients could use for acquisition, refinancing, and renovations. One advantage Richfield claims for its programme is that borrowers can operate their hotels as independent brands or under the national brand of their choice, whereas financing programmes offered by franchisors require that the borrower fly the franchisor's flag. Rates start at 290 basis points over the 20-year Treasury bill rate.

No deals had been closed in the Richfield programme as of mid-September, but several were in the pipeline, according to Roberta Griffin, senior director of corporate finance at Richfield. Industry observers reported that many conduits have yet to do a great deal of actual lending. Do conduits represent a threat to traditional lenders? Roderick Rohrbach of Credit Lyonnais doesn't see them as shutting banks out.

"Lenders such as ourselves will naturally cater to the borrower who seeks more of a customized approach than the conduits, which are less conducive to customized financing," says Rohrbach.

Richfield's Roberta Griffin acknowledges Rohrbach's point. "Right now, because the conduit programmes involve rated securities, there isn't a whole lot of room" for flexibility. However, she adds that investors' changing appetites might someday enable securitization programmes to become more adaptable.

Adaptable or not, right now conduit financing is expensive. Stephen Rushmore of Hospitality Valuation Services points out that a typical loan rate today is 9.5%; by contrast, the conduits are charging in the neighbourhood of 11%. "Conduits are very expensive," says Rushmore, "and you'd only use them if you had a gun to your head."

Chapter 10

Industrial Relations and Hotel Motel Professionals

INDUSTRIAL RELATIONS

'Human resource management' and the 'new industrial relations', like most terms in the field of management and organization, originated in the United States. Those using the terms were not doing so with a concern for precision; nor were they proposing any tight distinction between them. Rather, they were seeking to convey to a predominantly management audience a sense of innovation and change. There appear to be no compelling reasons why we should therefore seek to impose artificial boundaries of our own.

However, 'human resource management' generally conjures up an image of a high technology non-union environment while the use of the term 'industrial relations' inevitably implies that trade unions or some other form of workforce representation are involved. In considering human resource management and the new industrial relations, it is on this absence or presence of a trade union and its consequences for policy, practice, and performance that we will concentrate.

The 1981 *Newsweek* article which perhaps more than anything else proclaimed '*The New Industrial Relations*' in the USA suggested that it had arrived almost unnoticed, and until then unannounced, accelerating the demise of the traditional adversarial industrial relations and its replacement by a new collaborative system. In keeping with the spirit of the times, the article went on to claim that the influences on the new approach came not from Japan or from any European system of codetermination but from a uniquely American tradition with its roots in the work of Mayo, Maslow, and McGregor.

In the kind of system outlined in the *Newsweek* article, the role of trade unions was rather blurred. The work of Kochan, Katz, and McKersie presented a positive view of the trade union contribution by focusing on cases where successful union-management collaboration had resulted in significant change. They celebrated the 'new' by entitling their book *The Transformation of American Industrial Relations*. What they showed was the possibility of bringing about marked improvements through management-union cooperation. What they could not do was indicate if this yielded better performanace than nonunion arrangements.

Alongside the debate on the new industrial relations, human resource management was emerging in the 1980s in the United States as a possible solution to the challenge of an increasingly competitive national and international industrial environment. Although the concept had been around for some time, often as an alternative to the rather jaded image of personnel management, it was given a major boost by the rediscovery of the human side of enterprise in Peters and Waterman *In Search of Excellence*. In this book, trade unions scarcely merited a mention; unlike the debate on the new industrial relations, it relegated unions to a minor historical role. Certainly we are left with the impression that they played no significant part in any 'excellent' companies.

As human resource management gained prominence in the United States, it was possible to discern three main strands of work. The first, captured in the work of writers like Tichy, Fombrun, and Devanna, Miles and Snow and Schuler, was primarily concerned with the relationship between business strategy and human resource management strategy. This implies that the key issue in human resource management is the question of strategic choice and recognition of the importance of considering human resource management issues in terms of their integration with wider business strategy. Driven by business and market considerations, this perspective treats trade unions as irrelevant and they are rarely if ever mentioned.

The second strand of work is captured in what might be termed the Harvard view of human resource management. This is essentially a generic approach which attempts to make the subject area comprehensible and interesting to Harvard MBA students and to general managers who have often been more attracted by the quantitative, financial, and strategic aspects of business. It is therefore an approach which tries to capture and re-present the field of what by tradition had been personnel management.

Apart from providing a much more contemporary 'feel',) the resulting analytic and descriptive material does not differ significantly from a number of personnel texts. Furthermore it explicitly acknowledges the role of trade unions in its conceptual framework by introducing the concept of 'stakeholder interests' as one of the key contingent variables helping to shape policy choices. However, once the more detailed material and the case studies are presented, trade unions are relegated to a very minor role. It was left to Kochan and his colleagues at MIT to present a more comprehensive framework which made explicit both the influences in the wider economic system and the potential role of trade unions.

The third strand, which perhaps links in more directly to Peters and Waterman as well as to the non-union case studies of Foulkes (1980) and some of the work of academics such as Lawler presents human resource management as an approach which is concerned with the full integration and full utilization of the workforce. This overlaps with the initial new industrial relations interest in the work of people like Maslow and McGregor. Indeed it is captured perhaps best in the writing of Walton and his contrast between the old control philosophy and the preferred new philosophy of high commitment.

Both Lawler and Walton acknowledge that in high commitment organizations trade unions could have a role to play, but they tend to pass on quickly to consider non-union environments. Foulkes is explicitly writing about policies in large non-union companies. This perspective maps out the potentially distinctive features of human resource management which have been developed and presented elsewhere. With its focus on an integrative, unitarist perspective, in which emphasis is placed on commitment to the organization, the role of trade unions is called into question. Indeed, one of the key research questions which emerges is whether it is possible to display commitment to both company and trade union.

This discussion of the emergence of human resource management and the new industrial relations in the United States is relevant partly because, at a key period in the 1980s, the United States was held up as the model to emulate in the UK. This was reflected in the warm relationship between Reagan and Thatcher at a political level and in the interest in monetarist free market economies at a policy level. Another source of interest was the legislative framework for industrial relations which in the United States reflected the dominance given to the operation of the market economy and made it more difficult for the unions to act as a significant economic constraint. Of course, as Beardwell has emphasized, there are dangers in taking the comparison too far.

The context in the UK in the early 1980s was different in some important respects from the United States; in particular, the trade unions were more powerful and membership was much higher. However, there was a vacuum created by the apparent failure of the pluralist industrial relations strategy to deliver either good industrial relations or an efficient and productive industry. This resulted in a major policy debate about the need for new legislation and about the appropriate role for trade unions. As Beardwell acknowledges, much of the rhetoric of the debate was drawn from America.

What this meant was that the UK became susceptible to American ideas about human resource management and the new industrial relations. Beardwell has drawn a distinction between two approaches to the new industrial relations. He sees one as concerned with the reform)f industrial relations, manifested in interest in job control, single union agreements, pendulum arbitration, and the like. The second approach is concerned with the new ideology of human resource management, with its focus on individualism and therefore it's potential to replace the traditional pluralist system.

The typical illustration of the reformist approach is the new Japanese manufacturing site, perhaps Toshiba or Nissan where management appears willing to accept a single union on their own terms. The American high technology firms such as IBM, Hewlett-Packard, Texas Instruments, and DEC represent the stereotype of the second approach.

However, as Garrahan and Stewart have argued in the case of Nissan and McLoughlin has shown in the case of high technology companies, the two approaches overlap, implying that the idea of the two perspectives existing Janus-like is too sharply drawn. Recognition of overlap has also been apparent in some of the debates about industrial relations and human resource management. What this implies is that managements' broad policy choices are not about a reformist industrial relations or human resource management but about options along two dimensions.

The first dimension is concerned with industrial relations. Following the Beardwell analysis, the type of industrial relations sought by management may range from the unreconstructed pluralism still found in some corners of the public sector, through a reformist type of new industrial relations complete with single union deal and pendulum arbitration to an absence of trade unions.

The second dimension is concerned with human resource management. Managers must decide how far they wish to embrace it. If they consider the issue strategically, they may opt to pursue a full-utilization model through policies designed to generate employee commitment, flexibility, and quality; and they may choose to do this for all or part of their staff. Alternatively, they may deliberately set out to pursue a strategy of cost-minimization, seeking high flexibility through short-term contracts and a policy of hire and fire. In such contexts, there is no pretence of seeking workforce commitment to the organization.

Considering the policy choices using these two dimensions takes us away from the conventional debates about the new versus the old or industrial relations and trade unions versus human resource management. Instead it opens up a variety of possible arrangements including trade unions operating alongside a set of human resource management initiatives. Alternatively, management may try to abandon any semblance of either traditional or new industrial relations and at the same time avoid any of the mutual commitments implied by human resource management.

Any consideration of this wider set of choices forces us to look at the key contextual influences in the economy and the market place. It also requires a reconsideration of the ideological framework. The contrast between pluralism and unitarism may need to be replaced by notions of coexistence or complementarity. The possibility that some managers may choose to avoid both trade unions and human resource management opens up the question of the black hole of non-unionism, for too long neglected by researchers.

At present we know too little about the policy choices that managers actually make, about what influences them and about their consequences. In our view the debate about human resource management and the new industrial relations has probably gone on long enough and the best way to take the debate forward is to generate empirical data which can inform it. The kind of research required must be both sufficiently wide-ranging to detect key trends and developments and sufficiently detailed to explore beneath the surface. Both surveys and case studies are required.

We need to know more than whether unions survive; we need to know whether they play an active role or have become an empty shell. We need to know more than whether an organization has introduced single status or quality circles. To explore any comprehensive theory of human resource management we need to understand how these techniques combine to provide some sort of integrated approach.

Researchers have already embarked upon this task. The breadth is provided in the WIRS. WIRS3, carried out in 1990, can find little evidence of major advances in human resource management. Such advances as there have been are more likely to have occurred in unionized workplaces. Non-union workplaces apparently avoid human resource management practices, preferring, it seems, to treat the workforce harshly with consequent costs for both employer and employees.

Such evidence further reinforces scepticism about the value of debates about trade unions or human resource management. Looking at the impact of human resource management, Fernie*et al.*, in their analysis of WIRS3, have shown that those workplaces that adopt single status and employee involvement are more likely to report better performance. However we can only take the debate about human resource management and the new industrial relations forward a little with WIRS3 because the survey omitted large areas of human resource management policy and practice.

McLoughlin and Beardwell, in their research on non-union establishments, have met the research criteria spelt out above by combining survey and case study material to highlight the diversity of practice in the nonunion sector. They explore the question of whether a human resource management strategy reduces the propensity of workers to join a union. The conclusion appears to be that although this may contribute, a range of other factors, centring around the low perceived instrumental value of union membership and lack of encouragement from trade unions, are more important.

Whatever the reasons, only 5 per cent of the establishments in their sample of high technology companies in South-East England recognize a trade union. Useful as it is, their research concentrates on issues of union joining and related management strategy rather than the detailed application and impact of human resource management.

In many respects their work is reinforced and complemented by the findings of the CLIRS2. For example, this survey reports diversity of practice about trade union recognition at new sites. Recognition is more likely where there is centralized pay bargaining and less likely in companies which, strategically, can be classified as financial controllers. Perhaps predictably, the decision about whether or not to recognize a trade union at a new establishment is usually taken centrally. This survey also finds that only a few companies practice what can be described as 'sophisticated' human resource management, reflected in eight indicators, but those that do are more likely to recognize a trade union.

These major surveys, together with a certain amount of detailed case study work, help to shed some light on the relationship between aspects of the new industrial relations and human resource management. However, they are unable to explore in sufficient detail the issue of the impact of trade unions on human resource management policy, practice, and performance. If we take the range of practices associated with human resource management, are there any which are more likely to be found in union or non-union workplaces?

Are unions inhibitors or facilitators of human resource management initiatives and, keeping an eye on the new industrial relations, does it matter whether the presence of a union is based on traditional UK multi-unionism or a single union deal? The aim of the remainder of this is to report research which helps to answer these questions.

In seeking to answer the question of whether human resource management is compatible with trade-unionism, we will operationalize the two dimensions described above. Along the dimension concerned with industrial relations policy and the union role we group establishments into four categories according to whether they recognize no union, recognize a single union in the context of a single union deal, recognize a single union but without any special deal, and whether they recognize multiple unions. On the human resource management dimension, we identify four categories acccording to whether they have an explicit human resource management strategy and the extent to which they make use of a range of human resource management practices. This provides us with a classification which we have initially applied to non-union establishments but which can equally well be applied to any workplace.

Those with an explicit human resource strategy and a high use of human resource practices we label the Good. They adopt an approach close to the kind of 'high involvement' management espoused by Lawler. At the other extreme, those with no human resource strategy and a low adoption of human resource practices we label the Bad. This could be construed as cautious pragmatism, but it is more likely to be poor, ill-thought through management. Those with an explicit strategy but one which results in a low take-up of human resource practices we label the Ugly.

By implication, since they claim to have a strategy, they have thought through how they wish to manage their human resources and decided not to adopt a 'full utilization' approach. They fit the pattern outlined by Millward of bleak environments and limited rights. The Good and the Ugly have some parallels with the 'soft' and 'hard' versions of human resource management identified among others by Keenoy and Storey. Finally, those with no human resource strategy but a high use of human resource practices we label the Lucky. They are lucky in that they have stumbled on a set of practices, perhaps through outside guidance, perhaps through emulation or perhaps by following fads.

The potential value of a classification of this sort is that it explicitly takes into account the issue of strategic integration, emphasized by many writers on human resource management. Good human resource management should be based on a strategy and on extensive rather than narrowly focused application of human resource management practices. The research can explore the association between the two dimensions.

The second central research question is whether the trade unions act as a drag or a spur to performance. To explore this we will again use the same classification but add data on outcomes. Three types of outcome will be explored since they are the most central to the debates on the new industrial relations, the role of the unions, and the efficacy of human resource management.

These outcomes are those predicted as first level outcomes by human resource management theory such as levels of commitment, staff quality, and flexibility. The second are employee relations outcomes such as industrial conflict, labour turnover, and absence. The third are performance outcomes including resilience in the face of recession and benchmark estimates of establishment quality and productivity.

THE METHOD OF ANALYSIS

The data reported here are part of a larger study of human resource management in greenfield sites—new, often purpose-built factories and offices. The main study has three central aims; it examines what happens when greenfield sites turn brown; that is, as they age. The second part is concerned with the impact of ownership and in particular foreign ownership on the nature of human resource management.

The third question is concerned with the impact of human resource management. An overriding question is the extent to which human resource management has become established as a preferred management option, on the assumption that this will be most dearly manifested in new establishments where managers have greater freedom to express their preferred choice. There are three parts to the study; the first is a reanalysis of part of WIRS3; the second is a survey of greenfield sites in the UK; and the third is a number of case studies in some of the surveyed establishments.

For our present purposes we will use data collected from the survey of greenfield sites. The survey was conducted in mid-1993, when a postal questionnaire was sent to just over 1,000 establishments in the UK employing more than fifty staff, including about 800 set up since 1980. We received responses from 393 establishments, subsequently reduced to 344 since some had less than fifty employees. Of the 344, 96 are purpose-built greenfield sites, new plants or offices being used for the first time; 152 are 'refurbished' sites, where there had been a major change of ownership and usually of activity, often following a shut-down period for the refurbishment; and 96 were set up before 1980.

For this analysis, we have restricted the sample to the greenfield and refurbished sites set up after 1980. This cut-off date was chosen as it marks the point at which Thatcherism began to have an impact at work, launching the debate about the new industrial relations. Establishments started since then provide what is arguably the best setting in which to explore the choices managers make about how to operate in the new industrial relations environments.

At new establishments, unconstrained by history and tradition in the workplace, managers are most free to introduce the policies and practices of their choice. Equally, they provide the most exacting test of how far trade unions are able to respond to the challenges they face in the new industrial relations. If they can flourish in such settings, then we can be more confident about their ability to retain a viable long-term role. In operating with new establishments we recognize that there is a different argument that could be made about looking at processes of change in older establishments. However, we believe that the cutting edge of innovations and emerging patterns in human resource management and the new industrial relations is likely to be found in new establishments.

The sample therefore contains 248 post- 1980 establishments of which 166 (66.9 per cent) are non-union and 82 (33.1 per cent) are unionized. These figures are in line with what we might expect from the analysis of WIRS3. Analysis by ownership reveals 104 UK owned establishments, 45 American-owned, 52 Japanese-owned, 19 German owned, and the remaining 24 owned by companies from the rest of the world which in practice means predominantly European Union and EFTA countries. Comparison with WIRS3 shows that the sample is broadly representative in size, based on number of employees and allowing for exclusion of those employing less than fifty staff. It is weighted towards manufacturing industry; indeed 84 per cent are manufacturing establishments, 10 per cent are in financial services, and 6 per cent are other services.

The questionnaire contained four sections. The first asked for background information on issues such as size, ownership, sector, age, and location. The second contained items about the presence of mission statements, human resource management strategy, and the degree of 'parental' influence. The third contained twenty-six items describing a range of contemporary human resource management practices and asked whether they are currently in existence at the establishment and whether they were used one year after start-up. The final asked about a range of outcomes.

These fall into three groups concerned with human resource management, employee relations, and establishment performance. The vast majority of questionnaires were completed either by the head of personnel at the establishment or by the most senior line manager with special responsibility for personnel issues, which in practice often meant the Managing Director, General Manager, or Plant Manager.

MANAGEMENT AND UNIONS

In this subsection we examine the impact of trade unions on human resource management strategy and human resource management practices. We do this by comparing the establishments falling into the four trade union categories. These are those with no union (n = 166), those with a single union deal (n = 31), those with a single union but no single union deal (n = 18), and those with multiple-unionism (n = 33). In the questionnaire we were unable to explore the content of the single union deals, so there are risks in assuming that they are similar in nature. However, the question was quite explicit in asking whether there was a single union agreement.

How helpful is a union presence? One indirect way of exploring the impact of the unions was to gauge whether managers considered their presence to be helpful to the achievement of company goals. Sixty-six per cent of managers in establishments where unions were recognized considered the unions to be helpful. This ranged from 70 per cent in the case of single union deals to 55.6 per cent where there are single unions but no special deal.

Multi-union establishments fell between the others with 62.5 per cent considering them helpful. The differences are not significant so we must be cautious, despite the apparent trend, in concluding that unions in the context of single union deals are seen as more helpful. This is a somewhat surprising result if we accept the popular assumption that single union deals are explicitly designed to foster cooperation. It suggests that single union deals, assuming they have been correctly identified, do not have the clear-cut advantages sometimes claimed for them by their enthusiastic advocates.

On the other hand, with two-thirds of managers taking the view that the unions are helpful, it is possible that new establishments provide an opportunity for managers to develop the kind of cooperation they want irrespective of whether or not they have a single union deal.

Unions and human resource strategy The questionnaire contained a section of items on aspects of policy and strategy. The responses in this section are important in setting a key part of the context for human resource management. It is hypothesized that those who take strategy more seriously will have better outcomes.

However, as noted elsewhere the content of the strategy will be as important as having a strategy. The comparison of the 166 non-union establishments with those where various union arrangements were recognized. In this table we present the descriptive statistics, together with a Chi2 test of differences between the categories.

This controls for background variables and is a more rigorous test of differences between the categories. All types of unionized establishment are more likely to have a mission statement than non-union establishments. However, when we control for factors such as size and ownership, the difference is only significant for establishments with single union deals. Where there is a mission statement, it is more likely to include explicit reference to human resource issues in non-union establishments.

Although the Chi2 result falls just short of significance, the multivariate test is significant and reveals that once again the differences can be accounted for mainly by the establishments with a single union deal. The third key issue is the presence of a human resource strategy, formally endorsed and actively supported by the top management team at the establishment. Once again the unionized establishments are more likely to report the existence of such a strategy, although in both tables the results fall just short of significance.

The differences can be accounted for mainly by the establishments with single union deals. One indication of an effective strategy is that it is reasonably consistent over time. Although the differences are not significant, the results indicate that where a mission statement or a human resource management strategy exists, the nonunion establishments tend to be more likely to have altered both.

The results from this first set of data are reasonably clear-cut. Those new establishments where a union is recognized are more likely than non-union establishments to have a mission statement and to include in it specific reference to human resource issues, and more likely to have an explicit human resource strategy.

These differences remain when we control for a range of background factors so they cannot be accounted for by variations in size, sector, or ownership. However, the presence of all these reflections of a strategy varies within the unionized establishments and is much the most likely to be found where there is a single union deal.

We cannot establish cause and effect. It is possible that those who think strategically opt for a single union deal. Alternatively, agreement to consider a single union deal forces establishments to confront related strategic human resource issues.

It is probably most plausible to suggest that since we are dealing with new establishments, the development of human resource strategy and the planning of a single union deal go hand in hand. In this context, the role of the parent, as Marginson et al, have indicated, appears to be important in shaping attitudes towards trade union recognition and the form it takes. Whatever the reasons, the key finding is that it is the unionized rather than the non-union establishments that take the lead in developing human resource strategy.

Unions and Human Resource Practices

The data indicate that a union presence is associated with a greater likelihood of a human resource strategy and a mission statement. However, it is wise to be somewhat sceptical about both unless they are clearly reinforced by a set of relevant practices. This subsection therefore takes us a step further by examining the presence at the new sites of the sort of practices commonly associated with human resource management.

The list is not exhaustive and it concentrates on human resource practices rather than some of those that might be associated with the more narrowly defined industrial relations aspects of the new industrial relations. This reflected the key focus of the study and also our knowledge that most of the establishments in the sample would be non-union and therefore issues like pendulum arbitration would be irrelevant.

Perhaps the most interesting result is the lack of consistent differences between union and non-union establishments. In both sets of new establishments, the use of a majority of the innovative human resource management practices is now the norm. Nevertheless significant differences emerge on seven of the items. Two of these concern status and harmonization. Here the differences are not so much between union and non-union as between non-union and single union deals on the one hand and other forms of union recognition on the other. However, in both cases it is the non-union establishments that are most likely to report these practices; and, the differences between the non-union and single union deal establishments are significant.

Therefore, although establishments with single union deals are more like the non-union establishments, they still fall some way short on single status. The pattern is somewhat similar for two other items, merit pay and appraisal. Non-union establishments are well ahead of all forms of unionized establishment in the use of merit pay. The differences are much less marked on appraisal where it seems that the multi-union establishments are less likely to operate it.

The three remaining items are those where establishments with a single union deal stand out as most likely to have adopted a practice. One is the use of trainability as a major selection criterion; the others are concerned with integration of strategy. Establishments with single union deals are much more likely to claim that human resource policies are integrated with business strategy and that the various human resource policies are integrated with each other. This would fit with the earlier claims to be more likely to have a human resource strategy.

Taking the set of practices as a whole, it appears that they are most likely to be reported in establishments with a single union deal, closely followed by non-union establishments. However, the other unionized establishments are often little different, indicating that a union presence is no bar to most human resource practices.

Despite this, the exceptions may be important. Unionized establishments are less likely to have progressed towards single status and less likely to be using appraisal-linked merit pay. These touch on traditional trade union territory and it would seem that in this territory they are still able to exert some influence on workplace practices.

Unions and Types Strategy

There is some evidence from the preceding analysis that unionized workplaces, and more particularly those with a single union deal, are more likely to have developed a coherent human resource strategy. However, not all establishments have a strategy and not all have introduced human resource management practices. To explore whether a union presence is compatible with the kind of high utilization human resource strategy sometimes associated with best human resource practice but also often seen as inimical to a trade union presence, we can reclassify establishments.

The basis for this classification was introduced earlier. Those establishments labelled Good have a human resource strategy, defined in the questionnaire as being formally endorsed and actively supported by the top management at the site; and also a high use of human resource practices, defined arbitrarily as more than half of those listed. The Bad are the opposite in that they have no strategy and use less than half the practices listed. The Ugly have a strategy but use less than half the practices while the Lucky have no strategy but use more than half the practices.

If strategic integration is at all important, we would expect the Good to report better outcomes than the Bad. If strategic integration around a distinctive set of human resource practices confers an advantage then we would also expect to see the Good report better outcomes than the Ugly and Lucky. By comparing across the groups we can also identify whether adoption of practices without a strategy—the approach of the Lucky—also has an impact on outcomes. In our total sample of 245 establishments, 107 (43.7 per cent) were classified as Good, 70 (28.6 per cent) as Bad, 28 (11.4 per cent) as Ugly, and 40 (16.3 per cent) as Lucky.

The key question for the debate about human resource management and the new industrial relations is whether the Good are compatible with unionism.

The results confirm that a union presence is compatible with a high utilization model of human resource management. Indeed, if we examine the distribution, a higher proportion of union than non-union establishments fall in the good category. This is due to the greater likelihood that they will have a human resource strategy. In contrast, more of the non-union establishments fall into the lucky category.

They have adopted the practices but have not developed a strategy. The multivariate analysis confirms this pattern but reveals where the differences lie. It is the establishments with a single union deal that are significantly more likely to fall within the Good category while the non-union are significantly more likely to be Lucky. No group stands out as more likely to be Bad or Ugly, although, contrary to expectation, there is a slight tendency for them to be unionized rather than not.

Summarizing the results to date, we have shown that at new establishments, those set up in the 1980s or more recently, industrial relations, manifested in a trade union presence and human resource management are able to exist side by side. However, we can go further than this. It appears that, more particularly in the case of single union deals, it is less a matter of the systems coexisting as of being integrated through a coherent strategy.

Indeed, unionized workplaces are more likely than their non-union counterparts to have a human resource strategy. There do appear to be some differences between the types of union presence. Without a single union deal, there is a slightly lower use of human resource practices and slightly less evidence of the sort of strategic pursuit of a high utilization policy categorized as the Good.

We have shown that with perhaps two exceptions, represented by single status and appraisal-related merit pay, the unions do not inhibit human resource management practice. The next key question is whether they have any impact on performance.

The Impact of Unions

If we wish to conduct a rigorous test of the impact of unions on performance and other outcomes, it is firstly necessary to see if there are links between human resource policy and practice and outcomes. If there are, then it will be necessary to hold this factor constant in order to ascertain the effect which unions have on performance *per se,* irrespective of the policies which are being used. The wider and controversial literature concerning the impact of unions on performance suggests that on balance they act as a drag. However, it is plausible to hypothesize that where a union presence is part of a planned human resource strategy in a new workplace, this is less likely to be the case.

The first step is to examine the impact of human resource policy and practice on outcomes. This is an important and interesting topic in its own light. For this purpose, we retain the integrative distinction between the Good, the Bad, the Ugly, and the Lucky. These results show that there are consistent differences between the policy types and it will therefore be necessary to hold policy effects constant when testing for union effects.

It shows the strength of the links between the use of strategically integrated human resource policies and performance. Specifically, the good establishments, those with a human resource strategy and a high uptake of human resource practices, consistently report better outcomes. At the other extreme, those with the poorer outcomes, revealed most clearly are the Bad, those without a strategy or much use of human resource practices.

The Ugly and the Lucky both report consistently poorer performance than the Good on all three types of outcome. This result will be of great encouragement to those who are attempting to implement a high utilization human resource strategy. This is the first UK. study to date which demonstrates the benefits of such a strategy so clearly.

We can now hold the human resource policy variable constant while examining the impact of unions on outcomes. The resulting multivariate analysis is shown. First, however, we can examine the descriptive results.

The results reveal few significant differences between the various categories. There are some exceptions. Establishments with a single union deal claim to have weathered the recession more successfully than multi-union establishments. Industrial disputes are predictably less likely in non-union establishments. Finally there is a trend towards higher quality of staff in single union deal establishments compared with the multi-union.

Only when the controls are imposed do the differences become clearer. The unionized establishments, taken as a whole, report poorer outcomes on almost all variables.

On a number they are significant. However, as expected, there are variations according to the type of union arrangement. The rest indicates that the poorer outcomes are most likely to be found at the multi-union establishments. In particular, they appear to have poorer human resource outcomes. In contrast, the only significant factor among the single union establishments is the greater likelihood of industrial conflict compared with the non-union establishments. Indeed, on issues associated with flexibility they appear to be at an advantage.

What these results indicate is that the presence of a union still acts as a modest but sometimes significant drag on performance. The effects are greater for multi-unionism and least for single union deals. Despite the earlier evidence of a willingness on the part of union establishments to embrace human resource practices, it seems that the unions still exert some influence on workplace outcomes. Finally, it is worth noting that the human resource strategy types appear to exert more influence than the unions. Performance is poorer in the Bad establishments than in the multi-union establishments.

The first key question we set out to explore through the study of greenfield sites is whether human resource management and trade-unionism can coexist. The answer from this study is an unequivocal yes. Most human resource management practices are just as likely o exist at unionized establishments as at those without unions. There are some variations on this general pattern.

The first important variation is the finding that the presence of a trade union is associated with a greater use of a human resource management strategy and a mission statement, which, in addition, is more likely to refer explicitly to human resource issues. This needs to be qualified by the analysis of types of trade union presence. A strategy and mission statement is particularly likely to exist where there is a single union deal. We cannot tell from this cross-sectional data whether the union presence encourages managers to think strategically or whether those who think strategically opt for a single union deal.

Although we suspect that the causal direction varies from context to context, since the choice of whether to recognize a union is an increasingly open one, we suspect that management thinks strategically about both human resource management and the new industrial relations and decides to opt for a single union deal.

Multiple unionism, by contrast, may come into operation in those establishments where a parent company already has a central collective agreement with a number of unions. It follows that the majority of such cases are likely to be British-owned. Examination of the national ownership patterns confirms that this is indeed the case. The UK- and USA-owned establishments where any union is recognized are the least likely to report a single union deal.

The pattern across the range of human resource management practices also reveals some specific differences and helps to sharpen the distinction between the new industrial relations, reflected in single union deals, and the traditional industrial relations reflected in multi-unionism.

Any type of trade union presence is associated with less use of single status and use of performance appraisal and merit pay for all staff.

Single union deals on the other hand are associated with a set of practices broadly similar to non-union establishments but with the added advantage of having a more coherent human resource strategy. These results are strongly supported by Millward's analysis of the new industrial relations based on WIRS3. He finds that establishments with single union deals are consistently more likely to have a range of innovative practices, implying once again that they think strategically about single union deals and human resource management issues together.

The second major question we have explored is whether a union presence facilitates or constrains aspects of performance. The general conclusion is that unions inhibit performance and multi-unionism inhibits it more. However, this conclusion requires some qualification since single union deals have far less impact on performance, compared with non-union establishments.

The similarity between non-union establishments and those with a single union deal brings us back to the question of whether this type of unionism is an empty shell. It does not appear to constrain management. Indeed, it is associated with what managers believe to be greater commitment to the organization among lower level staff and with greater flexibility than even non-union establishments. In contrast, multi-unionism is associated with poorer outcomes on all variables except labour turnover and absenteeism; and on five of the outcomes, the differences with non-union establishments are significant. Thus multi-unionism is associated with poorer performance. This confirms the economic research on the impact of unions.

Before reaching the general conclusion that multi-unionism is bad for performance, we should recall the data on human resource management types. The Bad establishments are more clearly associated with poor outcomes than the multi-union establishments, implying that decisions about human resource strategy are more important for outcomes than decisions about multi-unionism—assuming that managers take decisions about these issues and that in practice the two can be disentangled. In one sense, this marginalizes the union issue. On the other hand, unions may always have been marginal to performance in the great majority of organizations although industrial relations specialists, with their distinctive focus on unions, have been understandably reluctant to acknowledge this.

To summarize, the new trade-unionism, reflected most strongly in single union deals, is compatible with human resource management. There is more of a question mark against multi-unionism. This raises the question of why any company will recognize a trade union at a new establishment. A single union deal has very little impact compared with non-union establishments suggesting that they turn unions into empty shells.

Multi-unionism has a somewhat negative impact. In our sample of post- 1980 establishments, approximately a third recognized one or more trade unions. However, this fell to 20 per cent in the 'pure' greenfield sites compared with 42 per cent in the refurbished sites. The great majority of managers have already decided that there is no value in recognizing a trade union. So why do others do so?

The evidence from our case studies supports the more extensive data from the CLIRS2. This indicates that unions will be recognized in those companies which have a centralized system of collective bargaining which they wish to retain. Secondly, as our comparison of greenfield and refurbished sites suggests, unions may be recognized at those workplaces which are taken over, even if shut down for a while and refurbished, and where a union was already recognized.]

It is possible that in some cases there may be scope for the operation of individual values. Some managers, including perhaps personnel managers in particular, may value the presence of a trade union as a counterweight to arbitrary management treatment. Since we have found little evidence of any trade union official presence in our case studies, it appears that the personnel manager may act as promoter and recruiter for the union. However, this is likely to become less common. The evidence from this study suggests that as we learn more about the impact of the new industrial relations, in the absence of any change towards a government that more actively encourages them, the outlook for trade unions is bleak.

The practices and process of 'new industrial relations' and human resource management have become the primary agenda of industrial relations research and teaching whether prescriptive or critical; notwithstanding this primacy new industrial relations and human resource management are of no use in themselves; they are propagated as mechanisms to rejuvenate the British economy, its manufacturing sector in particular, and connect with current dynamics in capitalist production. Without an evaluation of the problematic nature of the wider dynamics of capitalist production new industrial relations and human resource management are both abstract and decontextual.

In the period since 1945 the dynamics of capitalist production have been generalized under two broad headings. The post-war period is generalized as 'Fordism', centred on the mass production of standardized commodities, institutionalized collective bargaining, and Welfare State capitalism. The contemporary period is generalized as 'Post-Fordism' premissed on the demise of mass consumer markets, the rise of niche markets, and the erosion of social democracy in the institutional base of the State. In particular, it has rejected collective bargaining and trade union recognition as 'good' industrial relations.

If we accept that Fordism and Post-Fordism generalize periods in capitalist production it is equally necessary to question the degree to which national pathways in capitalist production measure up to the generalization. We contend that national pathways predominate over generalized descriptions in the development of capitalist production. In consequence we must evaluate the relationship between capital, labour, and the State within national pathways in order to illustrate how historical formation within particular nation states weakens the viability of generalized description.

We suggest that the British State has been subject to a formative influence of libertarian *laissez faire* which emphasizes freedom and liberty from centralized and institutionalized measures enacted by the State. In the post-war period plural industrial relations and voluntary regulation epitomize this influence. Equally during the post-war period the British State was subject to the contextual influence of social democracy and plural public policy manifest in 'good' industrial relations as collective bargaining and trade union recognition.

The contemporary erosion of social democracy and 'good' industrial relations has separated the State from an active interest in capitalist accumulation; in fact the disengagement of pluralism in industrial relations has wound up the contextual influence of social democracy and returned the formative influence of libertarian *laissez faire* as contemporary contextual influence in the State, its accumulation strategy, and public policy on industrial relations.

However, the disengagement of pluralism, an accumulation strategy based on flexibility, and redefined 'good' industrial relations are all caught in the permanent yet unfolding contradiction of libertarian *laissez faire*; that is, a continuity in historical formation within a particular nation state and the predominance of this over generalized pathways in capitalist production. We contend that new industrial relations is in the British case isolated and disengaged from contemporary material dynamics other than promoting what can be termed 'extra flexibility'.

This isolation illustrates the weakness of prescriptive generalization in capitalist production because Post-Fordism and Fordism are based on a presumed role for the State, which we suggest never developed in the British State. This seeks to illustrate the isolation of new industrial relations as informed by human resource management from market and production strategies which are portrayed as the (future) basis of capitalist production in the UK.

This develops a wide-ranging polemic and is eclectic in its discussion with references to the State and its current strategy of disengagement from active involvement in capitalist accumulation. Since 1945 'good' industrial relations have been a central feature of public policy. For much of the post-war period 'good' industrial relations was constituted in terms of plural State institutions presiding over an economy where collective bargaining and trade union recognition were functional elements within an accumulation strategy centred on Fordism. By 1979 'good' industrial relations had become 'bad' industrial relations; almost overnight the Thatcher Government rejected the pluralism in the post-war settlement between capital and labour.

More significantly the Thatcher Government came to power when the period of capitalist development generalized as Fordism was exhausted. The contemporary State has initiated a libertarian, that is individual accumulation, strategy, disengaged pluralism in industrial relations, and sought to roll back much of its previous social democratic orthodoxy in areas such as employment policy, the Welfare State, nationalized industry, and industrial relations. Good industrial relations have been reconstituted and now emphasize the managerial prerogative and less industrial action as the basis of good.

This contends that the contemporary State's method of operation, disengagement from social democracy, actively frustrates its efforts to generate a positive flexible Post-Fordism in the UK. This asserts that flexibility is a means to an end in the movement between stages of capitalist development whereas in the UK it has become an end in itself.

In consequence, in the UK, flexibility is not a bridge between Fordism and Post-Fordism but a method of making the entrails of Fordism more flexible, thereby contributing to the development of a neo-Fordist low wage, low productivity, yet flexible, economy. Hence our contention that sovereign national pathways to capitalist development predominate over generalized periodizations. In order to develop this overall argument the discussion which follows is divided into four sections.

In Section 2 formative and contextual influences on the British State are briefly introduced in order to specify the limited nature of the British State. Section 3 evaluates the process of contemporary State disengagement from the post-war social democratic orthodoxy; the strategy of Conservative governments and their attempts to reconstitute good industrial relations is located in the process of disengagement.

Section 4 evaluates new industrial relations, new market and production strategies, and suggests that institutional disengagement by the State isolates new (improved) industrial relations from new market and production strategies. In consequence typology-normative description of market and production strategies are removed from their actual constitution in the UK's national pathway.

Section 5 builds on the arguments of the previous sections to illustrate the limited nature of new industrial relations in the generation of flexibility and sustainable improvement in productivity.

Formative and Contextual Influences

As a precursor to a more detailed evaluation of new industrial relations we briefly discuss formative and contextual influences on the British State. The aim of this section is to illustrate how a renaissance of formative influences on the State in terms of its public policy actually frustrates overall economic performance. The formative influence on the development of the British State is libertarian *laissez faire*.

As an economic and political doctrine it eschews a centralized state and highlights voluntary regulation in all spheres through contract and status. Notwithstanding its formative influence, *laissez faire* was discredited as the industrial revolution progressed during the nineteenth century.

From the 1870s a contextual influence emerged on the State; social democracy and collectivism developed in response to industrialization and collective experience in the employment relationship. For example, between 1871 and 1906 trade unions were legalized so that their activities were given immunity from prosecution in specific instances. Additionally between 1832 and 1928 the franchise was extended to all adults over the age of 21. Lastly, between 1908 and 1911 the Liberal Government introduced the beginning of what later becomes a fully fledged Welfare State. In addition to these examples of collectivism and social democracy both concepts reached their height in the formulation of plural industrial relations as public policy in the post-war period.

For much of the period since 1945 industrial relations were worked out plurally between employers and employees free from substantive legislative interference by the State. In substance pluralism in industrial relations was extra-contractual and socio-political in its constitution.

By extra contractual we mean it operated beyond the influence of individual contract, in consequence its method centres on the negotiation of collective agreements on the individual enforcement of contract. Pluralism was socio-political in its constitution because in public policy it was geared towards collective bargaining, trade union recognition, and State absenteeism with minimal negative use of the law; Kahn-Freund referred to this as 'collective laissez faire'.

The formative influence of libertarian *laissez faire* on the British State facilitated the development of voluntary industrial relations, projecting freedom from the State in the institutional base of industrial relations. Voluntary method in industrial relations illustrates the political foundation of *laissez faire* which prescribes a preference for voluntary regulation over State regulation. In the post-war period this equated to autonomous collective bargaining between employers and employees.

The central point in the making is the contradictory effect the formative influence of libertarian *laissez faire* has had. In many respects voluntary industrial relations replicated the formative influence of libertarian *laissez faire* by limiting active and positive State regulation of industrial relations, in particular the negative use of the law. By this we mean that voluntarism, that is collective *laissez faire*, encouraged a form of decentralized production politics where capital, labour (and the State) sought to keep the State out of their internal affairs and relations.

Perkin argues that a pattern of preindustrial class-formation, emphasizing maximum material freedom from the State was reproduced in industrial society. Barrington-Moore refers to this as a peaceful bourgeois revolution expressing a continuity of interests in and between capital and free labour *vis-a-vis* the centralized State apparatus in the form of Monarchy or Parliament. I. Clark (forthcoming) illustrates this argument in relation to the development of State policy on productivity in the post-war period.

Notwithstanding the above, institutional freedom only extends to the method of industrial relations. Within a capitalist economy the State is always present in the institution of industrial relations; the State apparatus defends and maintains private property, capitalist reproduction, and the contractually determined employment relationship, that is the naturalized framework of capitalist production.

A contradiction in industrial relations is its complete separation from the dynamics of capitalist production. Rule-making in capitalist production is beyond economics but central to industrial relations, this defines the fictitious nature of voluntary industrial relations; their method may be voluntary but their institution results from the framework of capitalist production.

Since 1979 the State has not been rolled back *per se*, it is the contextual influence of social democracy and collectivism which has been curtailed. As a result the formative influence of libertarian *laissez faire* has been repopularized in order to halt socio-political advances made by labour during the post-war period.

In essence the Thatcher-Major Governments have sought to restructure capital by eroding social democracy and reconstituting public policy as individual and liberal. A major element in this policy has been the removal of 'market rigidities' such as trade unions, elements of the public sector, and within employment inflexible collective agreements constituted beyond contract.

A by-product of reconstituting public policy has been an effort to generate new industrial relations informed, initially by macho management and latterly by new management techniques amalgamated in 'human resource management'. In both cases individual contractual reward and regulation are highlighted. We now proceed to a more detailed discussion of new industrial relations.

Chapter 11

The Generation of New Industrial Relations

THE BASIS OF RELATIONS CHANGE

The previous argued that since 1979 the formative influence of libertarian *laissez faire* has been paramount in the State's efforts to restructure the UK's industrial capitalism. In addition it was argued that voluntary industrial relations, constituted collectively or individually, replicate the libertarian bias in the British State which emphasizes freedom from centralized State action and regulation. The absence of centralized State action and regulation has been projected as vital to the generation of new industrial relations; this in turn has led to a rejection of pluralism and social democracy in the institutional base of the State. Both of these were primary contextual influences on the post-war State and public policy on industrial relations. This section examines the State as a functional entity which seeks to structure class conflict and provide co-ordination for the market by facilitating capitalist accumulation.

The period of capitalist development which followed the Second World War is generalized as Fordism; within this, economic co-ordination and class struggle necessitated the promotion of plural industrial relations and a Welfare State. Such innovations accommodated the balance of class forces which were determined by full employment and a diffusion of social democracy in the State. Since 1979 the contemporary

State has disengaged this orthodoxy. It has been able to do this with such ease precisely because pluralism and social democracy were constituted beyond the formative influences on the State. One area where the pressure of disengagement has been most prominent is the generalization of new industrial relations.

In terms of our argument we suggest that new industrial relations represents three ideological images propagated by the contemporary State: first, the promotion of the managerial prerogative, employee compliance, and a low strike level; secondly, a rejection of collective bargaining and trade union recognition as public policy and their replacement with managerially determined regulation and individualism in the employment relationship; thirdly, a prescription for management labour use strategies centred on flexibility and extra-contractual commitment through human resource management. Each image evokes the formative influences of libertarian *laissez faire* informed by contract and status and rejects contextual influences centred on pluralism, collective bargaining, and trade unions.

Thatcherism emphasized the conservative nature of the British State and repopularized individualism and freedom from the State. Thatcherism sought to reduce financial and institutional dependence on the State and encourage self-reliance, both economically and socially. In so doing it attacked the contextual basis of the post-war State.

By promoting contractual individualism Thatcherism launched a supply side attack on 'obstacles' to productive efficiency such as public debt, State-spending on the products of social democracy, and the social democratic acceptance of privileged trade unions. As Gamble makes clear, Thatcherism unwound the coil of social democracy in the UK's State apparatus (a sociopolitical retreat designed to promote economic advance). A rapid change in public policy on industrial relations in the use of the law and the promotion of individualism became the leading edge of State disengagement from the postwar plural orthodoxy.

The rhetoric of new industrial relations attacks the acceptance of conflict in industrial relations; the failure of pluralist industrial relations as public policy. The substance of new industrial relations represents an effort to contextualize formative influences on the State. In consequence the State has sought to circumscribe or terminate key rights and immunities acquired by trade unions since the late nineteenth century. Pioneers of social democracy such as the Webbs saw the expansion of State activity and institutional recognition on behalf of labour as an imperative; that is, a functional response to the needs of industrial capitalism.

The political erosion of social democracy since 1979 is also propagated on the basis of current imperatives in capitalist development; in crude terms, the orthodox pluralism of 'old' industrial relations was based on the contextual influences of collectivism, union recognition and the absence of law: 'new' industrial relations is based in the formative influence of libertarian *laissez faire,* State individualism, and freedom from extra contractual institutional regulation. Collectivism sat easily with the functional requirements of Fordism, whereas market individualism is propagated as essential for a successful movement to a Post-Fordist stage in capitalist development.

In order to avoid the charge of functional determinism there are two caveats which illustrate the problematic of function. First, old and new industrial relations are constituted through public policy; in both cases the extent to which the reality measures up to constitution is questionable. The second caveat concerns the generation of new industrial relations and its role in the movement from Fordism to Post-Fordism. As Zeitlin points out, States are not rational actors operating as historical subjects in defined periods but complex and contradictory associations. Hence there can be no guarantee that action by the State can be coherent or strategic. If this were the case order in industrial relations would be the norm.

The interesting question is how public policy becomes dysfunctional; the role and motivation of the State is a key factor as are its formative limitations. In the post-war period contextual influences on the State, pluralism, and social democracy became almost exclusive. For example, the Donovan prescription for industrial relations reform had no linkage to economic performance other than the social democratic assertion that formalized procedures at company level would arrest the use of restrictive practices, unofficial industrial action, and informal sectionalism. Since 1979 public policy has sought to sweep away social democracy and pluralism in industrial relations precisely because it inhibited economic performance via its method of extra-contractual (collective) rigidity. In both periods public policy became dysfunctional; first, it failed to address the issue of management. In the 1960s management practice was largely ignored by the Donovan proposals.

Flanders argued that procedural reform would improve management; however, as Hyman point out management did not necessarily improve its own practice in terms of cost and production control or work study. In the contemporary period management is assumed to be improved by measures which promote the managerial prerogative. However, British management practice was not necessarily connected to the broader material dynamics of Fordism or Post-Fordism.

A second reason for State policy becoming dysfunctional centres on the form of the State; in the post-war period contextual influences were determined extra-contractually whereas in the contemporary period extra-contractual influences have been curtailed. The contradiction for the State is its limited form. In the era of pluralism the State could not structure an integration of formative and contextual influences, whereas today the State has rejected the latter and seeks to operate through the former. Hence human agency within the institutional base of the State has gone from social democracy without a consideration of economic performance to a singular consideration of capitalist accumulation without a consideration of social democracy or comparative economic performance.

Use of law and the rejection of anything approaching good industrial relations in public policy are the dysfunctional consequences of State policy: the absence of the latter and pivotal role of the former have enabled the State to go back to its formative influences of contract, status, and the market. All three now drive human agency within the State's institutional apparatus.

For example, in the pluralist era 'status rights' were determined extra-contractually through the acceptance of collective bargaining, trade unions, and the minimal use of the law. In the contemporary era 'status' is not attached to anything collective, but instead, the individual contract of employment, which the prescription behind human resource management encourages individual employees to go beyond in order to progress up a single status hierarchy.

By disengaging from an institutional interest in good industrial relations the State has no industrial relations or overall industrial strategy which can lever the UK economy into Post-Fordism other than the purported benefits of market-oriented flexibility and statistically engineered improvement in productivity. As Zeitlin points out, functional explanations become tautological if any development can (retrospectively) be advantageous or compatible with functional requirements in capitalism.

The critical issue is the disconnection of cause and positive effect. Changes in the use of law and the generation of new industrial relations as enterprisebased public policy are largely negative in their effect because in the UK they fail to connect with production and market strategies essential in a movement to positive Post-Fordism. In the main, new industrial relations operates in Fordist product and market strategies which in the majority of areas encourage low productivity and low wages.

Business operates in a climate of perennial uncertainty and instability which in the absence of an overall industrial strategy encourages short-term responses to marketing, production, and management in general. As enterprise responses such moves are expressions of rational self-interest; however, the absence of an overall industrial strategy, other than the pursuit of flexibility, provides no positive dynamic for employers to follow.

The first Thatcher administration visualized trade unions as operationally uncontrollable and restrictive. Trade unions were held to be uncontrollable in the sense that industrial action was often unofficial, secondary, and involved the use of mass picketing. In addition highly particular restrictive practices were generalized to be operative throughout the economy. Such practices created inflexibility and rigidity in the supply side of the economy blunting its efficiency. Inefficiency manifested itself in a failure to use new technology in a competitive manner.

Supply side measures attacked obstacles to productive efficiency such as trade unions. Early legislation was designed with two purposes in mind: first, to challenge established patterns of behaviour and conduct in industrial disputes, and secondly, to improve the managerial prerogative. The latter effect is a function of the former; measures such as secondary picketing and unofficial industrial action were often traditional responses to managerial unreasonableness and unilateralism. In the new legal environment of the trade union as legal personality, fines and possible sequestration make such action less likely. Hence in operational terms the likelihood of trade union financial loss facilitated a potential improvement in the managerial prerogative.

The Employment Acts of 1980 and 1982 were not primarily directed at the internal activity of unions or their (restrictive) practices but at their conduct within industrial disputes. The 1980 Act outlawed secondary industrial action and secondary picketing whereas the 1982 Act made the continuation of these now illegal activities more pressing by narrowing the definition of a trade dispute and restoring the legal personality of trade unions. As Brown and Wadhwani comment, these changes substantially weakened the position of unions which traditionally relied on secondary action.

Thus, the first attack on the working of established industrial relations was to weaken its mode of operation in times of dispute. The second attack can most effectively be seen within the wider attack on, and rejection of, elements within the supply side of the post-war settlement.

The attack on the post-war settlement and the supply side in particular was the Thatcher Government's response to the failure of economic and social regulation in the orthodoxy of the social democratic State; that is, the capacity of the State to manage this orthodoxy. The presence of near full employment was visualized as reducing pressures on employers to be efficient thereby resulting in uncompetitive productivity levels especially in manufacturing.

In addition the restrictive nature of trade unions stifled enterprise and the effective operation of market forces. Initially the strategy of attack was to shake out the manufacturing sector by severe deflation, an indirect effect of which was to promote the managerial prerogative on the basis of 'macho management' which later appeared more reasoned in 'new industrial relations' centred on the idea of human resource management.

By implication the Government argued that the manufacturing sector would re-emerge leaner, fitter, more flexible, and free of the rigidity imposed by previously acceptable restrictive practices. Crouch sees this as a 'rejection of compromise': what we have termed the social democratic orthodoxy in the post-war settlement. Crouch argues that the State has rejected the need for good industrial relations and failed to institute anything in its place.

Whilst Crouch is generally correct it must be pointed out that human agency which is driving the contemporary State does not want to institute anything in the place of good industrial relations; precisely because the basis of the comtemporary State's effort to generate new industrial relations is institutional disengagement from the employment relationship; an effect of which is a loss of political citizenship for trade unions.

Efforts to politically reconstitute good industrial relations are a response to the incapacity of the social democratic orthodoxy in the post-war State. It is best visualized as an effort to modify the working of market forces to counter the tendency for the rate of profit to fall. For sustainable success such a policy must be grounded in a solid industrial policy.

Lane has argued that since 1979 the State has disengaged itself from industry and the circuit of capital precisely because of its overt free market ideology which denies the need for an active industrial policy. This is exactly the case because current accumulation strategies and industrial policy express the contradiction of the formative influence on the State; that is, the libertarian bias of freedom from State regulation.

Jessop *et al.* has highlighted this as a central flaw in the libertarian accumulation strategy of the contemporary State. Dynamic efficiency within any accumulation strategy requires the active that is collective, cooperation of both parties in the employment relationship. The political reconstitution of good industrial relations expressly avoids this via its rejection of pluralism. This point can be amplified through a brief discussion of these changes at the level of the firm.

RELATIONS AT THE LEVEL OF THE FIRM

The rejection of the post-war settlement and higher levels of unemployment, together with the empty libertarian accumulation strategy, has placed economic uncertainty at the centre of corporate strategy. As Hyman argues the primary effect of this uncertainty is budgetary pressure supplemented by management empowerment-prerogative to introduce new initiatives in industrial relations centred on labour control under the label human resource management.

Hyman's point is reinforced by Streeck who highlights the attack on 'status rights' within the contract of employment which new industrial relations promotes via its location in the wider reassertion of market principles. The message of human resource management replaces the notion of social stability and extra-contractual status (in collective bargaining) with the promotion of cooperative 'extra' flexibility based on individual status and extra-contractual obligation, what Storey terms going beyond contract.

The template of so-called 'soft' human resource management focuses on the individual to legitimize more authoritarian employment practices which undermine the institutional framework of 'old' industrial relations. However, the devices of contractual regulation, extra-contractual obligation, and individual status are insufficient to raise productivity and counter the tendency for the rate of profit to fall. An active industrial strategy is essential to focus the material objectives behind greater flexibility and improved productivity; in the absence of this the pursuit of flexibility has become an end in itself not a means of capitalist regeneration.

The contemporary libertarian accumulation strategy centres on the deregulation of markets, especially the labour-market, privatization, the stimulation of small businesses, and the enterprise culture. It is based on a highly particular stereotypical image of private sector capitalism which the individualist and contractually bound State generalized as the norm.

In summary it can be concluded that elements of new industrial relations have been introduced but there are two caveats; first, if we evaluate new industrial relations in terms of the historical development of the British State and its formative influences, the disengagement of pluralism in industrial relations further separates the State from active involvement in capitalist production; that is, new industrial relations cannot by itself connect with contemporary material dynamics.

Secondly and relatedly, in the absence of an active industrial strategy new industrial relations largely operate in a vacuum; that is, the atomized firm and individual accumulation strategies. In the following section we can address the question of why we need new industrial relations by examining product, employment, and labour-market changes in more detail.

The Need for New Industrial Relations

The previous made clear that the generation of new industrial relations is of no use in itself. The management and regulation of employment; that is, its industrial relations is a requirement of industrial capitalism and its wider production dynamics. In consequence it is necessary to examine wider economic and social restructuring which are alleged to be the crucial impetus for the dissemination of new industrial relations.

The central components of economic and social restructuring are twofold: first, new forms of production and associated market strategies, and second, social restructuring. The former is generalized in terms of flexible specialization and a movement to 'Post-Fordism' whereas the latter is generalized as 'flexibility' in civil society and its prevailing attitude to work.

This section briefly details both flexible specialization and flexibility and then evaluates each in terms of the UK's contemporary accumulation strategy and the historical development of the State. It propagates an argument which suggests that, in the UK at least, flexibility does not measure up to either dominant model; as a result, we contend that in the UK flexibility is constituted in the entrails of Fordism.

In consequence the substance of new industrial relations cannot connect with market and production strategies on which it is premissed. Hence in large measure it is rhetorically based to justify deterioration in the quality of the employment relationship. However, because of its individual constitution new industrial relations do benefit some workers who are empowered to go beyond contract; that is, become more flexible.

Conventional Flexibility

As a theory of production flexible specialization concentrates on changes in the production process which result from the application of new technology and computerized production equipment. The demand side dynamic of flexible specialization is the saturation and collapse of mass Fordist markets together with the promulgation of more determined consumer sovereignty. The supply side dynamic of flexible specialization represents a market strategy based on the pursuit of niche markets.

The economics of flexible specialization are simple: improvements in the technological base of production enable niche markets to be pursued because the fixed costs of set-up times can be drastically reduced, thereby enabling small batch customized products to be profitably produced at standardized prices. The primary advocates of this strategy, Piore and Sabel, see flexible specialization facilitating the re-emergence of craft products and in consequence multi-skilled craft workers; for a critical review of evidence for the UK see Nolan and Walsh.

In the absence of stable accumulation and production strategies based in Fordism, alternatives such as flexible specialization are propagated as the harbingers of economic and social stability in a movement to Post-Fordism. We can now turn to flexibility as a labour utilization strategy at the level of the firm.

Flexibility as a management-use strategy for labour was first repopularized in a typology presented by Atkinson. This typology centred on management segmenting its labour force into a core, with structured internal labourmarkets and a periphery of plug-in-unplug jobs. Hutton refers to these groups as privileged: the 40 per cent of the labour-market whose market power has increased since 1979 and the marginalized and insecure whose market position has deteriorated since 1979, as a result of flexibility and new industrial relations.

Segmentation leads to the possibility of functional flexibility in the core and numerical flexibility in the peripheral groups. Hyman argues that flexibility has become the theme of the 1980s wherein industrial relations is integrated into business strategy in order for management to cope with economic uncertainty. If we accept that flexibility is the main theme in contemporary business strategies we must add that it represents one result of the State's disengaged accumulation strategy. This positions the management of macroeconomic uncertainty at the level of the individual firm.

It is important to make clear that in the UK flexibility is a management strategy (flexible firm) and more. Flexibility also refers to labour-market outcomes which result from deregulation, the enhanced managerial prerogative, human resource management, and the disengagement of the social democratic State. We term this 'extra flexibility' in order to distinguish it from flexibility inherent to the flexible firm and flexible specialization.

Jessop*et al.* generalize flexible specialization and flexibility into a post-recession settlement which forms the basis of a movement to Post Fordism in the UK; that is, it is a functional response to the needs of British capitalism. The effect of this movement, the success of which is highly uncertain, impacts on industrial relations in three ways. First, industrial relations have become less collective and more differentiable.

Core workers who presumably are the focus of new industrial relations are themselves integrated into the organization for which they work by their location in secure internal labour-markets. The mechanics of human resource management are prescribed to be the basis of this integration for a hopeful account of these developments).

Secondly, collective industrial relations are of declining significance; as a response to heightened uncertainty in market conditions, the wage relation itself is made more flexible for both the core and the periphery. WIRS3 data concludes that the majority of workers do not have their pay determined as a result of collective bargaining. For manual and non-manual workers in 1990 the figures were 45 per cent and 24 per cent respectively whereas in private services the figures for manual and non-manual workers were 32 per cent and 27 per cent. Only in the public sector did the majority of manual and nonmanual workers have their last pay increase determined by collective bargaining (78 per cent and 84 per cent respectively). Where pay was not determined through collective bargaining the most significant determinant was management at establishment level. A third effect of the post-recession settlement on industrial relations is the disappearance of many full-time jobs, some of which are reconstituted via subcontracting, or the use of non-standard labour in the form of agency workers and part-timers.

For Boyer these types of labour-market and industrial relations flexibility are essential because capitalism has moved beyond Fordism. In consequence methods of industrial relations regulation and the quasi-right to full-time employment are unsuitable in Post-Fordism or neo-Fordism stages of capitalist development. We can now evaluate flexible specialization and the generalized flexibility thesis within the UK's current accumulation strategy and the stance of the State.

Economic and Social Restructuring

The libertarian accumulation strategy espoused by the State during the 1980s and 1990s is centred on extra-flexibility popular (individualist) capitalism and the enterprise culture. It assumes social and economic stability will result from the stance of the State; that is, its disengagement from the economy and further separation from civil society.

Within the libertarian accumulation strategy flexible specialization and flexibility are more or less left as free-standing strategies with which the mechanics of new industrial relations can connect. In short the chimeric content of the contemporary accumulation strategy has generated an enterprise strategy based around numerical flexibility between core and peripheral workers. The potential benefits of flexible specialization have been relegated to a concentration on changes in current production and labour processes which in themselves create functional flexibility.

Hence both flexibility as a labour-use strategy and attempts at flexible specialization place the emphasis on labour input in isolation from the wider context of such movements. Lane argues that flexibility in the UK has been brought about by an overall reduction in terms and conditions of employment, with functional flexibility pushing more labour into the periphery. In consequence the potential benefits of new industrial relations and human resource management are irrelevant to large sections of the employed labour force because they are not in its locus.

Elger argues that flexibility in British manufacturing is based in job intensification and job enlargement not multi-skilling. Knell concludes that foreign-owned multinational firms who invest in British regions do not necessarily bring flexible specialization to such regions but adapt production to local flexibility as generalized by the accumulation strategy of the host State; that is, in the UK low productivity, low value production by marginalized and insecure labour. As a result flexibility becomes functional and rhetorical.

Flexibility is functional in the sense that its actual dissemination as distinct from prescribed type is seen by the State as a response to the imperative and pressures of capitalist accumulation in the movement to Post-Fordism. Such passive facilitation is rhetorical in that as a response it solves problems in a deterministic manner. In short the passive response of the State, evident in the absence of industrial strategy, coordinates production dynamics and resolves industrial relations conflict in civil society precisely because it meets the changing requirements of British capitalism as defined by the *laissez faire* State.

That is, an accumulation strategy based on flexibility and low wages is likely to reproduce a Hong Kong style economy with the worst traits of the deregulated US labour-market, wherein regions seek to attract foreign-owned non-European multinationals. Besides providing employment this is likely to reduce indigenous profitability in similar sectors by exposure to greater international competition (premissed on flexibility and low wages) creating pressure for further financial engineering to remain competitive via flexibility and reductions in labour numbers and standards. This is likely to reduce the level of capital stock per employee, reducing the need for investment in human capital.

Sadly, this course of action has led to an evaluation of economic performance solely in terms of the productivity of human labour in the absence of attention to longer term capital renewal, precisely because generalizing low wages (by European Union standards) but high (in comparison to the recent past) productivity is the basis of the contemporary accumulation strategy. The absence of the potential for class conflict or even a collective employee voice mechanism has resulted in extra flexibility being conflated and generalized as a direct result of flexibility as presented by Atkinson.

Storey describes the presence of human resource management under four headings: beliefs and assumptions, the pre-eminence of line managers, strategic aspects, and key levers. All four are premissed on a 'can do' outlook which eschews and goes beyond contract, a movement which empowers employees and management to become more committed to their organization. We term this an individual status-obligation fulcrum.

The fulcrum and its mechanisms listed under the four headings may well define an organization as one where human resource management philosophy prevails; however, the whole approach is premissed on the absence of employee interests, a benefit of which is greater flexibility. Clark argues that flexibility is only useful as a means, therefore it must be allied to existing procedures, not seen as an end which was absent in 'old' industrial relations.

The disengagement of the State at the level of the economy combines with the institutional prescription of individualism and individual values which permeate civil society; this combination is dysfunctional. It promotes the managerial prerogative together with entrepreneurialism without stimulating an active context for individualism to operate in. Storey and Sisson argue that much of the individualist prescription in the human resource management literature is decontextualized from the real world; in the case of the UK we can add to this that much of it is decontextualized from the way the State operates. For example, the voluntarist principle on apprenticeship training was virtually destroyed in the early 1980s as a result of the shake-out in manufacturing industry. Voluntary destruction illustrates a contradiction in new industrial relations as informed by human resource management; its prescription empowers commitment and multi- or re-skilling, but the absence of formally administered and regulated training systems promotes a logic of improving flexibility in current production systems and methods of work organization. The resultant trend of such inertia is the development of a low productivity, low value-added, low pay manufacturing sector.

Hence in respect of decontextualized position there is a double contradiction; new industrial relations and human resource management are decontextualized from the voluntary basis of much of the UK's industrial relations framework; equally and relatedly, management in the UK is unlikely to consider the benefits of human resource management and might prefer not to use it because of its resource demands.

The fact that this point is rarely made clearly indicates the organization specific pathway to new industrial relations and human resource management. The pathway rejects a collective employee voice mechanism as irrelevant because it is based only in input analysis. This is likely to be the case because of an absence of focused industrial strategy on economic and social restructuring, the basis of the State's industrial strategy: placing extra flexibility centre stage in the status-obligation fulcrum of new industrial relations and human resource management at the level of the firm; that is, flexibility based largely in the productivity of human labour.

Core workers are assumed to collaborate with management in the socioeconomic restructuring of the labour process through the mechanics of new industrial relations and human resource management. Individualism, trust, empowerment, quality circles, briefings, and improved communication encourage and empower workers to enter the restructuring process themselves.

Here we can see how flexible specialization, the flexible firm plus extra flexibility have been fused together to create an enterprise strategy derived from direct and indirect pressure on labour independent of market production pressures. This point illustrates the argument presented above that flexibility in the UK is itself an atomized concept and an end rather than a means.

Recent empirical evidence seems to confirm that the main thrust of flexibility as a labour-use strategy is not functional and numerical flexibility as prescribed in the Atkinson typology but an exercise driven by cost and financial pressures. In many cases this resulted in the continued use of nonstandard labour in the form of part-timers, agency or other temporary workers, and subcontracting. Another significant conclusion of the study suggested that many employers were now moving away from the use of non-standard labour and returning to a reliance on standard full-time labour because of the competitive and organizational benefits it brings.

In the UK the focus of economic and social restructuring through flexible specialization and flexibility has been politically mediated through the active disengagement of the State. As Jessop argues, it has resulted in a form of flexibility too flexible for the generation of Post-Fordism by the flexible specialization route. Nolan and O'Donnell assert that this results from a neglect of positive interventionary industrial policy which is essential to conduct and focus individual enterprise strategies.

This is the case because individualism permeates the current institutional framework of the State and informs human agency within the apparatus of the State. Both are crucial to the generation of extra flexibility and the avoidance of a centrally determined industrial policy. Libertarian *laissez faire*, that is freedom from the State, the basis of the current accumulation strategy, is a political leitmotiv, nothing more. It is a theme without substance which is replicated in much of new industrial relations and human resource management. Both are rhetorically based in the managerial prerogative and flexibility as an end in management labour-use strategies.

Human agency which drives the State has determined to separate the State, civil society, the locus of new industrial relations, and human resource management; in consequence the collective State apparatus cannot focus the accumulation strategy it has determined. The State has, however, succeeded in attaining increased extra flexibility within the employment relationship.

As Sisson shows, at the level of the firm, much of this rooting is at the 'soft' end of human resource management. The short-term benefits of new industrial relations and soft human resource management are likely to be constituted in improved productivity figures and tighter wages costs; however, it is as yet unclear what the economic benefits of this extra flexibility are (other than it being visualized as an end in itself).

We can follow Boyer in suggesting that flexibility within economic and social restructuring can be either positive or negative. In the UK's case it appears to be negative in the sense that flexibility represents movement within current structures and does not represent a transition to something new.

The form of the State and the absence of positive interventionary industrial and employment strategies are central to this process. In the light of this argument we can now proceed to discuss the limited potential of new industrial relations in the generation of increased flexibility and improved productivity in the wider context of the UK's neo-Fordism.

Index

M

N

O

P

Q

R

S